STUDY GUIDE

MW00893950

Corporations, Partnerships, Estates & Trusts

1999 Edition

General Editors

William H. Hoffman, Jr., J.D., Ph.D., C.P.A.   **William A. Raabe,** Ph.D., C.P.A.

James E. Smith., Ph.D., C.P.A.   **David M. Maloney,** Ph.D., C.P.A.

Prepared by Paul O'Brien, Governors State University

Contributing Authors

James H. Boyd
Ph.D., C.P.A.
Arizona State University

William H. Hoffman, Jr.
J.D., Ph.D., C.P.A.
*University of Houston
and State University*

W. Eugene Seago
J.D., Ph.D., C.P.A.
Virginia Polytechnic Institute

D. Larry Crumbley
Ph.D., C.P.A.
Louisiana State University

David M. Maloney
Ph.D., C.P.A.
University of Virginia

James E. Smith
Ph.D., C.P.A.
College of William and Mary

Steven C. Dilley
J.D., Ph.D., C.P.A.
Michigan State University

William A. Raabe
Ph.D., C.P.A.
Samford University

Eugene Willis
Ph.D., C.P.A.
University of Illinois at Urbana

Mary Sue Gately
Ph.D., C.P.A.
Texas Tech University

Boyd C. Randall
J.D., Ph.D.
Brigham Young University

WEST/SOUTH-WESTERN College Publishing

An International Thomson Publishing Company

Accounting Team Director: Richard K. Lindgren
Acquisitions Editor: Alex von Rosenberg
Developmental Editor: Esther Craig
Production Editor: Rebecca Glaab
Marketing Manager: Maureen L. Riopelle
Manufacturing Coordinator: Gordon Woodside

ISBN: 0-538-88583-1

1 2 3 4 5 6 7   WST   4 3 2 1 0 9 8

Printed in the United States of America

International Thomson Publishing
West/South-Western College Publishing is an ITP Company.
The ITP trademark is used under license.

Contents

To the Student

This Study Guide has been designed to be used as a supplement to the 1999 Annual Edition of *West's Federal Taxation: Corporations, Partnerships, Estates, and Trusts*. The purpose of this Study Guide is to aid you in mastering the textbook material, not to replace it.

Each Study Guide chapter contains:

- A list describing the Learning Objectives.

- A list of Key Terms discussed in the text chapter.

- A review, in outline form, of major points covered in the text.

- Test questions and solutions.

In addition, flowcharts describing the application of particular Code sections appear in various chapters. Problems covering corporate, partnership and S corporation tax return preparation have been inserted at the end of Chapters 3, 11, and 12 respectively.

Though no study technique is equally effective for all students, I suggest that you first review the list of Key Terms, read the textbook chapter, then review the Outline in the Study Guide.

Paul O'Brien
March, 1998

CHAPTER 1

UNDERSTANDING AND WORKING WITH THE FEDERAL TAX LAW

LEARNING OBJECTIVES

After completing Chapter 1, you should be able to:

1.   Realize the importance of revenue needs as an objective of Federal tax law.

2.   Appreciate the influence of economic, social, equity, and political considerations on the development of the tax law.

3.   Understand how the IRS, as the protector of the revenue, has affected tax law.

4.   Recognize the role of the courts in interpreting and shaping tax law.

5.   Identify tax law sources -- statutory, administrative, and judicial.

6.   Locate tax law sources.

7.   Assess the validity and weight of tax law sources.

8.   Make use of various tax planning procedures.

9.   Have an awareness of computer-assisted tax research.

KEY TERMS

Acquiescence	Determination letters	Revenue neutral
Arm's length concept	Indexation	Revenue Procedures
Business purposes concept	Letter rulings	Revenue Rulings
Certiorari	Nonacquiescence	Tax benefit rule
Continuity of interest concept	Proposed Regulations	Temporary Regulations
		Wherewithal to pay

OUTLINE

I.   THE WHYS OF THE TAX LAW

    A.   Revenue Needs
        1.   The major objective of the Federal tax law is raising revenue to absorb the cost of government operations.
        2.   In recent years, budget deficit considerations have emphasized the concept of revenue neutrality.
        3.   Revenue neutrality neither reduces nor increases the deficit, the net revenue raised remains the same.

    B.   Economic Considerations
        1.   Control of the economy
            a.   capital outlays for business property is
                1.   encouraged through shorter asset lives and accelerated methods of depreciation.
                2.   discouraged through longer asset lives and slower methods of depreciation.
            b.   spending is promoted by lower tax rates.
        2.   Encouragement of certain activities
            a.   technological progress is encouraged by favorable tax provisions concerning the treatment of
                1.   research and development expenditures.
                2.   inventors and patents.
            b.   a healthy environment is encouraged through amortization of pollution control facilities.
            c.   low income rental housing is encouraged through tax credits.
            d.   exports are encouraged through foreign sales corporations.
        3.   Encouragement of certain industries
            a.   farmers are allowed elections to
                1.   expense certain soil and water conservation expenditures.
                2.   defer gain recognition on crop insurance proceeds.
            b.   extractors of gas, oil and some minerals are allowed to use percentage depletion and may expense rather than capitalize some exploration costs.
        4.   Encouragement of small business
            a.   ordinary loss treatment allowed on certain small business corporation's stock encourages investments.
            b.   the S corporation election allow the corporation to pass through profits and losses to shareholders without a corporate level income tax.
            c.   provisions for corporate reorganizations allow corporations to combine without adverse tax consequences.

C. Social Considerations
1. Nontaxability of some employer sponsored insurance coverage encourages private sector financial support for employees and their families in the event of an employee's illness, injury, or death.
2. Deferred taxability of private retirement plans encourages saving to supplement social security benefits in post-employment years.
3. Qualified charitable contribution deductions encourages private sector support for socially desirable programs.
4. Child and dependent care tax credits encourages taxpayers to work.

D. Equity Considerations
1. To alleviate the effect of multiple taxation
    a. deductions are allowed for state and local income taxes.
    b. credits or deductions are allowed for foreign income taxes paid.
    c. corporations are allowed a deduction for certain dividends received.
2. The wherewithal to pay concept allows deferral of gain recognition in specific situations where a taxpayer's economic positions has not significantly changed.
3. To mitigate the effect of annual accounting periods
    a. provisions allow the carryback and carryover of net operating and capital losses.
    b. gain on installment sales is recognized over the payout period.

E. Political Considerations
1. Special interest legislation is an inevitable product of our political system; certain groups influence Congress to promote the enactment of laws providing special tax treatment for their particular business or interest.
2. Political expediency refers to tax provisions developed in response to popular opinion at the time of enactment.
3. State and local influences on Federal tax law developed in response to disparities in Federal income tax treatment based on state of residence.

F. Influence of the Internal Revenue Service
1. The IRS as protector of the revenue has been instrumental in securing passage of much legislation designed to close tax loopholes.
2. Administrative feasibility of the tax laws is aided by provisions which place taxpayers on a pay-as-you-go basis, and impose interest and penalties on taxpayers for noncompliance.

G. Influence of the Courts
1. Judicial concepts relating to tax law serve as guides in applying various tax provisions.
2. Judicial influence on statutory provisions came into being as a result of certain key court decisions.

II.   WORKING WITH THE TAX LAW - TAX SOURCES

    A.   Statutory Sources of the Tax Law
        1.   Origin of the Internal Revenue Code
            a.   The Internal Revenue Code of 1939 arranged all Federal tax provisions enacted by Congress prior to that time in a separate part of the Federal statutes.
            b.   The Internal Revenue Code of 1954 was a revision of the 1939 Code.
            c.   The Internal Revenue Code of 1986 adds to, deletes and amends the 1954 Code.
            d.   Statutory amendments to the tax law, such as the Taxpayer Relief Act of 1997, are integrated into the existing Code.
        2.   The Legislative Process
            a.   tax legislation generally originates in the House of Representatives
                1.   considered by the House Ways and Means Committee
                2.   if accepted, referred to entire House for a vote
                3.   if approved, referred to Senate Finance Committee
                4.   if accepted, referred to entire Senate for a vote
                5.   if approved, referred to the President
                6.   if accepted, the bill becomes law.
            b.   tax bill may originate in the Senate as riders to other legislation.
            c.   when the House and Senate versions of a bill differs, the Joint Conference Committee attempts to resolve the differences.

    B.   Administrative Sources of the Tax Law
        1.   Treasury Department Regulations
            a.   provide taxpayers with guidance on the meaning and application of the Code.
            b.   new Regulations are usually issued in proposed form before finalization to permit comment from taxpayers.
            c.   Temporary Regulations are issued when speed is critical.
            d.   Temporary Regulations are simultaneously issued as Proposed Regulations and automatically expire within three years.
            e.   Final Regulations are issued as Treasury Decisions.
        2.   Revenue Rulings and Revenue Procedures
            a.   Revenue Rulings provide interpretation of the tax law as it applies to a particular set of circumstances.
            b.   Revenue Procedures deal with the internal management practices and procedures of the IRS.
        3.   Other Administrative Pronouncements
            a.   Treasury Decisions are issued to make known Final Regulations, to change existing Regulations, or to announce the Government's position on selected court decisions.

      b.   Technical Information Releases are issued to announce the publication of various IRS pronouncements.

      c.   Letter rulings are issued, upon a taxpayer's request, to describe how a proposed transaction will be treated for tax purposes.
1. letter rulings generally apply only to the requesting taxpayer.
2. the issuance of letter rulings is limited to restricted, preannounced areas.

      d.   Technical advice memoranda are issued in response to IRS personnel during audits and give the IRS's determination of an issue.

      e.   Determination letters are issued at the request of taxpayers to provide guidance concerning the tax laws applicable to a completed transaction.

C.   Judicial Sources of the Tax Law
1. The judicial process
      a.   if no satisfactory settlement has been reached with the IRS, the dispute can be taken to Federal court.
      b.   the case is first considered by a court of original jurisdiction.
1. Federal District Court
2. U.S. Court of Federal Claims
3. Tax Court
4. Small Cases Division of the Tax Court
      c.   any appeal is taken to the appropriate appellate court.
1. Court of Appeals of appropriate jurisdiction
2. Court of Appeals for the Federal Circuit
3. Supreme Court
2. Judicial Citations
      a.   under the doctrine of stare decisis, each case has precedential value for future cases having the same controlling set of facts.
      b.   The U.S. Tax Court issues two types of decisions:
1. Regular decisions involve issues not previously resolved by the Court.
2. Memorandum decisions involve application of already established principles of law.
      c.   if the IRS loses in a decision, it usually indicates agreement: acquiescence, or disagreement: nonacquiescence.

III.   WORKING WITH THE TAX LAW - TAX RESEARCH

A.   Identify the Problem
1. Gather all of the facts that might have a bearing on the problem.

    2.   Refine the problem and determine the tax consequences of each possibility.

B.   Locate the Appropriate Tax Law Sources - be sure your information is up to date.

C.   Assess the Validity of Tax Law Sources
    1.   Assess the relevance of the tax law source in light of the facts and circumstances of the problem at hand.
    2.   Assess the weight of the tax law source in light of the facts and circumstances of the problem at hand.
    3.   Different sources have varying degrees of authority.

D.   Arrive at the Solution or at Alternative Solutions

E.   Communicate Tax Research
    1.   Present a clear statement of the issue.
    2.   Provide a short review of the factual pattern that raised the issue.
    3.   Provide a review of the controlling tax law sources consulted.
    4.   Describe any assumptions made in arriving at the solution.
    5.   State the recommended solution and the reasoning to support it.
    6.   List the references consulted.

IV.   WORKING WITH THE TAX LAW - TAX PLANNING

A.   The primary purpose of the effective tax planning is to reduce the taxpayer's total tax bill.

B.   Minimization of tax payments must
    1.   Be consistent with the taxpayer's legitimate business goals.
    2.   Consider the impact of a particular action over time, not just the current year.

C.   Tax Avoidance and Tax Evasion
    1.   Tax avoidance minimizes tax liabilities through legal techniques.
    2.   Tax evasion implies the use of subterfuge and fraud to reduce taxes.

TEST FOR SELF-EVALUATION

True or False

T F 1. Nonacquiescence by the Commissioner of Internal Revenue to an adverse decision in a regular Tax Court case means the Internal Revenue Service will NOT accept the decision and will NOT follow it in cases involving similar facts.

(IRS 96 4A-27)

T F 2. A Memorandum Decision is a report of a Tax Court decision thought to be of little value as a precedent because the issue has been decided many times.

(IRS 96 4A-28)

T F 3. An income tax case NOT resolved at an appeals conference can proceed to the United States Tax Court WITHOUT the taxpayer paying the disputed tax, but generally, the United States District Court and United States Claims Court hear tax cases ONLY after the tax is paid and a claim for credit or refund is filed by the taxpayer and is rejected by the IRS or the IRS has not acted on the taxpayer's claim within six months from the date of filing the claim for refund.

(IRS 95 4A-11)

T F 4. All courts except the Tax Court are bound by legislative regulations.

(IRS 95 4A-24)

T F 5. Proposed regulations automatically replace the temporary regulations.

(IRS 95 4A-25)

T F 6. Revenue rulings are the published conclusions of the IRS concerning the application of tax law to a specific set of facts.   (IRS 95 4A-26)

T F 7. The courts are NOT bound by Treasury Regulations.   (IRS 94 4A-27)

T F 8. Decisions of the courts other than the Supreme Court are binding on the Commissioner of Internal Revenue ONLY for the particular taxpayer and for the years litigated.   (IRS 94 4A-28)

T F 9. If the Supreme Court determines that various lower courts are deciding a tax issue in an inconsistent manner, it may review a decision and resolve the contradiction.

(IRS 94 4A-29)

Fill in the Blanks

1. _____, _____, _____, and _____ play a significant role in the development of Federal tax law.

2. _____, _____ and _____ are examples of political considerations.

3. The courts have influenced and formulated tax law through the two techniques of _____ and _____.

4. If the IRS loses in a Regular decision of the Tax Court, it will indicate _____ or _____ with the result reached by the Court.

5. Appeal to the U.S. Supreme Court is by _____.

6. _____ are issued at the request of taxpayers and provide guidance concerning the application of tax law to completed transactions.

7. Tax reform legislation which does not change net revenues raised is _____.

8. The _____ concept applies to situations in which a taxpayer's economic position has not significantly changed; gain recognition is postponed.

9. _____ is the method whereby one determines the best solution or series of solutions to a particular problem with tax ramifications.

10. _____ is the minimization of tax payments through legal means.

Multiple Choice

_____ 1.   With regard to revenue rulings and revenue procedures, all of the following statements are are correct except: (IRS 96 4B-69)

    a. A revenue ruling is a published official interpretation of tax law by the IRS that sets forth the conclusion of the IRS on how the tax law is applied to an entire set of facts.

    b. Revenue rulings have the force and effect of Treasury Regulations.

    c. A revenue procedure is a published official statement of procedure that either affects the rights or duties of taxpayers or other members of the public under the Internal Revenue Code and related statutes and regulations or, if not necessarily affecting the rights and duties of the public, should be a matter of public knowledge.

    d. Revenue procedures are directive and NOT mandatory so that a taxpayer has no vested right to the benefit of the procedures when the IRS deviates from its internal rules.

_____ 2.   Which of the following statements BEST describes the applicability of a constitutionally valid Internal Revenue Code section on the various courts?
(IRS 95 4B-70)

a. Only the Supreme Court is NOT bound to follow the code section. All other courts are bound to the Code section.
b. Only the Tax Court is bound to the Code section, all other courts may waiver from the Code section.
c. Only District, Claims and Appellate Courts are bound by the Code section, the Supreme and Tax Courts may waiver from it.
d. All courts are bound by the Code section.

_____ 3.   All of the following statements with respect to classes of regulations are CORRECT except: (IRS 95 4B-71)

a. All regulations are written by the Office of the Chief Counsel, IRS, and approved by the Secretary of the Treasury.
b. Public hearings are NOT held on temporary regulations.
c. Although IRS employees are bound by the regulations, the courts are NOT.
d. Public hearings are NOT held on proposed regulations.

_____ 4.   Which of the following is NOT one of the three classes of Treasury Regulations?
(IRS 95 4B-72)

a. Temporary
b. Judicial
c. Final
d. Proposed

_____ 5.   Which of the following statements is FALSE?   (IRS 95 4B-73)

a. The Tax Court will issue either a regular report or a memorandum decision depending upon the issues involved and the relative value of the decision being made.
b. The Commissioner of Internal Revenue does NOT isssue a public acquiescence or nonacquiescence on District or Claims court cases.
c. Interpretative regulations are issued under the general authority of Internal Revenue Code Section 7805(a) and legislative regulations are issued under the authority of the specific Internal Revenue Code section to which they relate.
d. The government prints the regular and memorandum Tax Court decisions in bound volumes.

_____ 6.   With regard to the small tax case procedures of the United States Tax Court, all of the following statements are correct except: (IRS 94 4B-41)

    a.   The amount of tax involved in the case must be $10,000 or less for any one tax year or period.
    b.   The taxpayer must request small case procedures and the Tax Court must approve the request.
    c.   The taxpayer must pay the tax and file a claim for credit or refund that the IRS rejects.
    d.   The Tax Court decision is final and you CANNOT appeal.

_____ 7.   With regard to Treasury Regulations, all of the following statements are correct except: (IRS 94 4B-69)

    a.   Notices of proposed rulemaking are REQUIRED for proposed regulations and are published in the Federal Register so that interested parties have an opportunity to participate in the rulemaking process.
    b.   Until final regulations are issued, temporary regulations have the same force and effect of law as final regulations.
    c.   Legislative regulations are those for which the IRS is specifically authorized by the IR Code to provide the details of the meaning and rules for particular Code sections.
    d.   Interpretative regulations, which explain the IRS's position on the various sections of the IR Code, are NOT accorded great weight by the courts.

_____ 8.   With regard to revenue rulings and revenue procedures, all of the following statements are correct except: (IRS 94 4B-70)

    a.   A revenue ruling is a published official interpretation of tax law by the IRS that sets forth the conclusion of the IRS on how the tax law is applied to an entire set of facts.
    b.   Revenue rulings have the force and effect of Treasury Regulations.
    c.   A revenue procedure is a published official statement of procedure that either affects the rights or duties of taxpayers or other members of the public under the Internal Revenue Code and related statutes and regulations or, if not necessarily affecting the rights and duties of the public, should be a matter of public record.
    d.   Revenue procedures are directive and NOT mandatory so that a taxpayer has no vested right to the benefit of the procedures when the IRS deviates from its internal rules.

_____ 9. If a taxpayer with a notice of deficiency wishes his/her case heard by a court before paying the tax, which court would the taxpayer petition?   (IRS 94 4B-71)

    a. United States Tax Court
    b. United States Claims Court
    c. United States District Court
    d. United States Court of Appeals

_____ 10. With regard to terminology relating to court decisions, all of the following statements are correct except: (IRS 94 4B-72)

    a. DECISION, the court's formal answer to the principal issue in litigation, has legal sanction and is enforceable by the authority of the court.
    b. DICTUM, a court's statement of opinion on a legal point NOT raised by the facts of the case, is NOT controlling, but may be persuasive to another court deciding the issue dealt with by the dictum.
    c. Acquiescence by the Commissioner of Internal Revenue Service on adverse regular Tax Court decisions, generally means the IRS will follow the Court's decision in cases involving similar facts.
    d. Writ of Certiorari is a petition issued by the lower appellate court to the Supreme Court to hear a case that is NOT subject to obligatory review by the Supreme Court.

SOLUTIONS

True or False

1. T (p. 1-31)
2. T (p. 1-29)
3. T (p. 1-26)
4. F (p. 1-36)
5. F (p. 1-22)
6. F (p. 1-22; interpretations not conclusions)
7. T (p. 1-37)
8. T (p. 1-27)
9. T (p. 1-29)

Fill in the Blanks

1. Economic, social, equity and political factors (p. 1-2)
2. Special interest legislation, political expediency, and state and local influences (p. 1-11)
3. Judicial concepts and key decisions (p. 1-14)
4. acquiescence, nonacquiescence (p. 1-31)
5. writ of certiorari (p. 1-28)
6. Determination Letters (p. 1-24)
7. revenue neutral (p. 1-3)
8. wherewithal to pay (p. 1-7)
9. Tax research (p. 1-32)
10. Tax avoidance (p. 1-42)

Multiple Choice

1. b (p. 1-22)
2. d (p. 1-16)
3. d (p. 1-22)
4. b (p. 1-22)
5. d (p. 1-29, 31)
6. c (p. 1-25)
7. d (p. 1-22, 37)
8. b (p. 1-22)
9. a (p. 1-26)
10. d (p. 1-25, 28, 30)

CHAPTER 2

CORPORATIONS: INTRODUCTION, OPERATING RULES, AND RELATED CORPORATIONS

LEARNING OBJECTIVES

After completing Chapter 2, you should be able to:

1. Summarize the various forms of conducting a business.

2. Compare the taxation of individuals and corporations.

3. Discuss the tax rules unique to corporations.

4. Compute the corporate income tax.

5. Explain the tax rules unique to multiple corporations.

6. Describe the reporting process for corporations.

7. Evaluate corporations for conducting a business.

KEY TERMS

Brother-sister controlled group
C corporation
Controlled group
Dividends received deduction
Limited liability company

Limited partnership
Organizational expenditures
Parent-subsidiary controlled group
Passive loss
Personal service corporation

Regular corporation
Related corporations
S corporation
Schedule M-1

OUTLINE

I.   TAX TREATMENT OF VARIOUS BUSINESS FORMS

    A.   Sole Proprietorships report all business activity on the individual owner's Schedule C, Form 1040.

    B.   Partnerships report all of the partner's business activity on Form 1065 and allocate to each partner their share on Schedule K-1, this information is then transferred to and included in each partner's Form 1040.

    C.   S corporations are similar to partnerships, the entity reports its activities on Form 1120S and K-1's are issued to each shareholder and included on their Form 1040.

    D.   Regular, C corporations report all business activity on Form 1120. These corporations are taxable entities separate and distinct from their owner, shareholders.

    E.   Limited liability companies may be taxed as partnerships. Check-the-box rules permit a domestic entity to elect taxation as a corporation or as a partnership regardless of its corporate or noncorporate characteristics.

II.   INCOME TAXATION OF CORPORATIONS

    A.   Overview
        1.   The gross income of a corporation, including gains and losses from property transactions is determined in much the same manner as it is for individuals.
        2.   Business deductions of corporations parallel those of individuals, deductions are allowed for all ordinary and necessary expenses paid or incurred in carrying on a trade or business.

    B.   Specific Provisions
        1.   Accounting periods and methods
            a.   regular corporations may choose a calendar or fiscal tax year.
            b.   a Personal Service Corporation must, generally, use a calendar year. A corporation is a PSC if:
                1.   the principal activity is the performance of personal services in the fields of: health, law engineering, architecture, accounting, actuarial science, performing arts or consulting;
                2.   services are substantially performed by owner-employees;
                3.   more than 10% of the value of the corporation's stock is held by owner-employees.

        c.   generally, a regular corporation must use the accrual method of accounting.

        d.   the cash method may be used by:

                1.   corporations engaged in the trade or business of farming and timber.

                2.   corporations having average annual gross receipts of $5 million or less.

                3.   qualified PSCs.

                4.   S Corporations.

2.   Capital gains and losses

        a.   net capital gain is fully included in a corporation's taxable income.

        b.   capital losses can offset only capital gains.

        c.   net capital losses may be carried back 3 years and forward 5 years.

        d.   when carried back or forward, all capital losses are treated as short-term.

3.   Recapture of depreciation

        a.   depreciation recapture for §1245 property is the same for corporations as for individuals.

        b.   20% of the excess of any amount treated as ordinary income under §1250 is treated as ordinary income for corporate sales of depreciable real estate that is §1250 property.

4.   Passive losses

        a.   closely held C corporations may offset passive losses against active income, but not against portfolio income.

        b.   a corporation is closely held if more than 50% of the value of the corporation's outstanding stock is held by 5 or fewer individuals at any time during the tax year.

        c.   PSCs cannot offset passive losses against either active income or portfolio income.

5.   Charitable contributions

        a.   the recipient must be a qualified charitable organization.

        b.   an accrual basis corporation may claim the deduction in the year preceding payment if:

                1.   the contribution has been authorized by the end of that year, and

                2.   the payment is made on or before the 15th day of the 3rd month of the next year.

        c.   property contributions

                1.   the deduction for long-term capital gain property donated is, generally, fair market value.

                2.   the deduction for ordinary income property donated is, generally, limited to its basis.

                3.   the flowchart following this chapter outline reviews exceptions for property contributions.

        d.   a corporate taxpayer's charitable contribution deduction for any one year is limited to 10% of taxable income.

6.   Net operating losses may be carried back 2 years and forward 20 years to offset taxable income.

7.   Deductions available only to corporations

    a.   the dividends received deduction is to prevent triple taxation

        1.   a corporation may deduct 70, 80 or 100% of the amount of dividends received from domestic corporations.

        2.   the percentage of ownership in the payor corporation determines the deductible percentage.

        3.   this deduction may be limited by the corporation's taxable income.

    b.   organizational expenditures

        1.   a corporation may elect to amortize organizational expenditures over a period of 60 months or more.

        2.   amortizable expenses include:

           a.   legal services incident to organization

           b.   necessary accounting services

           c.   expenses of temporary directors

           d.   expenses of organizational meetings of directors or shareholders

           e.   fees paid to the state of incorporation

        3.   the expenditures must be incurred before the end of the taxable year in which the corporation begins business.

III.   DETERMINING THE CORPORATION INCOME TAX LIABILITY

A.   1997 Corporate Income Tax Rates:

Taxable Income Over---	But Not Over---	Tax Is:	Of the Amount Over---
$ 0	$ 50,000	15%	$ 0
50,000	75,000	7,500 + 25%	50,000
75,000	100,000	13,750 + 34%	75,000
100,000	335,000	22,250 + 39%	100,000
335,000	10,000,000	113,900 + 34%	335,000
10,000,000	15,000,000	3,400,000 + 35%	10,000,000
15,000,000	18,333,333	5,150,000 + 38%	15,000,000
18,333,333	--	35%	0

B.   Qualified PSCs are taxed at a flat 35% rate on all taxable income.

C.   Corporations are subject to the Alternative Minimum Tax.

D.   A controlled group of corporations' taxable income is limited in the tax brackets below 35% to the amount the corporations in the group would have if they were one corporation.

IV.   PROCEDURAL MATTERS

A.   A corporation, whether or not it has taxable income, must file its return by the 15th day of the 3rd month after the close of its tax year.

B.   An automatic extension of six months for filing the corporate return may be requested on Form 7004.

C.   Estimated tax payments are required of corporations expecting a tax liability of $500 or more.

V.   TAX PLANNING CONSIDERATIONS

A.   Tax planning to reduce corporate income taxes should occur before year end.

B.   Particular attention should be focused on:
1.   Charitable contributions
2.   Timing capital gains and losses
3.   Net operating losses
4.   Dividends received deductions
5.   Organizational expenditures
6.   Shareholder-employee payment of corporate expense

Section 170-Charitable Contributions

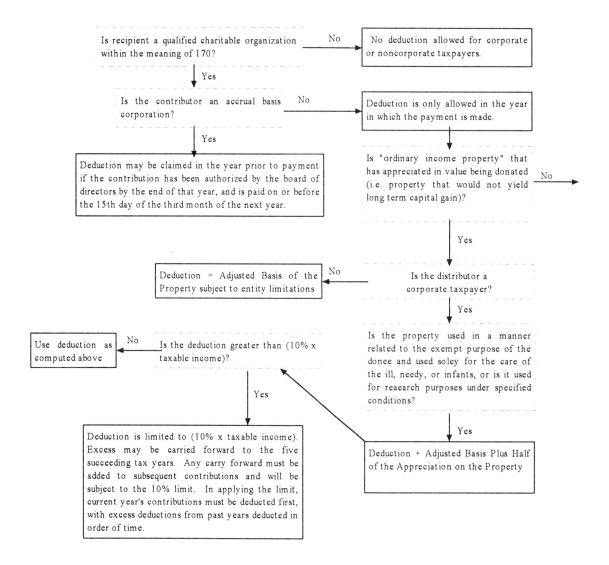

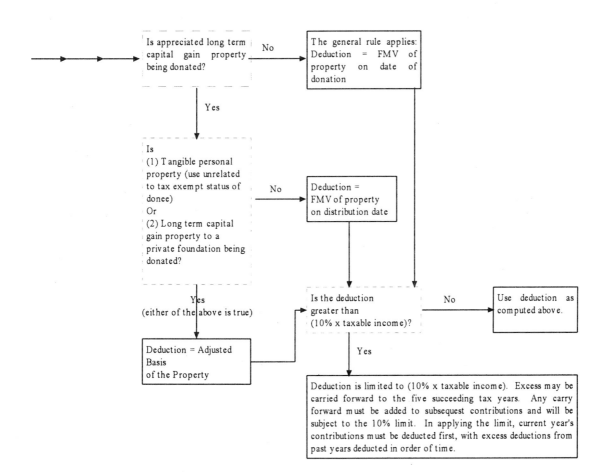

Section 243-Dividends Received Deductions

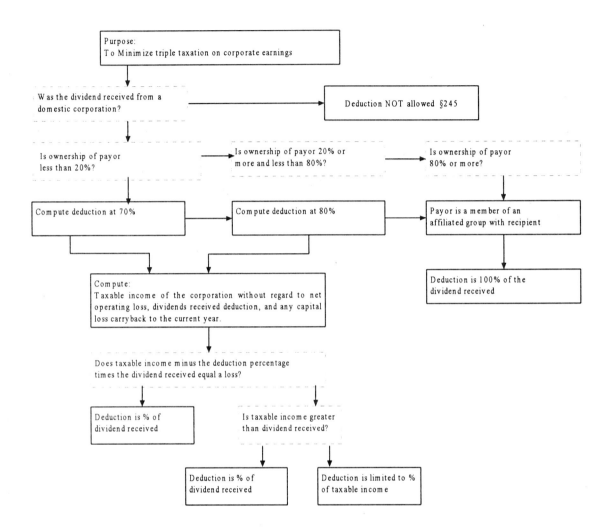

TEST FOR SELF-EVALUATION

True or False

T F 1. A corporation will receive an automatic 6-month extension of time for filing its return by submitting an application for extension on Form 7004. The IRS can terminate this extension at any time by mailing a notice of termination to the corporation. (IRS 96 3A-1)

T F 2. Corporation Y, a calendar year corporation, incurred qualifying organizational expenses of $7,000, and started business on January 1, 1995. Corporation Y may elect to deduct the organizational expenses in full in 1995 or treat them as deferred expenses and amortize them over a period of no less than 60 months. (IRS 96 3A-4)

T F 3. Advertising expenses for the opening of a business of a corporation that has not yet begun its business operations MUST be considered a start-up expense. (IRS 95 3A-3)

T F 4. In 1993, Rock Corporation incurred a net operating loss and elected to forgo the carryback period. Rock incurred another net operating loss in 1994. Since Rock elected to forgo the carryback period for 1993, it CANNOT carry the 1994 net operating loss back to 1991. (IRS 95 3A-7)

T F 5. Corporation W, a calendar year corporation, incurred organizational expenses of $1,000 and started business on January 1, 1990. It filed its return on March 20, 1991, without an extension. We can automatically amortize some of its organizational expenses in 1990. (IRS 91 3A-4)

T F 6. In 1992, a corporation has a net short-term capital gain of $3,000 and a net long-term capital loss of $9,000. The short-term capital gain offsets some of the long-term loss, leaving a net capital loss of $6,000. The corporation treats this $6,000 as a short-term loss when carried back or forward. (IRS 93 3A-5)

T F 7. Generally, the total deduction for dividends received is limited to 70% of the taxable income of a corporation. In figuring this limitation, taxable income is determined without regard to any capital loss carryback to the tax year. (IRS 90 3A-6)

T F 8. During 1992, a corporation set up a contingent liability on its books to take into account a customer's claim. The claim was NOT settled in 1992. The contingent liability is NOT deductible in determining the corporation's 1992 taxable income but it does REDUCE unappropriated retained earnings and is shown as an adjustment on Schedule M-2 of Form 1120. (IRS 93 3A-7)

T F 9.   The component members of a controlled group of corporations are generally limited to one apportionable $50,000 amount and one $25,000 amount (in that order) in each taxable income bracket below 35%. Unless the component members of the controlled group agree to a different allocation, the $50,000 and $25,000 (in that order) amount is to be divided equally among all members.

(IRS 91 3A-11)

T F 10.   If a corporation's capital losses from two or more years are carried to the same year, the loss from the earliest year is deducted first. When that loss is completely used up, the loss from the next earliest year is deducted, and so on.

(IRS 91 3A-9)

Fill in the Blanks

1.   Corporations are to include the amount of net long-term capital gain in _____ .

2.   Corporations may carryback capital losses to the _____ preceding years.

3.   Generally charitable contributions of long-term capital gain property are measured at their _____ on the date of their donation.

4.   The charitable deduction for "ordinary income property" that has appreciated in value is generally limited to the _____ of the property.

5.   For net operating losses of a corporation, the carryback period is _____ years and forward _____ years.

6.   A corporation is required to file its tax return on or before the 15th day of the _____ month following the close of its fiscal year.

7.   A group of corporations form a _____ if each corporation is a member of either a parent-subsidiary controlled group or a brother-sister controlled group, at least one of the corporations is a _____ of a parent-subsidiary controlled group and the parent corporation is also a member of a _____ .

Multiple Choice

_____ 1.   In 1995 Rock Corporation made contributions totaling $20,000 to qualified charitable organizations. Due to the 10% limit, Rock could only deduct $15,000 of the contributions on its return. Which of the following statements regarding the excess contributions of $5,000 is correct?   (IRS 96 3B-23)

    a.   Charitable contributions in excess of the limit may, subject to limitations, be carried back to each of the 3 prior years.
    b.   Charitable contributions in excess of the limit may, subject to limitations, be carried over to each of the following 10 years.
    c.   Charitable contributions in excess of the limit may, subject to limitations, be carried over to each of the following 15 years.
    d.   Charitable contributions in excess of the limit may, subject to limitations, be carried over to each of the following 5 years.

_____ 2.   Ace Corporation, a calendar year corporation, started business on May 1, 1995. The corporation incurred the following expenses related to the organization of the business:

Fee paid to state for incorporation	$2,400
Legal fees for drafting corporation charter and bylaws	$4,200
Cost of printing stock certificates	$1,200
Commission expense on sale of stock	$2,300
Expenses of temporary directors	$2,400

If Ace Corporation elects to amortize its organizational expenses, what is the maximum allowable deduction for 1995?   (IRS 96 3C-49)

    a. $880
    b. $1,040
    c. $1,200
    d. $1,667

_____ 3.   In 1995, Jeffers Corporation experienced a $30,000 loss from operations. It received $200,000 in dividends from a domestic corporation of which Jeffers owns 20% of its total stock outstanding. Jeffers' taxable income before the dividends received deduction was $170,000. What is the amount of Jeffers' dividends received deduction?   (IRS 96 3C-50)

    a. $119,000
    b. $136,000
    c. $140,000
    d. $160,000

_____ 4.   During 1995, PARD Corporation had the following income and expenses

Gross receipts	$350,000
Salaries	$175,000
Contributions to qualified charitable organizations	$ 20,000
Capital gains	$ 3,000
Capital loss carryback	$ 3,000
Depreciation expense	$ 14,000
Dividend income	$ 30,000
Dividend deduction	$ 21,000

What is PARD's charitable contribution deduction for 1995?

(IRS 96 3C-51)

a. $15,000
b. $17,000
c. $19,400
d. $20,000

_____ 5.   During 1995 Page Corportation reported gross income from operations of $200,000 and operating expenses of $300,000. Page Corporation also received dividend income of $180,000 from Taylor, Inc., a domestic corporation, of which Page is a 10% shareholder. What is the amount of Page Corporation's net operating loss?   (IRS 96 3C-52)

a. $0
b. $46,000
c. $64,000
d. $100,000

_____ 6.   WEB Corporation, a calendar-year corporation, estimated its income tax for 1995 will be $20,000. WEB deposited the first two estimated tax installments on April 15 and June 15, 1995 in the amount of $5,000 each (25% of $20,000). On July 1, WEB estimated its tax will be $40,000. How much estimated tax should WEB Corporation pay on September 15?   (IRS 96 3C-54)

a. $20,000
b. $15,000
c. $10,000
d. $5,000

_____ 7.   For tax year 1995, Sting Corporation had net income per books of $65,000, tax exempt interest of $1,500, excess contributions of $3,000, excess tax depreciation over book depreciation of $4,500, premiums paid on term life insurance on corporate officers of $10,000 (Sting is the beneficiary) and accrued federal income tax of $9,700. Based on this information, what is Sting Corporation's taxable income as would be shown on Schedule M-1 of its 1995 corporate tax return?
(IRS 96 3C-56)

a. $58,700
b. $61,700
c. $81,700
d. $93,700

_____ 8.   Which of the following statements concerning the extension of time to file a corporate tax return is FALSE?   (IRS 95 3B-21)

a. A corporation will receive an automatic 6-month extension of time for filing by submitting Form 7004.
b. The Internal Revenue Service can terminate the extension to file at any time by mailing a notice of termination to the corporation.
c. Form 7004 must be filed by the due date of the corporation's income tax return.
d. An automatic extension of time for filing a corporate income tax return also extends the time for paying the tax due on the return.

_____ 9.   An accrual basis corporation's organizational expenses are amortizable
(IRS 95 3B-24)
a. starting with the month the corporation incurred the expenses.
b. starting with the month the corporation paid the expenses.
c. starting with the month the corporation actively engages in business.
d. NEVER, they MUST be capitalized and later deducted when the corporation liquidates.

_____ 10.   Which of the following statements concerning the charitable contribution deduction by a corporation is CORRECT?   (IRS 95 3B-25)

a. A corporation cannot deduct contributions that exceed 10% of its taxable income.
b. A corporation can only deduct contributions to charitable organizations if they are made in cash.
c. A corporation utilizing the accrual basis of accounting must have made the charitable donation by the close of its tax year.
d. A corporation is not permitted to carryover any charitable contributions that were not deducted in the current year.

_____ 11.   Which of the following statements concerning capital losses by corporations other than S corporations is CORRECT?   (IRS 95 3B-26)

a.   Assuming no capital gains to offset the corporation's capital losses, the maximum deduction is $3,000.
b.   A capital loss may NEVER be carried forward.
c.   A net capital loss may be carried back 3 years and carried forward for up to 15 years.
d.   Capital losses can be deducted only up to the amount of capital gains.

_____ 12.   With regard to a controlled corporate group, all of the following statements are CORRECT except: (IRS 95 3B-27)

a.   The controlled group is allowed only ONE set of graduated income tax brackets.
b.   Controlled groups are allowed ONE $40,000 exemption amount for alternative minimum tax purposes.
c.   The controlled group is allowed a $250,000 accumulated earnings credit for EACH member.
d.   The tax benefits of the graduated rate schedule are to be allocated equally among the members of the group unless they all consent to a different apportionment.

_____ 13.   During 1994, XYZ Corporation had the following income and expenses:

Gross receipts	$1,000,000
Salaries	350,000
Contributions to qualified charitable organizations	75,000
Operating Expenses	395,000
Dividend income from a 20% owned corporation	65,000
Dividends received deduction	52,000

What is the amount of XYZ's charitable contribution carryover to 1995?
                    (IRS 95 3C-54)
a. $32,000
b. $43,000
c. $51,000
d. $75,000

_____ 14.   McCormick, Inc., a C corporation, had the following transactions during 1994:

Long-term gain from sale of land	$ 10,000
Long-term gain from sale of stock	20,000
Long-term loss from sale of securities	(40,000)

What is the amount of long-term capital loss that may be taken as a deduction by McCormick in 1994?   (IRS 95 3C-55)

a. $0
b. $10,000
c. $30,000
d. $40,000

_____ 15.   For the tax year ended December 31, 1994, ABC Corporation had gross income of $300,000 and operating expenses of $450,000. Contributions of $2,500 were included in the expenses. In addition to the expenses, ABC Corporation had a net operating loss carryover of $8,000. What is the amount of ABC Corporation's net operating loss for 1994?   (IRS 95 3C-57)

a. $147,500
b. $150,000
c. $152,500
d. $156,500

_____ 16.   Blitz, an accrual method C corporation, had unappropriated retained earnings of $50,000 as of December 31, 1993. For its 1994 tax year, Blitz's books and records reflect the following:

Net income per books (after federal income taxes)	$125,000
Cash distributions	12,500
Federal income tax refund - 1993	17,000

Based on the above, what is Blitz Corporation's unappropriated retained earnings as of December 31, 1994?   (IRS 95 3C-61)

a. $204,500
b. $192,000
c. $179,500
d. $175,500

_____ 17.   For tax year 1994, Ace Corporation had net income per books of $76,000, tax-exempt interest of $4,000, excess contributions of $2,000, meals in excess of 50% limitation of $8,000, and federal income taxes of $18,000. What is the amount of Ace Corporation's taxable income as it would be shown on Schedule M-1 of its corporate income tax return?   (IRS 95 3C-62)

    a. $92,000
    b. $100,000
    c. $104,000
    d. $108,000

_____ 18.   Estimated tax payments must be made if a corporation's estimated tax is at least:
    (IRS 96 3B-24)

    a. $500
    b. $1,000
    c. $1,500
    d. $2,000

SOLUTIONS

True or False

1. T (p. 2-27)
2. F (p. 2-20; amortize or capitalize, not deductible)
3. T (p. 2-21)
4. F (p. 2-18; the election is made on a year by year basis)
5. F (p. 2-20; the election must be timely made)
6. T (p. 2-11)
7. T (p. 2-18)
8. T (p. 2-29)
9. T (p. 2-22)
10. T (p. 2-12)

Fill in the Blanks

1. ordinary income (p. 2-12)
2. three (p. 2-12)
3. fair market value (p. 2-15)
4. adjusted basis (p. 2-15)
5. two; twenty (p. 2-17)
6. third (p. 2-21)
8. combined group; parent; brother-sister controlled group (p. 2-22)

Multiple Choice

1. d (p. 2-16)
2. c (p. 2-20; (2,400 +4,200+2,400)/60 x 8)
3. b (p. 2-18; 80% of 170,000)
4. c (p. 2-16; (350,000+3,000+30,000-175,000-14,000) x 10%)
5. b (p. 2-18; NOL rule)
6. a (p. 2-28; 75% of $40,000 - $10,000)
7. c (p. 2-28; 65,000 - 1,500 + 3,000 - 4,500 + 10,000 + 9,700)
8. d (p. 2-27)
9. c (p. 2-20)
10. a (p. 2-17)
11. d (p. 2-12)
12. c (p. 2-23)
13. b (p. 2-16; 1,000,000 - 350,000 - 395,000 + 65,000 = 320,000; 10% of 320,000 allowed)
14. c (p. 2-12; capital losses offset capital gains)
15. a (p. 2-16; 300,000 - 450,000 + 2,500)
16. c (p. 2-29; 50,000 + 125,000 + 17,000 - 12,500)
17. b (p. 2-28; 76,000 - 4,000 + 2,000 + 8,000 + 18,000)
18. a (p. 2-28)

CHAPTER 3

CORPORATIONS:
ORGANIZATION AND CAPITAL STRUCTURE

LEARNING OBJECTIVES

After completing Chapter 3, you should be able to:

1. Identify the tax consequences of incorporating a business.

2. Understand the special rules that apply when liabilities are assumed by a corporation.

3. Recognize the basis issues relevant to the shareholder and the corporation.

4. Appreciate the tax aspects of the capital structure of a corporation.

5. Recognize the tax differences between debt and equity investments.

6. Handle the tax treatment of shareholder debt and stock losses.

7. Identify tax planning opportunities associated with organizing and financing a corporation.

KEY TERMS

Assumption of liabilities	Liabilities in excess of basis	Qualified small business stock
Capital contribution	Nonbusiness bad debt	Section 1244 stock
Control	Property	Securities
Investor losses	Qualified small business corporation	Thin capitalization

OUTLINE

I.   ORGANIZATION OF AND TRANSFERS TO CONTROLLED CORPORATIONS

    A.   In General
        1.   Normally, gain or loss is recognized on a property transfer.
        2.   The Code provides exceptions where:
            a.   a taxpayer's economic status has not changed, and
            b.   the wherewithal to pay is lacking.
        3.   Section 351 provides nonrecognition of gain or loss when:
            a.   property is transferred for
            b.   stock, and
            c.   the transferors are in control of the transferee corporation.
        4.   Section 351 is mandatory.

    B.   Property Defined
        1.   The Code specifically excludes services rendered.
        2.   With the above exception, the definition of property is comprehensive.

    C.   Stock Transferred
        1.   Common and preferred stock are included in this definition.
        2.   Stock rights or warrants are not included in this definition.
        3.   Any property, other than stock, received in the exchange, by the transferor, is considered boot.
        4.   All corporate debt constitutes boot.
        5.   Boot is taxable to the extent of any gain realized.

    D.   Control of the Corporation
        1.   80% stock ownership
            a.   80% of the total combined voting power, and
            b.   80% of the total number of shares of all other classes of stock.
        2.   Control immediately after the transfer
            a.   may refer to one person or several individuals.
            b.   all transfers need not be made simultaneously.
            c.   for transfers involving more than one person:
                1.   the rights of the persons should be defined, in a written agreement, prior to any transfers.
                2.   the transfers should occur close together in time.
                3.   Transfers for property and services
                    a.   persons who transfer property and perform services for stock are considered members of the transferring group, generally, the value of the property must be at least 10% of the value of the service provided.

        b.   that person is taxed on the value of stock issued for services.

        c.   all the stock received by that person is counted to determine whether or not the control requirement is met.

E.   Assumption of Liabilities

1.   Generally, a corporation's assumption of a liability or acceptance of property subject to a liability does not result in boot to the transferor shareholder.

2.   Liabilities assumed by the corporation are treated as boot for determining the shareholder's basis in the stock received.

3.   Liabilities in excess of basis cause taxable gain because, without this provision, the stock basis would be negative.

F.   Basis Determination

1.   Basis of stock to shareholder

        a.   basis held in the property transferred, plus

        b.   gain recognized on the exchange, minus

        c.   boot received, including any liabilities transferred.

2.   Basis of property to corporation

        a.   transferor's basis, plus

        b.   gain recognized by the transferor shareholder.

3.   Holding period for shareholder's stock received for

        a.   transfer of a capital asset or §1231 property, includes the holding period of the property transferred.

        b.   transfer of inventory, begins the day after the exchange.

4.   Holding period for corporate property received is the holding period of the transferor shareholder.

II.   CAPITAL STRUCTURE OF A CORPORATION

A.   Capital Contributions

1.   The basis of property received by a corporation from a shareholder is the transferor's basis plus gain recognized by the transferor/shareholder.

2.   The basis of property received by a corporation from a nonshareholder is zero.

3.   Money received by a corporation from a nonshareholder

        a.   reduces the basis of any property acquired with the money during the 12 months following receipt of such contribution.

        b.   any excess over the cost of new property reduces the basis of other corporate property in proportion to the relative bases of the properties, in the following order

1. depreciable property
2. amortizable property
3. depletable property
4. all other remaining property.

B. Debt in the Capital Structure
1. Advantages of debt
   a. interest is deductible by the corporation, dividends are not.
   b. shareholders are not taxed on loan repayments.
   c. a stock investment cannot be withdrawn tax-free while the corporation has earnings and profits.
2. Reclassification of debt as equity
   a. a debt instrument having too many features of stock may be treated as a form of stock.
   b. factors to be considered include:
      1. the form of the debt instrument
      2. a definite maturity date and reasonable interest rate
      3. timely payment
      4. subordination to other liabilities
      5. the ratio of debt to equity.

C. Investor Losses
1. Stock and security losses
   a. for stocks and bonds held as capital assets, capital losses materialize as of the last day of the year in which the stocks or bonds become completely worthless.
   b. no deduction is allowed for partial worthlessness.
2. Business versus nonbusiness bad debts
   a. business bad debts are deducted as ordinary losses.
   b. nonbusiness bad debts are treated as short-term capital losses and limited to noncorporate taxpayers.
   c. partial worthlessness can be deducted only for business bad debts.
   d. all corporate bad debts qualify as business bad debts.
3. Section 1244 stock
   a. §1244 allows ordinary loss treatment for losses on the sale or worthlessness of a small business corporation's stock.
   b. the amount of loss deductible in any one year is limited to $50,000 or $100,000 for a jointly filed return.
   c. only the original holder of §1244 stock qualifies for ordinary loss treatment.
   d. to qualify as §1244 stock
      1. the total stock offered cannot exceed $1 million.
      2. more than 50% of the corporation's gross receipts must be derived from the active conduct of a trade or business.

D.   Gain from Qualified Small Business Stock
       1.   Is stock in a C corporation
              a.   issued after August 10, 1993, whose aggregate gross assets did not exceed $50 million on August 10, 1993, through the date the stock was issued.
              b.   who used at least 80% of its assets in the active conduct of a trade or business.
       2.   Noncorporate shareholders may exclude 50% of the gain on a sale or exchange of qualified small business stock.
              a.   the taxpayer must have held the stock for more than 5 years.
              b.   the taxpayer must have acquired the stock as part of an original issue.
       3.   The 50% exclusion can apply to the greater of
              a. $10 million, $5 million for married filing separately, or
              b.   10 times the shareholder's aggregate adjusted basis in the qualified stock disposed of during the year.

III.   TAX PLANNING CONSIDERATIONS

A.   Working with §351
       1.   Does compliance with §351 yield the desired tax result?
       2.   Utilizing §351
              a.   ensure all parties transferring property receive control.
              b.   be sure later transfers of property satisfy the control requirement if gain recognition is to be avoided.

B.   Determine which assets and liabilities should be transferred to the corporation.

C.   The debt to equity ratio of the corporation's capital structure
              a.   thin capitalization and potential reclassification,
              b.   investor losses and §1244 attributes.

TEST FOR SELF-EVALUATION

True or False

T F 1. Mike transferred money and property to Growth Corporation solely in exchange for stock in Growth. Immediately after the exchange, Mike owned 80% of the total combined voting power of all classes of stock entitled to vote and 51% of all other classes of stock. No gain or loss will be recognized by Mike or Growth.
(IRS 96 3A-2)

T F 2. A corporation does not recognize gain or loss if you transfer property and money to the corporation in exchange for the corporation's stock (including treasury stock).
(IRS 96 3A-3)

T F 3. If you acquire an asset in exchange for another asset and your basis for the new asset is figured, in whole or in part, by your basis in the old property, the holding period of the new property begins the day after the date of the exchange.
(IRS 96 3A-5)

T F 4. If the sole shareholder of a corporation receives no additional shares for a contribution of property to the corporation, the basis of the property received by the corporation is the same as it was to the shareholder.   (IRS 96 3A-7)

T F 5. In order to protect her investment, Beth, an officer and principal shareholder of Turbo Corporation, guaranteed payment of a bank loan Turbo received. During 1994, Turbo defaulted on the loan and Beth made full payment. Beth is entitled to a business bad debt deduction.   (IRS 95 2A-9)

T F 6. Steve transferred his services to a corporation in exchange for 85% of all classes of the corporation's stock. Steve will NOT have to report the fair market value of the stock as taxable compensation.   (IRS 95 3A-1)

T F 7. If an individual transfers mortgaged property to a corporation he or she controls, the individual generally will NOT have to recognize gain as a result of the corporation's assumption of a liability unless the liability is greater than the individual's adjusted basis in the property.   (IRS 95 3A-2)

T F 8. On January 1, 1994, Mr. Kitars transferred property he had originally acquired on July 1, 1991, to Westco Corporation in a nontaxable exchange for Westco's stock. After the transfer, Mr. Kitars had control of the corporation. On October 1, 1994, Westco Corporation sold the property for a gain. Westco's holding period does NOT include the period it was held by Mr. Kitars.   (IRS 95 3A-4)

T F 9.   Mr. Oak and Mr. Willow each transferred money and property to newly formed Corporation X. Immediately after this exchange Mr. Oak and Mr. Willow each owned 50% of Corporation X's only class of stock. Mr. Oak and Mr. Willow will NOT recognize a gain or loss on this transaction.   (IRS 93 3A-1)

T F 10.   During 1991, Mrs. Grace sold all her section 1244 stock in two small business corporations. Her loss on Corporation X was $120,000, and her loss on Corporation Y stock was $10,000. Mrs. Grace, who files jointly with her husband, has a deductible $130,000 ordinary loss for 1991.   (IRS 92 2A-9)

Fill in the Blanks

1.   _____ in a §351 transaction does not result in boot to the transferor shareholder.

2.   For _____ of property received from a nonshareholder, the corporation's basis is zero.

3.   _____ immediately after §351 exchange requires _____ stock ownership in the transferee corporation.

4.   _____ transferred, without taxable gain recognition, would cause the transferor shareholder to have a _____ basis in the stock received.

5.   _____ are treated as short-term capital losses of noncorporate taxpayers.

6.   Property for purposes of §351 specifically excludes _____.

7.   _____ allows ordinary loss treatment on the sale or worthlessness of small business corporation's stock.

8.   _____ are long-term debt instruments.

9.   _____ situations arise when shareholder debt is high relative to shareholder equity.

Multiple Choice

_____ 1.   Which of the following factors is NOT taken into account when determining if a gain or loss should be recognized on the transfer of property to a corporation in exchange for a controlling interest in stock of the corporation?

(IRS 96 3B-21)

a.   Receipt of money in addition to the stock.
b.   Fair market value of the property transferred to the corporation.
c.   Ownership of at least 80% of the total combined voting power of all stock entitled to vote.
d.   Ownership of at least 80% of the total number of shares of all other classes of stock.

_____ 2.   During 1995, Randy and Audra formed a corporation to which Randy transferred equipment that had a fair market value of $25,000 and zero adjusted basis. Audra transferred a building that had a fair market value of $100,000 and an adjusted basis to her of $80,000. In return, Randy received 200 shares and Audra received 800 shares of the corporation's outstanding shares of its only class of stock. As a result of this transaction, Audra should report: (IRS 96 3B-22)

a.   Neither a gain or loss.
b.   A section 1250 gain of $20,000.
c.   An ordinary gain of $20,000.
d.   A capital gain of $20,000.

_____ 3.   In exchange for Thunder Corporation stock, Sydney performed legal services for Thunder valued at $7 000 and paid Thunder $18,000 cash. The stock received by Sydney had a fair market value at the time of the exchange of $25,000. What is the amount of Sydney's recognized gain from this exchange? (IRS 96 3C-46)

a. $25,000
b. $18,000
c. $7,000
d. $0

_____ 4.   During 1995, Shelly transferred property having an adjusted basis to her of $20,000 and a fair market value of $27,000 to DLW Corporation. In exchange for the property she received $6,000 cash and 100% of DLW's only class of stock. If the stock received by Shelly had a fair market value of $21,000 at the time of the transfer, what is the amount of her recognized gain?   (IRS 96 3C-47)

a. $0
b. $6,000
c. $7,000
d. $21,000

_____ 5.   Andrew transferred an office building that had an adjusted basis of $180,000 and a fair market value of $350,000 to Dickens Corporation in exchange for 80% of Dickens' only class of stock. The building was subject to a mortgage of $200,000, which Dickens assumed for valid business reasons. The fair market value of the stock on the date of the transfer was $150,000. What is the amount of Andrew's recognized gain?   (IRS 96 3C-48)

    a. $0
    b. $20,000
    c. $170,000
    d. $350,000

_____ 6.   Ms. Witherby purchased 100 shares of qualifying small business (Section 1244) stock for $10,000 on January 2, 1994. On July 1, 1994, Ms Witherby had to make an additional $2,000 contribution to capital which increased her total basis in the 100 shares to $12,000. On November 9, 1994, Ms. Witherby sold the 100 shares for $9,000 to an unrelated party. What is the amount and character of the gain or (loss) Ms. Witherby may claim on her 1994 income tax return? (IRS 95 2C-59)

	Ordinary Loss	Capital Gain or (Loss)
a.	($12,000)	$9,000
b.	($ 3,000)	$ 0
c.	($2,500)	($ 500)
d.	$ 0	($3,000)

_____ 7.   Ferdinand and Isabella transferred money and a business sailing ship for stock in Columbus Corporation. Immediately after the exchange, Ferdinand owned 30% of the voting power and 49% of the total shares of each of the other classes of stock and Isabella owned 55% of the voting power and 36% of the total shares of each of the other classes of stock. Ferdinand and Isabella are not otherwise related. Assuming Ferdinand and Isabella each realized gains on the transaction, which of the following statements would apply?   (IRS 95 3B-22)

    a.   Only Ferdinand will recognize gain on the exchange.
    b.   Only Isabella will recognize gain on the exchange.
    c.   Both Ferdinand and Isabella will recognize gains on the exchange.
    d.   Neither Ferdinand nor Isabella will recognize gain on the exchange.

_____ 8.   The basis of stock received in exchange for property transferred to a corporation is the same as the basis of the property transferred with certain adjustments. Which one of the following would NOT decrease the basis of the stock received?

(IRS 95 3B-23)

a.   The fair market value of other property received.
b.   Any amount treated as a dividend.
c.   Any money received.
d.   Any loss recognized on the exchange.

_____ 9.   Mr. Carroll transferred the title of a condo he owned in Mexico to his 100% owned accounting corporation in exchange for stock worth $5,000. Carroll used the condo for personal purposes and there was no bona fide business reason for the transfer. At the time of the transfer, the condo had an adjusted basis of $160,000, and a mortgage of $165,000 (which was assumed by the corporation). What is the amount of Mr. Carroll's recognized gain?   (IRS 95 3C-47)

a. $165,000
b. $10,000
c. $5,000
d. $0

_____ 10.   Kim transferred property with an adjusted basis of $16,000 and a fair market value of $25,000, to Corporation K in exchange for 90% of K's only class of stock and $3,000 cash. The stock received by Kim had a fair market value of $22,000 at the time of the exchange. What is Corporation K's basis in the property received from Kim?   (IRS 95 3C-48)

a. $25,000
b. $22,000
c. $19,000
d. $16,000

_____ 11.   Anthony, Bill and Chester decided to form Paradise Corporation. Anthony transferred property with an adjusted basis of $35,000 and a fair market value of $44,000 for 440 shares of stock. Bill exchanged $33,000 cash for 350 shares of stock. Chester performed services valued at $33,000 for 330 shares of stock. The fair market value of Paradise Corporation's stock is $100 per share. What is Paradise's basis in the property received from Anthony?   (IRS 95 3C-49)

a. $0
b. $9,000
c. $35,000
d. $44,000

_____ 12.   Ms. R transferred property with an adjusted basis of $60,000 and a fair market value of $55,000 to Rain Corporation. She received in exchange 60% of Rain Corporation's only class of stock. At the time of the transfer, the stock Ms. R received had a fair market value of $65,000. What is Rain Corporation's basis in the property after the exchange?   (IRS 95 3C-50)

    a. $0
    b. $55,000
    c. $60,000
    d. $65,000

_____ 13.   Scott Corporation transferred stock with a fair market value of $20,000 to its creditor in satisfaction of indebtedness of $30,000. The stock's book value was $15,000. How much income from this transaction should Scott include in its 1994 income tax return?   (IRS 95 3C-51)

    a. $0
    b. $5,000
    c. $10,000
    d. $15,000

_____ 14.   In exchange for his old stretch limo that had a fair market value of $50,000 and an adjusted basis of $35,000, Jeeves received 100% of the stock of Wegofast Corporation. The Wegofast stock had a fair market value at the time of the transaction of $40,000. Jeeves also received a used limo that had an adjusted basis to Wegofast of $8,000 and a fair market value at the time of the the transaction of $10,000. What is the amount of Jeeves' recognized gain on this transaction?   (IRS 95 3C-46)

    a. $0
    b. $10,000
    c. $13,000
    d. $15,000

_____ 15.   Frank, an attorney, performed legal services, valued at $2,000, for Joey Corporation, a newly formed corporation in exchange for 1% of the issued and outstanding stock. The fair market value of the shares received was $2,000. Frank would recognize: (IRS 94 3B-22)

    a.   A short term capital gain of $2,000.
    b.   Compensation of $2,000.
    c.   No income until the stock is sold.
    d. $2,000 as ordinary income ratably over 60 months.

SOLUTIONS

True or False

1. F (p. 3-6; 80% of all other classes required)
2. T (p. 3-14)
3. F (p. 3-14; includes the holding period of the asset transferred)
4. F (p. 3-14; additional price paid for shares held)
5. F (p. 3-19; non-business, to protect her investment)
6. F (p. 3-4)
7. T (p. 3-10)
8. F (p. 3-14; holding period does carry over)
9. T (p. 3-3)
10. F (p. 3-20; the loss is limited)

Fill in the Blanks

1. liabilities assumed (p. 3-9)
2. capital contributions (p. 3-15)
3. control, 80% (p. 3-6)
4. liabilities in excess of basis, negative (p. 3-10)
5. nonbusiness bad debts (p. 3-18)
6. services (p. 3-4)
7. §1244 (p. 3-19)
8. bonds (p. 3-5)
9. thin capitalization (p. 3-16)

Multiple Choice

1. b (p. 3-3)
2. a (p. 3-6; combined controlling power)
3. c (p. 3-4; stock for services are compensation)
4. b (p. 3-3; boot received)
5. b (p. 3-10; excess of liabilities over basis)
6. c (p. 3-20; 2,000/12,000(3,000) = 500 capital loss)
7. d (p. 3-6; combined controlling power)
8. b (p. 3-12)
9. b (p. 3-9; no bona fide business purpose)
10. c (p. 3-12; adjusted basis, 16,000 + gain recognized, 3,000)
11. d (p. 3-6; control requirement is not met, FMV of stock & property)
12. d (p. 3-6; control requirement is not met)
13. c (p. 3-14; debt, 30,000 - FMV of stock, 20,000 = income, 10,000)
14. b (p. 3-3; FMV of boot received)
15. b (p. 3-4)

Return Problem

Given the following data, prepare Form 1120, U.S. Corporation Income Tax Return, Form 4562, Depreciation and Amortization and any required schedules.

Name:	ABC Corporation
Address:	123 School Street, Joslin, IL 60838
EIN:	36-6135404
Business Activity:	Manufacture toys for pre-schoolers
Officers:	President, Mary Robert 336-58-5900
	Secretary-Treasurer, Michael Williams 382-31-8401

ABC Corporation was formed on January 2, 1996, by Michael Williams and Mary Robert. Michael and Mary each own ½ of the outstanding common stock; no other class of stock is authorized. Both Michael and Mary are full-time employees of the corporation and each receives a salary of $35,000. Michael handles all paperwork as well as sales and deliveries. Mary designs the toys and supervises production.

ABC rents space for $5,000 per month; the factory and inventory storage areas occupy 85% of this space. The corporation uses the accrual method of accounting and has adopted a calendar year. The specific charge-off method is used for bad debts. Depreciation is calculated under MACRS for both book and tax purposes; no new assets were purchased in 1997. The following amounts represent selected book balances at December 31, 1997.

Gross Sales	$750,000	Machinery		$75,000
Sales returns	2,500	Office equipment		4,500
Raw materials	56,000	Delivery truck		11,000
*Wages: factory	150,000	Accumulated Depreciation		
office	15,000	machinery		29,085
Payroll taxes: factory	15,650	office		1,745
office	4,225	truck		5,720
Insurance: factory	10,000	Advertising		5,000
office	2,000	Telephone		4,800
Heat & electric	16,000	Packaging		7,000
Small tools	1,200	Delivery		2,400
Machinery maintenance	2,200	Dues & subscriptions		725
Materials & supplies	5,000	Office supplies		2,500
Dividends	12,000	Legal & accounting		1,000
Estimated tax payments	15,000	Entertainment		750

*Wages do not include officer salaries.
Portions of the Schedule L, Balance Sheet have been completed for you.

Form **1120**	**U.S. Corporation Income Tax Return**	OMB No. 1545-0123
Department of the Treasury Internal Revenue Service	For calendar year 1997 or tax year beginning _____ , 1997, ending _____ , 19 ____ ▶ Instructions are separate. See page 1 for Paperwork Reduction Act Notice.	**1997**

A Check if a:
1 Consolidated return (attach Form 851) ☐
2 Personal holding co. (attach Sch. PH) ☐
3 Personal service corp. (as defined in Temporary Regs. sec. 1.441-4T— see instructions) ☐

Use IRS label. Otherwise, print or type.

Name

Number, street, and room or suite no. (If a P.O. box, see page 5 of instructions.)

City or town, state, and ZIP code

B Employer Identification number

C Date incorporated

D Total assets (see page 5 of instructions)

E Check applicable boxes: (1) ☐ Initial return   (2) ☐ Final return   (3) ☐ Change of address $

Income

1a	Gross receipts or sales _____ **b** Less returns and allowances _____ **c** Bal ▶	1c	
2	Cost of goods sold (Schedule A, line 8)	2	
3	Gross profit. Subtract line 2 from line 1c	3	
4	Dividends (Schedule C, line 19)	4	
5	Interest	5	
6	Gross rents	6	
7	Gross royalties	7	
8	Capital gain net income (attach Schedule D (Form 1120))	8	
9	Net gain or (loss) from Form 4797, Part II, line 18 (attach Form 4797)	9	
10	Other income (see page 6 of instructions — attach schedule)	10	
11	**Total income.** Add lines 3 through 10 ▶	11	

Deductions (See instructions for limitations on deductions.)

12	Compensation of officers (Schedule E, line 4)	12	
13	Salaries and wages (less employment credits)	13	
14	Repairs and maintenance	14	
15	Bad debts	15	
16	Rents	16	
17	Taxes and licenses	17	
18	Interest	18	
19	Charitable contributions (see page 8 of instructions for 10% limitation)	19	
20	Depreciation (attach Form 4562) ... 20		
21	Less depreciation claimed on Schedule A and elsewhere on return ... 21a	21b	
22	Depletion	22	
23	Advertising	23	
24	Pension, profit-sharing, etc., plans	24	
25	Employee benefit programs	25	
26	Other deductions (attach schedule)	26	
27	**Total deductions.** Add lines 12 through 26 ▶	27	
28	Taxable income before net operating loss deduction and special deductions. Subtract line 27 from line 11	28	
29	**Less:** **a** Net operating loss deduction (see page 9 of instructions) ... 29a		
	b Special deductions (Schedule C, line 20) ... 29b	29c	

Tax and Payments

30	**Taxable income.** Subtract line 29c from line 28	30	
31	**Total tax** (Schedule J, line 10)	31	
32	Payments: **a** 1996 overpayment credited to 1997 ... 32a		
b	1997 estimated tax payments ... 32b		
c	Less 1997 refund applied for on Form 4466 ... 32c ( ) **d** Bal ▶ 32d		
e	Tax deposited with Form 7004 ... 32e		
f	Credit for tax paid on undistributed capital gains (attach Form 2439) ... 32f		
g	Credit for Federal tax on fuels (attach Form 4136). See instructions ... 32g	32h	
33	Estimated tax penalty (see page 10 of instructions). Check if Form 2220 is attached ▶ ☐	33	
34	**Tax due.** If line 32h is smaller than the total of lines 31 and 33, enter amount owed	34	
35	**Overpayment.** If line 32h is larger than the total of lines 31 and 33, enter amount overpaid	35	
36	Enter amount of line 35 you want: **Credited to 1998 estimated tax** ▶ _____ Refunded ▶	36	

Sign Here

Under penalties of perjury, I declare that I have examined this return, including accompanying schedules and statements, and to the best of my knowledge and belief, it is true, correct, and complete. Declaration of preparer (other than taxpayer) is based on all information of which preparer has any knowledge.

▶ _____ Signature of officer   Date   ▶ _____ Title

Paid Preparer's Use Only

Preparer's signature ▶	Date	Check if self-employed ☐	Preparer's social security number
Firm's name (or yours if self-employed) and address ▶		EIN ▶	
		ZIP code ▶	

ISA
STF FED3903F.1

Form 1120 (1997) Page **2**

Schedule A Cost of Goods Sold (See page 10 of instructions.)

1	Inventory at beginning of year	**1**
2	Purchases	**2**
3	Cost of labor	**3**
4	Additional section 263A costs (attach schedule)	**4**
5	Other costs (attach schedule)	**5**
6	**Total.** Add lines 1 through 5	**6**
7	Inventory at end of year	**7**
8	**Cost of goods sold.** Subtract line 7 from line 6. Enter here and on page 1, line 2	**8**

9a Check all methods used for valuing closing inventory:
- (i) ☐ Cost as described in Regulations section 1.471-3
- (ii) ☐ Lower of cost or market as described in Regulations section 1.471-4
- (iii) ☐ Other (Specify method used and attach explanation.) ▶ _____

b Check if there was a writedown of subnormal goods as described in Regulations section 1.471-2(c) .... ▶ ☐

c Check if the LIFO inventory method was adopted this tax year for any goods (if checked, attach Form 970) .... ▶ ☐

d If the LIFO inventory method was used for this tax year, enter percentage (or amounts) of closing inventory computed under LIFO **9d**

e If property is produced or acquired for resale, do the rules of section 263A apply to the corporation? .... ☐ Yes ☐ No

f Was there any change in determining quantities, cost, or valuations between opening and closing inventory? If "Yes," attach explanation .... ☐ Yes ☐ No

Schedule C Dividends and Special Deductions (See page 11 of instructions.)

		(a) Dividends received	(b) %	(c) Special deductions (a) × (b)
1	Dividends from less-than-20%-owned domestic corporations that are subject to the 70% deduction (other than debt-financed stock)		70	
2	Dividends from 20%-or-more-owned domestic corporations that are subject to the 80% deduction (other than debt-financed stock)		80	
3	Dividends on debt-financed stock of domestic and foreign corporations (section 246A)		see instructions	
4	Dividends on certain preferred stock of less-than-20%-owned public utilities		42	
5	Dividends on certain preferred stock of 20%-or-more-owned public utilities		48	
6	Dividends from less-than-20%-owned foreign corporations and certain FSCs that are subject to the 70% deduction		70	
7	Dividends from 20%-or-more-owned foreign corporations and certain FSCs that are subject to the 80% deduction		80	
8	Dividends from wholly owned foreign subsidiaries subject to the 100% deduction (section 245(b))		100	
9	**Total.** Add lines 1 through 8. See page 12 of instructions for limitation			
10	Dividends from domestic corporations received by a small business investment company operating under the Small Business Investment Act of 1958		100	
11	Dividends from certain FSCs that are subject to the 100% deduction (section 245(c)(1))		100	
12	Dividends from affiliated group members subject to the 100% deduction (section 243(a)(3))		100	
13	Other dividends from foreign corporations not included on lines 3, 6, 7, 8, or 11			
14	Income from controlled foreign corporations under subpart F (attach Form(s) 5471)			
15	Foreign dividend gross-up (section 78)			
16	IC-DISC and former DISC dividends not included on lines 1, 2, or 3 (section 246(d))			
17	Other dividends			
18	Deduction for dividends paid on certain preferred stock of public utilities			
19	**Total dividends.** Add lines 1 through 17. Enter here and on line 4, page 1 ▶			
20	**Total special deductions.** Add lines 9, 10, 11, 12, and 18. Enter here and on line 29b, page 1 ▶			

Schedule E Compensation of Officers (See instructions for line 12, page 1.)

Complete Schedule E only if total receipts (line 1a plus lines 4 through 10 on page 1, Form 1120) are $500,000 or more.

(a) Name of officer	(b) Social security number	(c) Percent of time devoted to business	Percent of corporation stock owned (d) Common	(e) Preferred	(f) Amount of compensation
1		%	%	%	
		%	%	%	
		%	%	%	
		%	%	%	
		%	%	%	

2	Total compensation of officers	
3	Compensation of officers claimed on Schedule A and elsewhere on return	
4	Subtract line 3 from line 2. Enter the result here and on line 12, page 1	

STF FED3903F.2

Form 1120 (1997)   Page **3**

Schedule J — Tax Computation (See page 12 of instructions.)

1   Check if the corporation is a member of a controlled group (see sections 1561 and 1563) . . . . ▶ ☐

   Important: Members of a controlled group, see instructions on page 12.

2a If the box on line 1 is checked, enter the corporation's share of the $50,000, $25,000, and $9,925,000 taxable income brackets (in that order):

   (1) $ _____   **(2)** $ _____   **(3)** $ _____

b   Enter the corporation's share of:

   (1) Additional 5% tax (not more than $11,750) $ _____

   (2) Additional 3% tax (not more than $100,000) $ _____

3   Income tax. Check this box if the corporation is a qualified personal service corporation as defined in section 448(d)(2) (see instructions on page 13) . . . . ▶ ☐ | **3** |

4a Foreign tax credit (attach Form 1118) . . . . | **4a** |

b   Possessions tax credit (attach Form 5735) . . . . | **4b** |

c   Check: ☐ Nonconventional source fuel credit   ☐ QEV credit (attach Form 8834) | **4c** |

d   General business credit. Enter here and check which forms are attached: ☐ 3800

   ☐ 3468   ☐ 5884   ☐ 6478   ☐ 6765   ☐ 8586   ☐ 8830   ☐ 8826

   ☐ 8835   ☐ 8844   ☐ 8845   ☐ 8846   ☐ 8820   ☐ 8847   ☐ 8861 | **4d** |

e   Credit for prior year minimum tax (attach Form 8827) . . . . | **4e** |

5   **Total credits.** Add lines 4a through 4e . . . . | **5** |

6   Subtract line 5 from line 3 . . . . | **6** |

7   Personal holding company tax (attach Schedule PH (Form 1120)) . . . . | **7** |

8   Recapture taxes. Check if from: ☐ Form 4255   ☐ Form 8611 . . . . | **8** |

9   Alternative minimum tax (attach Form 4626) . . . . | **9** |

10 **Total tax.** Add lines 6 through 9. Enter here and on line 31, page 1 . . . . | **10** |

Schedule K — Other Information (See page 14 of instructions.)

1   Check method of accounting: **a** ☐ Cash   **b** ☐ Accrual   **c** ☐ Other (specify) ▶ _____

2   See page 16 of the instructions and state the principal:

a   Business activity code no. ▶ _____

b   Business activity ▶ _____

c   Product or service ▶ _____

3   At the end of the tax year, did the corporation own, directly or indirectly, 50% or more of the voting stock of a domestic corporation? (For rules of attribution, see section 267(c).) . .

   If "Yes," attach a schedule showing: **(a)** name and identifying number, **(b)** percentage owned, and **(c)** taxable income or (loss) before NOL and special deductions of such corporation for the tax year ending with or within your tax year.

4   Is the corporation a subsidiary in an affiliated group or a parent-subsidiary controlled group? . . . .

   If "Yes," enter employer identification number and name of the parent corporation ▶ _____

5   At the end of the tax year, did any individual, partnership, corporation, estate or trust own, directly or indirectly, 50% or more of the corporation's voting stock? (For rules of attribution, see section 267(c).) . . . .

   If "Yes," attach a schedule showing name and identifying number. (Do not include any information already entered in **4** above.) Enter percentage owned ▶ _____

6   During this tax year, did the corporation pay dividends (other than stock dividends and distributions in exchange for stock) in excess of the corporation's current and accumulated earnings and profits? (See secs. 301 and 316.) . . . .

   If "Yes," file Form 5452. If this is a consolidated return, answer here for the parent corporation and on **Form 851,** Affiliations Schedule, for each subsidiary.

7   Was the corporation a U.S. shareholder of any controlled foreign corporation? (See sections 951 and 957.) . . . .

   If "Yes," attach Form 5471 for each such corporation. Enter number of Forms 5471 attached ▶ _____

8   At any time during the 1997 calendar year, did the corporation have an interest in or a signature or other authority over a financial account (such as a bank account, securities account, or other financial account) in a foreign country?

   If "Yes," the corporation may have to file Form TD F 90-22.1.

   If "Yes," enter name of foreign country ▶ _____

9   During the tax year, did the corporation receive a distribution from, or was it the grantor of, or transferor to, a foreign trust? If "Yes," see page 15 of the instructions for other forms the corporation may have to file . . . .

10 At any time during the tax year, did one foreign person own, directly or indirectly, at least 25% of: **(a)** the total voting power of all classes of stock of the corporation entitled to vote, or **(b)** the total value of all classes of stock of the corporation? If "Yes,"

a   Enter percentage owned ▶ _____

b   Enter owner's country ▶ _____

c   The corporation may have to file Form 5472. Enter number of Forms 5472 attached ▶ _____

11 Check this box if the corporation issued publicly offered debt instruments with original issue discount . . . . ▶ ☐

   If so, the corporation may have to file Form 8281.

12 Enter the amount of tax-exempt interest received or accrued during the tax year ▶ $ _____

13 If there were 35 or fewer shareholders at the end of the tax year, enter the number ▶ _____

14 If the corporation has an NOL for the tax year and is electing to forego the carryback period, check here . . . . ▶ ☐

15 Enter the available NOL carryover from prior tax years (Do not reduce it by any deduction on line 29a.) ▶ $ _____

Form 1120 (1997)   Page **4**

Schedule L	Balance Sheets per Books	Beginning of tax year		End of tax year	
	Assets	**(a)**	**(b)**	**(c)**	**(d)**
1	Cash		11,338		32,408
2a	Trade notes and accounts receivable	23,100		65,595	
b	Less allowance for bad debts	( )	23,100	( )	65,595
3	Inventories		61,621		46,718
4	U.S. government obligations				
5	Tax-exempt securities (see instructions)				
6	Other current assets (attach schedule)				
7	Loans to stockholders				
8	Mortgage and real estate loans				
9	Other investments (attach schedule)				
10a	Buildings and other depreciable assets	90,500			
b	Less accumulated depreciation	(13,561)	76,939	( )	
11a	Depletable assets				
b	Less accumulated depletion	( )		( )	
12	Land (net of any amortization)				
13a	Intangible assets (amortizable only)				
b	Less accumulated amortization	( )		( )	
14	Other assets (attach schedule)				
15	Total assets		172,998		144,721
	Liabilities and Stockholders' Equity				
16	Accounts payable		48,810		23,325
17	Mortgages, notes, bonds payable in less than 1 year				
18	Other current liabilities (attach schedule)				
19	Loans from stockholders				
20	Mortgages, notes, bonds payable in 1 year or more				
21	Other liabilities (attach schedule)				
22	Capital stock: a Preferred stock				
	b Common stock	100,000	100,000	100,000	100,000
23	Additional paid-in capital				
24	Retained earnings — Appropriated (attach schedule)				
25	Retained earnings — Unappropriated		24,188		
26	Adjustments to shareholders' equity (attach schedule)				
27	Less cost of treasury stock		( )		( )
28	Total liabilities and stockholders' equity		172,998		123,325

Note: *You are not required to complete Schedules M-1 and M-2 below if the total assets on line 15, column (d) of Schedule L are less than $25,000.*

Schedule M-1	Reconciliation of Income (Loss) per Books With Income per Return (See page 15 of instructions.)

1	Net income (loss) per books		7	Income recorded on books this year not included on this return (itemize):
2	Federal income tax			Tax-exempt interest $ _____
3	Excess of capital losses over capital gains			_____
4	Income subject to tax not recorded on books this year (itemize): _____		8	Deductions on this return not charged against book income this year (itemize):
	_____		a	Depreciation ...... $ _____
5	Expenses recorded on books this year not deducted on this return (itemize):		b	Contributions carryover $ _____
a	Depreciation .... $ _____			_____
b	Contributions carryover $ _____			_____
c	Travel and entertainment $ _____			_____
	_____		9	Add lines 7 and 8
	_____		10	Income (line 28, page 1) — line 6 less line 9
6	Add lines 1 through 5			

Schedule M-2	Analysis of Unappropriated Retained Earnings per Books (Line 25, Schedule L)

1	Balance at beginning of year		5	Distributions: a Cash
2	Net income (loss) per books			b Stock
3	Other increases (itemize): _____			c Property
	_____		6	Other decreases (itemize): _____
	_____		7	Add lines 5 and 6
4	Add lines 1, 2, and 3		8	Balance at end of year (line 4 less line 7)

Form **4562**	**Depreciation and Amortization**	OMB No. 1545-0172
Department of the Treasury Internal Revenue Service (99)	(Including Information on Listed Property) ▶ See separate instructions. ▶ Attach this form to your return.	**1997** Attachment Sequence No. **67**

Name(s) shown on return	Business or activity to which this form relates	Identifying number

Part I   Election To Expense Certain Tangible Property (Section 179) (Note: *If you have any "listed property," complete Part V before you complete Part I.*)

1	Maximum dollar limitation. If an enterprise zone business, see page 2 of the instructions	**1**	$18,000
2	Total cost of section 179 property placed in service. See page 2 of the instructions	**2**	
3	Threshold cost of section 179 property before reduction in limitation	**3**	$200,000
4	Reduction in limitation. Subtract line 3 from line 2. If zero or less, enter -0-	**4**	
5	Dollar limitation for tax year. Subtract line 4 from line 1. If zero or less, enter -0-. If married filing separately, see page 2 of the instructions	**5**	

(a) Description of property	(b) Cost (business use only)	(c) Elected cost	
6			

7	Listed property. Enter amount from line 27 . . . . [**7**]		
8	Total elected cost of section 179 property. Add amounts in column (c), lines 6 and 7	**8**	
9	Tentative deduction. Enter the smaller of line 5 or line 8	**9**	
10	Carryover of disallowed deduction from 1996. See page 3 of the instructions	**10**	
11	Business income limitation. Enter the smaller of business income (not less than zero) or line 5 (see instructions) . .	**11**	
12	Section 179 expense deduction. Add lines 9 and 10, but do not enter more than line 11	**12**	
13	Carryover of disallowed deduction to 1998. Add lines 9 and 10, less line 12 . . . . . ▶ [**13**]		

Note: Do not use Part II or Part III below for listed property (automobiles, certain other vehicles, cellular telephones, certain computers, or property used for entertainment, recreation, or amusement). Instead, use Part V for listed property.

Part II   MACRS Depreciation For Assets Placed in Service ONLY During Your 1997 Tax Year (Do Not Include Listed Property.)

Section A — General Asset Account Election

14	If you are making the election under section 168(i)(4) to group any assets placed in service during the tax year into one or more general asset accounts, check this box. See page 3 of the instructions . . . . ▶ ☐

Section B — General Depreciation System (GDS) (See page 3 of the instructions.)

(a) Classification of property	(b) Month and year placed in service	(c) Basis for depreciation (business/investment use only — see instructions)	(d) Recovery period	(e) Convention	(f) Method	(g) Depreciation deduction
15a 3-year property						
b 5-year property						
c 7-year property						
d 10-year property						
e 15-year property						
f 20-year property						
g 25-year property			25 yrs.		S/L	
h Residential rental			27.5 yrs.	MM	S/L	
property			27.5 yrs.	MM	S/L	
i Nonresidential real			39 yrs.	MM	S/L	
property				MM	S/L	

Section C — Alternative Depreciation System (ADS) (See page 6 of the instructions.)

(a) Classification of property	(b)	(c)	(d) Recovery period	(e) Convention	(f) Method	(g)
16a Class life					S/L	
b 12-year			12 yrs.		S/L	
c 40-year			40 yrs.	MM	S/L	

Part III   Other Depreciation (Do Not Include Listed Property.) (See page 6 of the instructions.)

17	GDS and ADS deductions for assets placed in service in tax years beginning before 1997	**17**	
18	Property subject to section 168(f)(1) election	**18**	
19	ACRS and other depreciation	**19**	

Part IV   Summary (See page 7 of the instructions.)

20	Listed property. Enter amount from line 26	**20**	
21	**Total.** Add deductions on line 12, lines 15 and 16 in column (g), and lines 17 through 20. Enter here and on the appropriate lines of your return. Partnerships and S corporations — see instructions	**21**	
22	For assets shown above and placed in service during the current year, enter the portion of the basis attributable to section 263A costs . . . . [**22**]		

For Paperwork Reduction Act Notice, see the separate instructions.   ISA

Form **4562** (1997)

Part V   Listed Property — Automobiles, Certain Other Vehicles, Cellular Telephones, Certain Computers, and Property Used for Entertainment, Recreation, or Amusement

Note: For any vehicle for which you are using the standard mileage rate or deducting lease expense, complete only 23a, 23b, columns (a) through (c) of Section A, all of Section B, and Section C if applicable.

Section A — Depreciation and Other Information (Caution: See page 8 of the instructions for limits for passenger automobiles.)

23a Do you have evidence to support the business/investment use claimed? ☐ Yes ☐ No   23b If "Yes," is the evidence written? ☐ Yes ☐ No

(a) Type of property (list vehicles first)	(b) Date placed in service	(c) Business/ investment use percentage	(d) Cost or other basis	(e) Basis for depreciation (business/investment use only)	(f) Recovery period	(g) Method/ Convention	(h) Depreciation deduction	(i) Elected section 179 cost
24 Property used more than 50% in a qualified business use (See page 7 of the instructions.):								
		%						
		%						
		%						
25 Property used 50% or less in a qualified business use (See page 7 of the instructions.):								
		%				S/L –		
		%				S/L –		
		%				S/L –		

26 Add amounts in column (h). Enter the total here and on line 20, page 1 . . . . | 26 |
27 Add amounts in column (i). Enter the total here and on line 7, page 1 . . . . | 27 |

Section B — Information on Use of Vehicles

Complete this section for vehicles used by a sole proprietor, partner, or other "more than 5% owner," or related person.
If you provided vehicles to your employees, first answer the questions in Section C to see of you meet an exception to completing this section for those vehicles.

	(a) Vehicle 1		(b) Vehicle 2		(c) Vehicle 3		(d) Vehicle 4		(e) Vehicle 5		(f) Vehicle 6	
28 Total business/investment miles driven during the year (DO NOT include commuting miles)												
29 Total commuting miles driven during the year												
30 Total other personal (noncommuting) miles driven												
31 Total miles driven during the year. Add lines 28 through 30												
	Yes	No	Yes	No	Yes	No	Yes	No	Yes	No	Yes	No
32 Was the vehicle available for personal use during off-duty hours?												
33 Was the vehicle used primarily by a more than 5% owner or related person?												
34 Is another vehicle available for personal use?												

Section C — Questions for Employers Who Provide Vehicles for Use by Their Employees

Answer these questions to determine if you meet an exception to completing Section B for vehicles used by employees who **are not** more than 5% owners or related persons.

	Yes	No
35 Do you maintain a written policy statement that prohibits all personal use of vehicles, including commuting, by your employees?		
36 Do you maintain a written policy statement that prohibits personal use of vehicles, except commuting, by your employees? See page 9 of the instructions for vehicles used by corporate officers, directors, or 1% or more owners		
37 Do you treat all use of vehicles by employees as personal use?		
38 Do you provide more than five vehicles to your employees, obtain information from your employees about the use of the vehicles, and retain the information received?		
39 Do you meet the requirements concerning qualified automobile demonstration use? See page 9 of the instructions.		

Note: *If your answer to 35, 36, 37, 38, or 39 is "Yes," you need not complete Section B of the covered vehicles.*

Part VI   Amortization

(a) Description of costs	(b) Date amortization begins	(c) Amortizable amount	(d) Code section	(e) Amortization period or percentage	(f) Amortization for this year
40 Amortization of costs that begins during your 1997 tax year:					
41 Amortization of costs that began before 1997			41		
42 **Total.** Enter here and on "Other Deductions" or "Other Expenses" line of your return			42		

STF FED5085F 2

Form 1120 — U.S. Corporation Income Tax Return

Department of the Treasury / Internal Revenue Service

For calendar year 1997 or tax year beginning _____ , 1997, ending _____ , 19 ___

► Instructions are separate. See page 1 for Paperwork Reduction Act Notice.

OMB No. 1545-0123 — **1997**

A Check if a:
1 Consolidated return (attach Form 851) ☐
2 Personal holding co. (attach Sch. PH) ☐
3 Personal service corp. (as defined in Temporary Regs. sec. 1.441-4T— see instructions) ☐

Use IRS label. Otherwise, print or type.

Name: ABC CORPORATION
Number, street, and room or suite no. (If a P.O. box, see page 5 of instructions.): 123 SCHOOL STREET
City or town, state, and ZIP code: JOSLIN IL 60838

B Employer Identification number: 36-6135404
C Date incorporated: 01/02/96
D Total assets (see page 5 of instructions): $ 198,720

E Check applicable boxes: (1) Initial return ☐ (2) Final return ☐ (3) Change of address ☐

Income

Line	Description	Amount
1a	Gross receipts or sales 750,000 b Less returns and allowances 2,500 c Bal ► 1c	747,500
2	Cost of goods sold (Schedule A, line 8)	572,920
3	Gross profit. Subtract line 2 from line 1c	174,580
4	Dividends (Schedule C, line 19)	
5	Interest	
6	Gross rents	
7	Gross royalties	
8	Capital gain net income (attach Schedule D (Form 1120))	
9	Net gain or (loss) from Form 4797, Part II, line 18 (attach Form 4797)	
10	Other income (see page 6 of instructions — attach schedule)	
11	**Total income.** Add lines 3 through 10 ►	174,580

Deductions (See instructions for limitations on deductions.)

Line	Description	Amount
12	Compensation of officers (Schedule E, line 4)	35,000
13	Salaries and wages (less employment credits)	15,000
14	Repairs and maintenance	
15	Bad debts	
16	Rents	9,000
17	Taxes and licenses	4,225
18	Interest	
19	Charitable contributions (see page 8 of instructions for 10% limitation)	
20	Depreciation (attach Form 4562) [20] 22,989	
21	Less depreciation claimed on Schedule A and elsewhere on return [21a] 18,367 21b	4,622
22	Depletion	
23	Advertising	5,000
24	Pension, profit-sharing, etc., plans	
25	Employee benefit programs	
26	Other deductions (attach schedule)	23,200
27	**Total deductions.** Add lines 12 through 26 ►	96,047
28	Taxable income before net operating loss deduction and special deductions. Subtract line 27 from line 11	78,533
29	Less: a Net operating loss deduction (see page 9 of instructions) [29a] b Special deductions (Schedule C, line 20) [29b] 29c	
30	**Taxable income.** Subtract line 29c from line 28	78,533
31	**Total tax** (Schedule J, line 10)	14,951

Tax and Payments

Line	Description	Amount
32	Payments: a 1996 overpayment credited to 1997 [32a]	
b	1997 estimated tax payments [32b] 15,000	
c	Less 1997 refund applied for on Form 4466 [32c] ( ) d Bal ► [32d] 15,000	
e	Tax deposited with Form 7004 [32e]	
f	Credit for tax paid on undistributed capital gains (attach Form 2439) [32f]	
g	Credit for Federal tax on fuels (attach Form 4136). See instructions [32g] 32h	15,000
33	Estimated tax penalty (see page 10 of instructions). Check if Form 2220 is attached ► ☐	
34	**Tax due.** If line 32h is smaller than the total of lines 31 and 33, enter amount owed	0
35	**Overpayment.** If line 32h is larger than the total of lines 31 and 33, enter amount overpaid	49
36	Enter amount of line 35 you want: **Credited to 1998 estimated tax** ► **Refunded** ►	49

Sign Here

Under penalties of perjury, I declare that I have examined this return, including accompanying schedules and statements, and to the best of my knowledge and belief, it is true, correct, and complete. Declaration of preparer (other than taxpayer) is based on all information of which preparer has any knowledge.

Signature of officer _____ Date _____ Title _____

Paid Preparer's Use Only

Preparer's signature _____ Date _____ Check if self-employed ☐ Preparer's social security number _____
Firm's name (or yours if self-employed) and address _____ EIN ► _____ ZIP code ► _____

ISA
STF FED3903F.1

Form 1120 (1997)   Page **2**

Schedule A — Cost of Goods Sold (See page 10 of instructions.)

1	Inventory at beginning of year	1	61,621
2	Purchases	2	256,000
3	Cost of labor	3	185,000
4	Additional section 263A costs (attach schedule)	4	
5	Other costs (attach schedule)	5	117,017
6	**Total.** Add lines 1 through 5	6	619,638
7	Inventory at end of year	7	46,718
8	**Cost of goods sold.** Subtract line 7 from line 6. Enter here and on page 1, line 2	8	572,920

9a Check all methods used for valuing closing inventory:

(i) ☐ Cost as described in Regulations section 1.471-3

(ii) ☐ Lower of cost or market as described in Regulations section 1.471-4

(iii) ☐ Other (Specify method used and attach explanation.) ▶ _____

b Check if there was a writedown of subnormal goods as described in Regulations section 1.471-2(c) .... ▶ ☐

c Check if the LIFO inventory method was adopted this tax year for any goods (if checked, attach Form 970) .... ▶ ☐

d If the LIFO inventory method was used for this tax year, enter percentage (or amounts) of closing inventory computed under LIFO .... | 9d | |

e If property is produced or acquired for resale, do the rules of section 263A apply to the corporation? .... ☐ Yes ☐ No

f Was there any change in determining quantities, cost, or valuations between opening and closing inventory? If "Yes," attach explanation .... ☐ Yes ☐ No

Schedule C — Dividends and Special Deductions (See page 11 of instructions.)

		(a) Dividends received	(b) %	(c) Special deductions (a) × (b)
1	Dividends from less-than-20%-owned domestic corporations that are subject to the 70% deduction (other than debt-financed stock)		70	
2	Dividends from 20%-or-more-owned domestic corporations that are subject to the 80% deduction (other than debt-financed stock)		80	
3	Dividends on debt-financed stock of domestic and foreign corporations (section 246A)		see instructions	
4	Dividends on certain preferred stock of less-than-20%-owned public utilities		42	
5	Dividends on certain preferred stock of 20%-or-more-owned public utilities		48	
6	Dividends from less-than-20%-owned foreign corporations and certain FSCs that are subject to the 70% deduction		70	
7	Dividends from 20%-or-more-owned foreign corporations and certain FSCs that are subject to the 80% deduction		80	
8	Dividends from wholly owned foreign subsidiaries subject to the 100% deduction (section 245(b))		100	
9	**Total.** Add lines 1 through 8. See page 12 of instructions for limitation			
10	Dividends from domestic corporations received by a small business investment company operating under the Small Business Investment Act of 1958		100	
11	Dividends from certain FSCs that are subject to the 100% deduction (section 245(c)(1))		100	
12	Dividends from affiliated group members subject to the 100% deduction (section 243(a)(3))		100	
13	Other dividends from foreign corporations not included on lines 3, 6, 7, 8, or 11			
14	Income from controlled foreign corporations under subpart F (attach Form(s) 5471)			
15	Foreign dividend gross-up (section 78)			
16	IC-DISC and former DISC dividends not included on lines 1, 2, or 3 (section 246(d))			
17	Other dividends			
18	Deduction for dividends paid on certain preferred stock of public utilities			
19	**Total dividends.** Add lines 1 through 17. Enter here and on line 4, page 1 ▶			
20	**Total special deductions.** Add lines 9, 10, 11, 12, and 18. Enter here and on line 29b, page 1 ▶			

Schedule E — Compensation of Officers (See instructions for line 12, page 1.)

Complete Schedule E only if total receipts (line 1a plus lines 4 through 10 on page 1, Form 1120) are $500,000 or more.

(a) Name of officer	(b) Social security number	(c) Percent of time devoted to business	(d) Common	(e) Preferred	(f) Amount of compensation
1 Michael Williams	382-31-8401	100 %	50 %	%	35,000
Mary Roberts	336-58-5900	100 %	50 %	%	35,000
		%	%	%	
		%	%	%	
		%	%	%	

2	Total compensation of officers	70,000
3	Compensation of officers claimed on Schedule A and elsewhere on return	35,000
4	Subtract line 3 from line 2. Enter the result here and on line 12, page 1	35,000

STF FED3903F.2

Form 1120 (1997)   Page **3**

Schedule J	Tax Computation (See page 12 of instructions.)

1   Check if the corporation is a member of a controlled group (see sections 1561 and 1563) .... ▶ ☐
   Important: Members of a controlled group, see instructions on page 12.

2a If the box on line 1 is checked, enter the corporation's share of the $50,000, $25,000, and $9,925,000 taxable income brackets (in that order):

   (1) |$ _____   (2) |$ _____   (3) |$ _____

 b Enter the corporation's share of:

   (1) Additional 5% tax (not more than $11,750) $ _____
   (2) Additional 3% tax (not more than $100,000) $ _____

3   Income tax. Check this box if the corporation is a qualified personal service corporation as defined in section 448(d)(2) (see instructions on page 13) .... ▶ ☐ | **3** | 14,951

4a Foreign tax credit (attach Form 1118) .... | **4a** |
 b Possessions tax credit (attach Form 5735) .... | **4b** |
 c Check: ☐ Nonconventional source fuel credit ☐ QEV credit (attach Form 8834) | **4c** |
 d General business credit. Enter here and check which forms are attached: ☐ 3800
   ☐ 3468 ☐ 5884 ☐ 6478 ☐ 6765 ☐ 8586 ☐ 8830 ☐ 8826
   ☐ 8835 ☐ 8844 ☐ 8845 ☐ 8846 ☐ 8820 ☐ 8847 ☐ 8861 | **4d** |
 e Credit for prior year minimum tax (attach Form 8827) .... | **4e** |

5   **Total credits.** Add lines 4a through 4e .... | **5** |
6   Subtract line 5 from line 3 .... | **6** | 14,951
7   Personal holding company tax (attach Schedule PH (Form 1120)) .... | **7** |
8   Recapture taxes. Check if from: ☐ Form 4255 ☐ Form 8611 .... | **8** |
9   Alternative minimum tax (attach Form 4626) .... | **9** |
10 **Total tax.** Add lines 6 through 9. Enter here and on line 31, page 1 .... | **10** | 14,951

Schedule K	Other Information (See page 14 of instructions.)

                                                                  Yes | No

1   Check method of accounting: a ☐ Cash
    b ☒ Accrual   c ☐ Other (specify) ▶ _____

2   See page 16 of the instructions and state the principal:
 a Business activity code no. ▶ 3998
 b Business activity ▶ Manufacturing
 c Product or service ▶ Toys

3   At the end of the tax year, did the corporation own, directly or indirectly, 50% or more of the voting stock of a domestic corporation? (For rules of attribution, see section 267(c).) .. | | X
    If "Yes," attach a schedule showing: (a) name and identifying number, (b) percentage owned, and (c) taxable income or (loss) before NOL and special deductions of such corporation for the tax year ending with or within your tax year.

4   Is the corporation a subsidiary in an affiliated group or a parent-subsidiary controlled group? .... | | X
    If "Yes," enter employer identification number and name of the parent corporation ▶ _____

5   At the end of the tax year, did any individual, partnership, corporation, estate or trust own, directly or indirectly, 50% or more of the corporation's voting stock? (For rules of attribution, see section 267(c).) .... | X |
    If "Yes," attach a schedule showing name and identifying number. (Do not include any information already entered in 4 above.) Enter percentage owned ▶ 50.

6   During this tax year, did the corporation pay dividends (other than stock dividends and distributions in exchange for stock) in excess of the corporation's current and accumulated earnings and profits? (See secs. 301 and 316.) .... | | X
    If "Yes," file Form 5452. If this is a consolidated return, answer here for the parent corporation and on **Form 851,** Affiliations Schedule, for each subsidiary.

                                                                  Yes | No

7   Was the corporation a U.S. shareholder of any controlled foreign corporation? (See sections 951 and 957.) .... | | X
    If "Yes," attach Form 5471 for each such corporation. Enter number of Forms 5471 attached ▶ _____

8   At any time during the 1997 calendar year, did the corporation have an interest in or a signature or other authority over a financial account (such as a bank account, securities account, or other financial account) in a foreign country? | | X
    If "Yes," the corporation may have to file Form TD F 90-22.1.
    If "Yes," enter name of foreign country ▶ _____

9   During the tax year, did the corporation receive a distribution from, or was it the grantor of, or transferor to, a foreign trust? If "Yes," see page 15 of the instructions for other forms the corporation may have to file .... | | X

10 At any time during the tax year, did one foreign person own, directly or indirectly, at least 25% of: (a) the total voting power of all classes of stock of the corporation entitled to vote, or (b) the total value of all classes of stock of the corporation? If "Yes," | | X
 a Enter percentage owned ▶ _____
 b Enter owner's country ▶ _____
 c The corporation may have to file Form 5472. Enter number of Forms 5472 attached ▶ _____

11 Check this box if the corporation issued publicly offered debt instruments with original issue discount .... ▶ ☐
    If so, the corporation may have to file Form 8281.

12 Enter the amount of tax-exempt interest received or accrued during the tax year ▶ $ _____ 0

13 If there were 35 or fewer shareholders at the end of the tax year, enter the number ▶ 2

14 If the corporation has an NOL for the tax year and is electing to forego the carryback period, check here .... ▶ ☐

15 Enter the available NOL carryover from prior tax years (Do not reduce it by any deduction on line 29a.) ▶ $ _____ 0

STF FED3903F.3

Form 1120 (1997)   Page **4**

Schedule L	Balance Sheets per Books	Beginning of tax year		End of tax year	
Assets		**(a)**	**(b)**	**(c)**	**(d)**
1	Cash		11,338		32,408
2a	Trade notes and accounts receivable	23,100		65,595	
b	Less allowance for bad debts	( )	23,100	( )	65,595
3	Inventories		61,621		46,718
4	U.S. government obligations				
5	Tax-exempt securities (see instructions)				
6	Other current assets (attach schedule)				49
7	Loans to stockholders				
8	Mortgage and real estate loans				
9	Other investments (attach schedule)				
10a	Buildings and other depreciable assets	90,500		90,500	
b	Less accumulated depreciation	(13,561)	76,939	(36,550)	53,950
11a	Depletable assets				
b	Less accumulated depletion	( )		( )	
12	Land (net of any amortization)				
13a	Intangible assets (amortizable only)				
b	Less accumulated amortization	( )		( )	
14	Other assets (attach schedule)				
15	Total assets		172,998		198,720
	Liabilities and Stockholders' Equity				
16	Accounts payable		48,810		23,325
17	Mortgages, notes, bonds payable in less than 1 year				
18	Other current liabilities (attach schedule)				
19	Loans from stockholders				
20	Mortgages, notes, bonds payable in 1 year or more				
21	Other liabilities (attach schedule)				
22	Capital stock: **a** Preferred stock				
	b Common stock	100,000	100,000	100,000	100,000
23	Additional paid-in capital				
24	Retained earnings — Appropriated (attach schedule)				
25	Retained earnings — Unappropriated		24,188		75,395
26	Adjustments to shareholders' equity (attach schedule)				
27	Less cost of treasury stock		( )		( )
28	Total liabilities and stockholders' equity		172,998		198,720

Note: *You are not required to complete Schedules M-1 and M-2 below if the total assets on line 15, column (d) of Schedule L are less than $25,000.*

Schedule M-1	Reconciliation of Income (Loss) per Books With Income per Return (See page 15 of instructions.)				
1	Net income (loss) per books	63,207	7	Income recorded on books this year not included on this return (itemize):	
2	Federal income tax	14,951		Tax-exempt interest $ _____	
3	Excess of capital losses over capital gains			_____	
4	Income subject to tax not recorded on books this year (itemize): _____			_____	
	_____		8	Deductions on this return not charged against book income this year (itemize):	
5	Expenses recorded on books this year not deducted on this return (itemize):		a	Depreciation ...... $ _____	
a	Depreciation .... $ _____		b	Contributions carryover $ _____	
b	Contributions carryover $ _____			_____	
c	Travel and entertainment $ _____ 375			_____	
	_____			_____	
	_____	375	9	Add lines 7 and 8	
6	Add lines 1 through 5	78,533	10	Income (line 28, page 1) — line 6 less line 9	78,533

Schedule M-2	Analysis of Unappropriated Retained Earnings per Books (Line 25, Schedule L)				
1	Balance at beginning of year	24,188	5	Distributions: **a** Cash	12,000
2	Net income (loss) per books	63,207		**b** Stock	
3	Other increases (itemize): _____			**c** Property	
	_____		6	Other decreases (itemize): _____	
	_____		7	Add lines 5 and 6	12,000
4	Add lines 1, 2, and 3	87,395	8	Balance at end of year (line 4 less line 7)	75,395

STF FED3903F.4

Form **4562**

Department of the Treasury
Internal Revenue Service   (99)

Depreciation and Amortization
(Including Information on Listed Property)

▶ See separate instructions.   ▶ Attach this form to your return.

OMB No. 1545-0172

1997

Attachment
Sequence No. **67**

Name(s) shown on return	Business or activity to which this form relates	Identifying number
ABC CORPORATION	FORM 1120	36-6135404

Part I Election To Expense Certain Tangible Property (Section 179) (Note: *If you have any "listed property," complete Part V before you complete Part I.*)

1	Maximum dollar limitation. If an enterprise zone business, see page 2 of the instructions	**1**	$18,000
2	Total cost of section 179 property placed in service. See page 2 of the instructions	**2**	
3	Threshold cost of section 179 property before reduction in limitation	**3**	$200,000
4	Reduction in limitation. Subtract line 3 from line 2. If zero or less, enter -0-	**4**	
5	Dollar limitation for tax year. Subtract line 4 from line 1. If zero or less, enter -0-. If married filing separately, see page 2 of the instructions	**5**	

(a) Description of property	(b) Cost (business use only)	(c) Elected cost
6		

7	Listed property. Enter amount from line 27	**7**	
8	Total elected cost of section 179 property. Add amounts in column (c), lines 6 and 7	**8**	
9	Tentative deduction. Enter the smaller of line 5 or line 8	**9**	
10	Carryover of disallowed deduction from 1996. See page 3 of the instructions	**10**	
11	Business income limitation. Enter the smaller of business income (not less than zero) or line 5 (see instructions)	**11**	
12	Section 179 expense deduction. Add lines 9 and 10, but do not enter more than line 11	**12**	
13	Carryover of disallowed deduction to 1998. Add lines 9 and 10, less line 12 ▶	**13**	

Note: *Do not use Part II or Part III below for listed property (automobiles, certain other vehicles, cellular telephones, certain computers, or property used for entertainment, recreation, or amusement). Instead, use Part V for listed property.*

Part II MACRS Depreciation For Assets Placed in Service ONLY During Your 1997 Tax Year (Do Not Include Listed Property.)

Section A — General Asset Account Election

14 If you are making the election under section 168(i)(4) to group any assets placed in service during the tax year into one or more general asset accounts, check this box. See page 3 of the instructions .... ▶ ☐

Section B — General Depreciation System (GDS) (See page 3 of the instructions.)

(a) Classification of property	(b) Month and year placed in service	(c) Basis for depreciation (business/investment use only — see instructions)	(d) Recovery period	(e) Convention	(f) Method	(g) Depreciation deduction
15a 3-year property						
b 5-year property						
c 7-year property						
d 10-year property						
e 15-year property						
f 20-year property						
g 25-year property			25 yrs.		S/L	
h Residential rental property			27.5 yrs.	MM	S/L	
			27.5 yrs.	MM	S/L	
i Nonresidential real property			39 yrs.	MM	S/L	
				MM	S/L	

Section C — Alternative Depreciation System (ADS) (See page 6 of the instructions.)

16a Class life					S/L	
b 12-year			12 yrs.		S/L	
c 40-year			40 yrs.	MM	S/L	

Part III Other Depreciation (Do Not Include Listed Property.) (See page 6 of the instructions.)

17	GDS and ADS deductions for assets placed in service in tax years beginning before 1997	**17**	19,469
18	Property subject to section 168(f)(1) election	**18**	
19	ACRS and other depreciation	**19**	

Part IV Summary (See page 7 of the instructions.)

20	Listed property. Enter amount from line 26	**20**	3,520
21	**Total.** Add deductions on line 12, lines 15 and 16 in column (g), and lines 17 through 20. Enter here and on the appropriate lines of your return. Partnerships and S corporations — see instructions	**21**	22,989
22	For assets shown above and placed in service during the current year, enter the portion of the basis attributable to section 263A costs	**22**	

For Paperwork Reduction Act Notice, see the separate instructions.   ISA
STF FED5085F.1

Form **4562** (1997)

Form 4562 (1997)   Page **2**

Part V	Listed Property — Automobiles, Certain Other Vehicles, Cellular Telephones, Certain Computers, and Property Used for Entertainment, Recreation, or Amusement

Note: *For any vehicle for which you are using the standard mileage rate or deducting lease expense, complete only 23a, 23b, columns (a) through (c) of Section A, all of Section B, and Section C if applicable.*

Section A — Depreciation and Other Information (Caution: *See page 8 of the instructions for limits for passenger automobiles.***)**

23a Do you have evidence to support the business/investment use claimed? ☒ **Yes** ☐ **No**   **23b** If "Yes," is the evidence written? ☒ **Yes** ☐ **No**

(a) Type of property (list vehicles first)	(b) Date placed in service	(c) Business/ investment use percentage	(d) Cost or other basis	(e) Basis for depreciation (business/investment use only)	(f) Recovery period	(g) Method/ Convention	(h) Depreciation deduction	(i) Elected section 179 cost
24 Property used more than 50% in a qualified business use (See page 7 of the instructions.):								
TRUCK	1/2/94	100 %	11,000	11,000	5	HY/DDB	3,520	
		%						
		%						
25 Property used 50% or less in a qualified business use (See page 7 of the instructions.):								
		%				S/L –		
		%				S/L –		
		%				S/L –		
26 Add amounts in column (h). Enter the total here and on line 20, page 1						**26**	3,520	
27 Add amounts in column (i). Enter the total here and on line 7, page 1.						**27**		

Section B — Information on Use of Vehicles

Complete this section for vehicles used by a sole proprietor, partner, or other "more than 5% owner," or related person.

If you provided vehicles to your employees, first answer the questions in Section C to see of you meet an exception to completing this section for those vehicles.

		(a) Vehicle 1		(b) Vehicle 2		(c) Vehicle 3		(d) Vehicle 4		(e) Vehicle 5		(f) Vehicle 6	
28	Total business/investment miles driven during the year (DO NOT include commuting miles)												
29	Total commuting miles driven during the year												
30	Total other personal (noncommuting) miles driven												
31	Total miles driven during the year. Add lines 28 through 30												
		Yes	No	Yes	No	Yes	No	Yes	No	Yes	No	Yes	No
32	Was the vehicle available for personal use during off-duty hours?												
33	Was the vehicle used primarily by a more than 5% owner or related person?												
34	Is another vehicle available for personal use?												

Section C — Questions for Employers Who Provide Vehicles for Use by Their Employees

Answer these questions to determine if you meet an exception to completing Section B for vehicles used by employees who are not more than 5% owners or related persons.

		Yes	No
35	Do you maintain a written policy statement that prohibits all personal use of vehicles, including commuting, by your employees?		
36	Do you maintain a written policy statement that prohibits personal use of vehicles, except commuting, by your employees? See page 9 of the instructions for vehicles used by corporate officers, directors, or 1% or more owners		
37	Do you treat all use of vehicles by employees as personal use?		
38	Do you provide more than five vehicles to your employees, obtain information from your employees about the use of the vehicles, and retain the information received?		
39	Do you meet the requirements concerning qualified automobile demonstration use? See page 9 of the instructions.		

Note: *If your answer to 35, 36, 37, 38, or 39 is "Yes," you need not complete Section B of the covered vehicles.*

Part VI	Amortization

(a) Description of costs	(b) Date amortization begins	(c) Amortizable amount	(d) Code section	(e) Amortization period or percentage	(f) Amortization for this year
40 Amortization of costs that begins during your 1997 tax year:					
41 Amortization of costs that began before 1997				**41**	
42 **Total.** Enter here and on "Other Deductions" or "Other Expenses" line of your return				**42**	

STF FED5085F.2

ABC Corporation   36-6135404
Form 1120   12/31/97

Page 2, Schedule A, Line 5, Other Costs:

Depreciation	18,367
Heat & electric 85% (16,000)	13,600
Insurance	10,000
Maintenance	2,200
Materials & supplies	5,000
Payroll taxes	15,650
Rent	51,000
Small tools	1,200
	117,017

Page 1, Line 26, Other Deductions:

Delivery	2,400
Dues & subscriptions	725
Entertainment 50% (750)	375
Heat & electric 15% (16,000)	2,400
Insurance	2,000
Legal & accounting	1,000
Office supplies	2,500
Packaging	7,000
Telephone	4,800
	23,200

CHAPTER 4

CORPORATIONS: EARNINGS & PROFITS AND DIVIDEND DISTRIBUTIONS

LEARNING OBJECTIVES

After completing Chapter 4, you should be able to:

1. Identify and understand the concept of earnings and profits.

2. Recognize the importance of earnings and profits in measuring the recipient shareholder's dividend income.

3. Understand the tax impact of property dividends, on both the recipient shareholder and the corporation making the distribution.

4. Understand the nature and treatment of constructive dividends.

5. Distinguish between taxable and nontaxable stock dividends and stock rights.

KEY TERMS

Accumulated earnings and profits	Earnings and profits	Stock rights
Constructive dividend	Property dividend	Unreasonable compensation
Current earnings and profits	Stock dividend	

OUTLINE

I.   TAXABLE DIVIDENDS - IN GENERAL

    A.   Distributions are presumed to be dividends unless the parties can show otherwise.

    B.   Dividend income is limited to the amount of E & P of the distributing corporation.

    C.   Distributions not taxed as dividends, because of insufficient E & P, are return of capital to the extent of stock basis and any remainder is gain.

    D.   E & P represents the corporation's economic ability to pay a dividend without impairing its capital.

II.   EARNINGS AND PROFITS

    A.   Computation of E & P
        1.   E & P is increased by:
            a.   all items of income
            b.   deferred gain on installment sales, in the year of sale
        2.   E & P is decreased by:
            a.   tax deductible items
                1.   depreciation, for E & P, must be computed using the straight-line method over the assets ADR midpoint life, units of production, or machine hours.
                2.   depletion, for E & P, must be computed using the cost depletion method.
            b.   excess capital losses.
            c.   expenses to produce tax-exempt income.
            d.   Federal income taxes.
            e.   non-deductible insurance premiums, fines, and penalties.
            f.   related party losses
        3.   Other adjustments
            a.   the percentage completion method of accounting for long-term contracts is required for E & P purposes.
            a.   intangible drilling costs, for E & P, are amortized over 60 months.
            b.   mine exploration and development costs, for E & P, are amortized over 120 months.

    B.   E & P measures the earnings of the corporation that are treated as available for distribution to shareholders as dividends.

C. Current versus Accumulate E & P
    1. Current E & P is determined by making a series of adjustments to the corporation's taxable income.
    2. Current E & P is allocated on a pro rata basis to distributions made during the year.
    3. Accumulated E & P is the total of all previous years' current E & P, since February 28, 1913, as computed on the first day of each tax year, reduced by distributions made.
    4. Accumulated E & P is applied, to the extent necessary, in chronological order beginning with the earliest distribution.

D. Allocating E & P To Distributions
    1. Positive current E & P + positive accumulated E & P = dividend.
    2. Positive current E & P + deficient accumulated E & P = dividend to extent of current E & P.
    3. Deficient current E & P + positive accumulated E & P = Net E & P.
        a. if positive, distribution is a dividend, to the extent of the balance;
        b. if negative, distribution is return of capital.

III. PROPERTY DIVIDENDS

A. Property Dividends - Effect on the Shareholder
    1. The amount of the distribution is the fair market value of the property on the date of distribution, reduced by liabilities of the corporation assumed by the shareholder.
    2. The shareholder's basis in the property is the fair market value of the property on the date of distribution.

B. Property Dividends - Effect on the Corporation
    1. All distributions of appreciated property cause gain recognition, the property is treated as sold for its fair market value.
    2. On distributions of property having a tax basis in excess of its fair market value the corporation cannot recognize a loss.
    3. If distributed property is subject to a liability in excess of basis, the fair market value of the property for determining gain on the distribution cannot be less than the liability.

C. Effect of Corporate Distributions on E & P
    1. E & P is reduced by the amount of money, or, if property, the greater of the fair market value or the adjusted basis minus any liability.
    2. E & P is increased by gain recognized on appreciated property distributions.

3.   Under no circumstances can a distribution generate or add to a deficit in E&P.

IV.   CONSTRUCTIVE DIVIDENDS

A.   Types of Constructive Dividends
1.   The key factor determining dividend status is that a measurable economic benefit is conveyed to the shareholder.
2.   The most frequent constructive dividend situations are:
   a.   shareholder use of corporate-owned property,
   b.   bargain sale of corporate property to a shareholder,
   c.   bargain rental of corporate property,
   d.   payments for the benefit of a shareholder,
   e.   unreasonable compensation,
   f.   loans to shareholders,
   g.   loans to a corporation by shareholders.

B.   Tax Treatment of Constructive Dividends
1.   Constructive distributions are, for tax purposes, treated the same as actual distributions.
2.   The constructive distribution is taxable dividend income to the extent of the corporation's current and accumulated E & P.

V.   STOCK DIVIDENDS AND STOCK RIGHTS

A.   Stock Dividends
1.   Stock dividends are not taxable if they are pro rata distributions on common stock.
2.   Five exceptions to nontaxability of stock dividends apply for distributions which can change proportionate ownership:
   a.   distributions payable either in stock or property.
   b.   distributions resulting in the receipt of property by some shareholders and an increase in the proportionate interest of other shareholders in the assets or E & P of the distributing corporation.
   c.   distributions of preferred stock to some common stock shareholders and common stock to other common shareholders.
   d.   distributions on preferred stock other than an increase in the conversion ratio of convertible preferred stock made solely to account for a stock dividend or stock split with respect to stock into which the preferred stock is convertible.

> e. distributions of convertible preferred stock, unless it can be shown that the distribution will not result in a disproportionate distribution.
>
> 3. E & P is not reduced for nontaxable stock dividends.
> 4. Taxable stock dividends are treated, by the corporation, the same as any other property distribution.
> 5. The shareholder's basis in a taxable stock dividend is fair market value.
> 6. The shareholder's basis in the stock on which a nontaxable stock dividend is distributed is reallocated to all the shares.

B. Stock Rights are subject to the same rules as stock dividends for determining taxability.

VI. TAX PLANNING CONSIDERATIONS

A. Corporation Distributions
1. An E & P account should be established and maintained because E & P is the measure of dividend income to shareholders.
2. There is no statute of limitations on the computation of E & P.

B. Constructive Dividends
1. Shareholders should try to structure their dealings with the corporation on an arm's length basis.
2. Dealings between shareholders and closely held corporations should be as formal as possible.

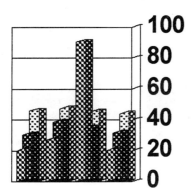

Section 301-Property Distributions Effect on the Shareholder

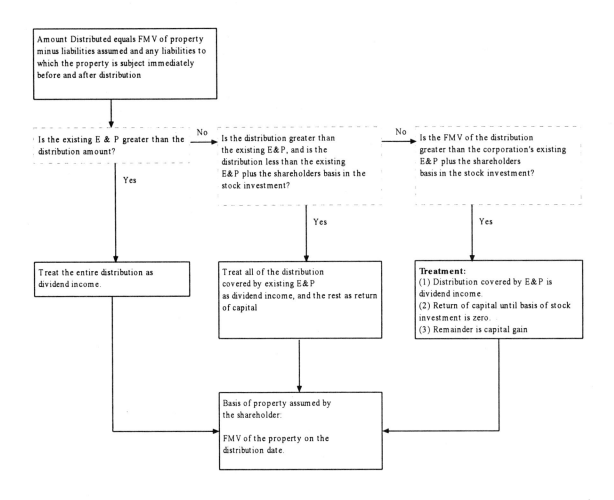

Section 305-Stock Dividends

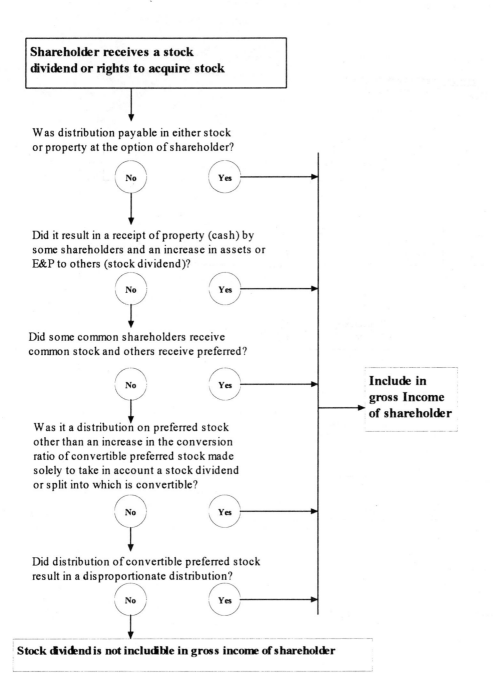

Section 311-Property Distributions Effect on the Corporation

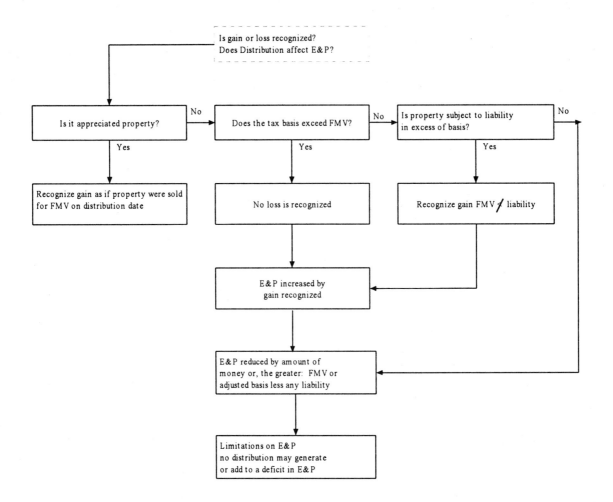

╭ ─ ─ ─ ─ ─ ─ ─ ─ ─ ─ ─ ─ ─ ─ ─ ─ ─ ─ ─
│ Is gain or loss recognized?
│ Does Distribution affect E&P?
└ ─ ─ ─ ─ ─ ─ ─ ─ ─ ─ ─ ─ ─ ─ ─ ─ ─ ─ ─

| Is it appreciated property? | No → | Does the tax basis exceed FMV? | No → | Is property subject to liability in excess of basis? | No → |

Yes ↓   Yes ↓   Yes ↓

| Recognize gain as if property were sold for FMV on distribution date | No loss is recognized | Recognize gain FMV ∤ liability |

E&P increased by
gain recognized

E&P reduced by amount of
money or, the greater: FMV or
adjusted basis less any liability

Limitations on E&P
no distribution may generate
or add to a deficit in E&P

∤ means is not less than

TEST FOR SELF-EVALUATION

True or False

T   F   1.   Gem Corporation has two classes of stock, Class A common and Class B preferred. Class B preferred stock CANNOT be converted into Class A common stock. If Gem declares a common stock dividend on the Class A stock pro rata among the shareholders, Class A shareholders must include the dividend in gross income.   (IRS 96 3A-9)

T   F   2.   The current earnings and profits of a corporation at the time of a distribution by the corporation, do NOT necessarily determine whether the distribution is a taxable dividend.   (IRS 95 3A-9)

T   F   3.   Generally, a shareholder will NOT include in gross income a distribution of stock or stock rights in a corporation if it is a distribution on preferred stock.   (IRS 95 3A-10)

T   F   4.   If a corporation distributes property subject to a liability which is greater than the property's adjusted basis, the fair market value of the property is treated as NOT less than the liability assumed or acquired by the shareholder. (IRS 95 3A-11)

T   F   5.   A shareholder holding solely common stock does NOT include a distribution of common stock in gross income if other common shareholders received preferred stock in the same distribution.   (IRS 94 3A-4)

T   F   6.   Corporation Y has a dividend reinvestment plan that allows its shareholders to use its dividends to buy more shares of stock in Corporation Y rather than receiving the dividend in cash. If shareholder W uses his dividends to buy more stock at a price equal to its fair market value, he does NOT report the dividends as income.   (IRS 94 1A-7)

T   F   7.   A shareholder does NOT include in gross income a distribution of stock or rights to acquire stock in the distributing corporation if any shareholder may elect to receive money in lieu of the stock or rights.   (IRS 93 3A-9)

T   F   8.   Generally, additional shares of stock received from nontaxable stock dividends or stock splits results in a per share reduction in the basis of the original stock.   (IRS 93 1A-10)

Fill in the Blanks

1.   The key factor in determining whether a dividend has in fact been paid is the measure of _____ conveyed to the shareholder.

2. Distributions by a corporation are presumed to be _____ unless the parties can prove otherwise.

3. When stock dividends are taxable, the basis to the shareholder-distributee is the _____.

4. The rules for determining the taxability of _____ are identical to those for determining taxability of stock dividends.

Multiple Choice

_____ 1.   For 1995, Roberts Corporation had a beginning balance of unappropriated retained earnings of $100,000 and net income per books of $125,000. During 1995 it paid cash dividends of $60,000, had a loss on sale of securities of $3,600, and received a refund of 1994 income taxes of $6,000. What is its ending balance of unappropriated retained earnings for 1995?   (IRS 96 3C-55)

   a. $225,000
   b. $174,600
   c. $171,000
   d. $161,400

_____ 2.   Camden, Inc., a calendar year C corporation that began conducting business in 1983, had accumulated earnings and profits of $20,000 as of January 1, 1995. On October 1, 1995, Camden distributed $25,000 in cash to Beaufort, Camden's sole shareholder. Camden had a $20,000 DEFICIT in earnings and profits for 1995. Beaufort had an adjusted basis of $8,000 in his stock before the distribution. What is the amount of Beaufort's ordinary dividend income and capital gain as of the date of the distribution?   (IRS 96 3C-57)

	Dividend Income	*Capital Gain*
a.	$0	$25,000
b.	$25,000	$0
c.	$5,000	$12,000
d.	$5,000	$8,000

_____ 3.   Elk Corporation, a calendar year C corporation, had accumulated earnings and profits of $60,000 as of January 1, 1995, the beginning of its tax year. Elk had an operating loss of $70,000 for the first 6 months of 1995, but had earnings and profits of $6,000 for the entire tax year 1995. Elk distributed $15,000 to its shareholders on July 1, 1995. What portion of the $15,000 distribution would be an ordinary dividend?   (IRS 96 3C-58)

    a. $15,000
    b. $10,600
    c. $6,000
    d. $0

_____ 4.   Ball, a calendar year C corporation, had accumulated earnings and profits of $50,000 as of January 1, 1995. Ball had a deficit in earnings and profits for 1995 of $65,000. Ball distributed $25,000 to its shareholders on July 1, 1995. What is Ball Corporation's accumulated earnings and profits as of December 31, 1995?   (IRS 96 3C-59)

    a. $0
    b.   ($15,000)
    c.   ($32,500)
    d.   ($40,000)

_____ 5.   Which of the following statements is CORRECT?   (IRS 95 1B-30)

    a.   Stock dividends are distributions made by a corporation of another corporation's stock.
    b.   In computing basis for new stock received as a result of a nontaxable dividend, it is immaterial whether the stock received is identical or not to the old stock.
    c.   If a stock dividend is taxable, the basis of the old stock does NOT change.
    d.   If you receive nontaxable stock rights and allow them to expire, you have a loss equal to the fair market value of the rights.

_____ 6.   E-Z Corporation, which has a dividend reinvestment plan, paid dividends of $20 per share during 1994. Carlos, who owned 100 shares of E-Z Corporation prior to the distribution, participated in the plan by using ALL the dividends to purchase 20 additional shares of stock. He purchased the stock for $100 per share when the fair market value was $125 per share. How much dividend income must Carlos report on his 1994 income tax return?   (IRS 95 1C-48)

    a. $2,500
    b. $2,000
    c. $500
    d. $0

_____ 7.   In 1992, Chim purchased 100 shares of preferred stock of Donald Corporation for $5,000. In 1994, she received a stock dividend of 20 additional shares of preferred stock in Donald. On the date of the distribution, the preferred stock had a fair market value of $40 per share. What is Chim's basis in the new stock she received as a result of the stock dividend?   (IRS 95 1C-60)

     a. $1,000
     b. $833
     c. $800
     d. $0

_____ 8.   Dublin, a calendar-year C corporation, had accumulated earnings and profits of $32,000 as of January 1, 1994. Dublin had a deficit in earnings and profits for 1994 of $40,000. On October 1, 1994, Dublin distributed $15,000 to one of its shareholders, Mr. Murphy. The adjusted basis of Murphy's stock before the distribution was $2,000. What is the amount of Murphy's ordinary dividend income and capital gain as of the date of the distribution?   (IRS 95 3C-63)

	Dividend Income	Capital Gain
a.	$0	$13,000
b.	$2,000	$13,000
c.	$2,000	$11,000
d.	$15,000	$0

_____ 9.   On July 1, 1994, VAL, a calendar-year C corporation, distributed an auto used 100% in its business to its sole shareholder. At the time of the distribution, the auto, which originally cost $18,000, had an adjusted basis of $6,000 and a fair market value of $5,000. There were no liabilities attached to the auto. No other distributions were made during 1994. As of January 1, 1994, VAL's accumulated earnings and profits was ($5,000). For 1994, VAL's earnings and profits was $8,000. By what amount will VAL reduce its earnings and profits as a result of the distribution of the auto?   (IRS 95 3C-64)

     a. $3,000
     b. $4,000
     c. $5,000
     d. $6,000

_____ 10.   Vernon Corporation, a calendar-year C corporation, had accumulated earnings and profits of $100,000 as of January 1, 1994. Vernon had a deficit in earnings and profits for 1994 in the amount of ($140,000). Vernon distributed $35,000 cash to its shareholders on July 1, 1994. Vernon Corporation's accumulated earnings and profits as of December 31, 1994 is: (IRS 95 3C-65)

a. $0
b. ($40,000)
c. ($70,000)
d. ($75,000)

____ 11. Yappa Corporation distributed depreciable personal property having a fair market value of $9,500 to its shareholders. The property had an adjusted basis of $2,000 to the corporation. Yappa had correctly deducted $7,000 in depreciation on the property. What is the amount of Yappa's ORDINARY INCOME due to this distribution? (IRS 95 3C-66)

a. $9,500
b. $7,500
c. $7,000
d. $0

____ 12. Rally Corporation distributed a sailboat to its sole shareholder, Ms. H. At the time of the distribution, the sailboat had a fair market value of $175,000 and an adjusted basis to Rally of $150,000. The sailboat was subject to a loan of $190,000, which Ms. H assumed. What is the amount of Rally's gain or (loss) on the distribution? (IRS 95 3C-67)

a. ($15,000)
b. $0
c. $25,000
d. $40,000

____ 13. In 1993, Corey bought 200 shares of ABC stock at $10 a share. In 1994, Corey bought an additional 100 shares of ABC stock at $20 a share. In 1995, ABC declared a 2-for-1 stock split. How many shares of ABC stock does Corey own and what is the basis of the stock? (IRS 96 1C-58)

a. 400 shares at $5 a share and 200 shares at $10 a share
b. 400 shares at $10 a share and 200 shares at $20 a share
c. 200 shares at $20 a share and 100 shares at $40 a share
d. 600 shares at $6.67 per share

_____ 14.   On January 3, 1995, Susan purchased 300 shares of common stock in Corporation Y for $120 per share. Four months later she purchased 100 additional shares at $180 per share. On December 10, 1995, Susan received a 20% nontaxable stock dividend. The new and the old stock are identical. What is the amount of Susan's basis in each share of Corporation Y stock after the stock dividend?

(IRS 96 1C-59)

a.   480 shares at $112.50 a share
b.   360 shares at $120 a share and 120 shares at $180 a share
c.   360 shares at $120 a share and 120 shares at $150 a share
d.   360 shares at $100 a share and 120 shares at $150 a share

_____ 15.   In 1993, Nancy bought 100 shares of Trauna, Inc. for $5,000 or $50 a share. In 1994, Nancy bought 100 shares of Trauna stock for $8,000 or $80 a share. In 1995, Trauna declared a 2-for-1 stock split. Nancy sold 50 shares of the stock she received from the stock split for $2,000. She could NOT definitely identify the shares she sold. What is the amount of Nancy's net capital gain from this sale for 1995?

(IRS 96 1C-68)

a. $0
b. $750
c. $1,625
d. $2,000

Comprehensive Problem

In its financial statements for 1997, JD Corporation showed $300,000 of pre-tax accounting income. Indicate any adjustments for the following recorded transactions and determine JD Corporation's taxable income and net increase (decrease) in E & P for the year.

	Per Book	Taxable	E & P
Pre-tax accounting income:	$300,000		
1. Insurance Premium Expense:			
a. fire & casualty	15,000		
b. employee group life (employee named beneficiary)	20,000		
c. term life on John Doe, Pres. (JD Corp. is beneficiary)	7,000		
2. Interest Income:			
a. University City bonds	15,000		
b. CD, National Bank	10,000		
3. Dividend Income:			
a. Fuji Photo, Tokyo	3,000		
b. Sears Roebuck, Chicago	8,000		
4. Charitable Contributions:			
a. United Way	7,000		
b. bowling team shirts	350		
c. University City Park District (unimproved land, FMV $50,000; cost $35,000)	35,000		
5. Depreciation (straight-line for book accelerated for tax)	40,000	70,000	
6. Dividend Payments:			
a. cash 20,000			
b. common stock, 1 for 3 $12 par value			
TAXABLE INCOME		_____	
7. Federal Income Taxes:		_____	_____
NET CHANGE IN E & P		_____	

SOLUTIONS

True or False

1. F (p. 4-14; distribution does not change proportionate common interest)
2. T (p. 4-7)
3. F (p. 4-14; distributions on preferred stock are generally taxable)
4. T (p. 4-11)
5. F (p. 4-14; distribution changes proportionate common interest)
6. F (p. 4-14)
7. F (p. 4-14)
8. T (p. 4-14)

Fill in the Blanks

1. economic benefit (p. 4-3)
2. dividends (p. 4-2)
3. fair market value (p. 4-14)
4. stock rights (p. 4-14)

Multiple Choice

1. c (100.000 + 125,000 - 60,000 + 6,000)
2. c (20,000 accumulated - 75%(20,000 current) = 5,000 dividend, 8,000 return of captial (to extent of basis) remaining 12,000 is capital gain)
3. a (sufficient accumulated E & P)
4. c (50,000 accumulated - 50% current = dividend, 32,500 remaining current E & P)
5. c (p. 4-14)
6. a (p. 4-14)
7. c (taxable dividend, 20 shares at $40 per share)
8. c (32,000 - 75%(40,000) = 2,000 dividend, 2,000 return of capital, 11,000 gain)
9. d (adjusted basis of property distributed, current E & P > basis)
10. c (100,000 - ½(140,000) = dividend, 70,000 is remaining current deficit)
11. c (depreciation recapture)
12. d (not less than the liability)
13. a (p. 4-14)
14. d (p. 4-14)
15. b (FIFO)

Comprehensive Problem

For tax:

1.	+ 7,000	expense to produce tax-exempt income
2.	- 15,000	tax-exempt municipal
3.	- 5,600	dividend received 70% (8,000) unrelated, domestic corporation
4.	+ 11,600 is	contribution before limitation is 7,000 + 50,000 the 10% limitation

applied to taxable income before dividends received deduction or any charitable deduction, in this problem, $30,400; $57,000 - $30,400 results in a $26,600 carry forward; the $350 could be deducted as a promotional expense.

5.	- 30,000	net change

TAXABLE INCOME: $268,000

7. $87,770; .15(50,000) + .25(25,000) + .34(193,000) + .05(168,000)

For E & P

4.	-15,000	57,000 allowable - 42,000 taken
5.	-20,000	dividend payment
7.	-87,770	federal income tax

NET CHANGE IN E & P: 177,230 increase

CHAPTER 5

CORPORATIONS:
REDEMPTIONS AND LIQUIDATIONS

LEARNING OBJECTIVES

After completing Chapter 5, you should be able to:

1. Identify stock redemptions that are treated as sales or exchanges of stock rather than as dividend income.

2. Recognize that some redemption transactions do not qualify for sale or exchange treatment.

3. Understand the tax consequences when a parent corporation distributes stock and securities of its subsidiary.

4. Understand the tax consequences of complete liquidations for both the corporation and its shareholders.

5. Identify tax planning opportunities available to minimize the tax impact in stock redemptions and complete liquidations.

KEY TERMS

Attribution	Meaningful reduction test	Redemption to pay death taxes
Business purpose	Not essentially equivalent	Residual method
Complete termination redemption	redemption	Section 338 election
Corporate liquidation	Partial liquidation	Stock redemption
Disproportionate redemption	Preferred stock bailout	

OUTLINE

I.   STOCK REDEMPTIONS - IN GENERAL

    A.   In a stock redemption, a corporation buys or exchanges property for its own stock, from a shareholder.

    B.   Only qualifying stock redemptions are treated as a sale or exchange for tax purposes; other redemptions are treated as dividend distributions.
        1.   Qualifying stock redemptions are defined in the Code.
        2.   Generally, in a qualified stock redemption, a substantial reduction in the shareholder's ownership of the corporation must occur.

II.   STOCK REDEMPTIONS - SALE OR EXCHANGE TREATMENT

    A.   Five major types of stock redemptions qualify for exchange treatment:
        1.   Not essentially equivalent to a dividend
        2.   Substantially disproportionate in terms of shareholder effect
        3.   Complete termination of a shareholder's interest
        4.   Partial liquidation of a corporation
        5.   To pay death taxes.

    B.   Stock Attribution Rules
        1.   Stock attribution rules treat a shareholder as the owner of stocks held by certain related parties, in addition to the stocks owned personally.
        2.   For an individual, redeeming stock, the following are related parties:
            a.   <u>family</u>: spouse, children, grandchildren, parents = deemed 100% owned by the individual.
            b.   <u>Partnership</u>:   partnership's stock times the partner's proportionate share in the partnership = % deemed owned by the individual.
            c.   <u>estate or trust</u>: estate or trust's stock times the beneficiary's proportionate interest in the estate or trust = % deemed owned by the individual.
            d.   <u>corporation</u>:   if a more than 50% shareholder, corporate stock times the shareholder's proportionate interest in the corporation = % deemed owned by the individual.
        3.   Stock attribution rules also apply to partnerships, estates, trusts and corporations redeeming stock:
            a.   <u>partnership</u>   stock of partner is deemed 100% owned.
            b.   <u>estate or trust</u>   stock of beneficiary is deemed 100% owned.
            c.   <u>corporation</u>   stock of 50% or more shareholder, is deemed 100% owned.

C.   Not Essentially Equivalent Redemptions
1.   A meaningful reduction in the shareholder's proportionate ownership must take place.
2.   A decrease in the redeeming shareholder's voting control is considered the most important factor in determining whether or not a meaningful reduction has occurred.

D.   Disproportionate Redemptions
1.   After the distribution, the shareholder must own less than 80% of his interest in the corporation before the redemption.
2.   After the distribution, the shareholder must own less than 50% of the total combined voting power of all classes of stock entitled to vote.

E.   Complete Termination Redemptions
1.   Family attribution rules do not apply if both the following conditions are met:
   a.   the former shareholder has no interest, other than as a creditor, in the corporation for at least 10 years after the redemption, and
   b.   the former shareholder files an agreement to notify the IRS of any acquisition of a disallowed interest within the 10 year period.
2.   The former shareholder may reacquire an interest in the corporation through a bequest or inheritance but in no other manner.

F.   Redemptions in Partial Liquidation
1.   A noncorporate shareholder is allowed exchange treatment when:
   a.   the distribution is not essentially equivalent to a dividend, or
   b.   an active business is terminated.
2.   The not essentially equivalent to a dividend requirement tests the effect of the distribution on the corporation, not the shareholder; there must be a genuine contraction of the business of the corporation.
3.   The complete termination of a business test requires:
   a.   the corporation has more than one trade or business and two or more of the businesses have been in existence for at least 5 years.
   b.   the corporation terminates one trade or business that has been in existence for at least 5 years while continuing a remaining business that has been in existence for at least 5 years.
   c.   the terminated trade or business was not acquired in a taxable transaction within the 5 year period.
4.   Any distribution must be made within the taxable year in which the plan is adopted or within the succeeding taxable year.

G. Redemptions to Pay Death Taxes
1. A redemption which qualifies as a redemption to pay death taxes is not subject to the not essentially equivalent to a dividend or substantially disproportionate tests.
2. The value of the stock in the gross estate of a decedent must exceed 35% of the value of the adjusted gross estate.
3. The distribution is limited to the sum of death taxes, funeral, and certain estate administration expenses.

H. Effect on the Corporation Redeeming Its Stock
1. Loss is not recognized on purchases or repurchases of stock, these are capital transactions.
2. The E & P account of a corporation is reduced by a stock redemption in proportion to the amount of the corporation's outstanding stock that is redeemed. The amount of the reduction cannot exceed the ratable share of the E & P attributable to the stock redeemed.

III. STOCK REDEMPTIONS - NO SALE OR EXCHANGE TREATMENT

A. Redemptions that do not qualify for exchange treatment as provided for in the Code are considered dividends to the extent of the corporation's E & P.

B. §306 Stock is stock other than common that:
1. is received as a nontaxable stock dividend.
2. is received tax-free in a corporate reorganization which is substantially the same as a stock dividend.
3. is received in exchange for §306 stock.
4. has a basis determined by reference to §306 stock.
5. If a corporation has no E & P on the date of a nontaxable preferred stock dividend, the stock will not be §306 stock.

C. The Problem
1. Clever taxpayers devised a scheme to bail out corporate profits.
    a. A corporation would issue a nontaxable, nonvoting preferred stock dividend on common stock.
    b. The shareholder would assign a portion of his common stock basis to the preferred stock.
    c. The shareholder would then sell the preferred stock to a third party.
2. The sale of the preferred stock bailed out corporate profits as capital gains without reducing the shareholder's percentage ownership of the corporation.

D. §306 Stock Bailout Solution
1. The shareholder has ordinary income on the sale of the preferred stock to a third party, to the extent that, the fair market value of the preferred stock, on the date of distribution, would have been a dividend.
2. No loss is recognized on the sale of the preferred stock by the shareholder.
3. If the corporation redeems the preferred stock, the proceeds constitute dividend income to the extent of the corporation's E & P on the date of the redemption.

E. Redemption Through Use of Related Corporations
1. When a shareholder controls two corporations and sells stock of one corporation to the other corporation, the sale may be treated as a redemption subject to the not essentially equivalent and disproportionate redemption rules.
   a. control is 50% of the combined voting power, or 50% of the total value of all classes of stock.
   b. constructive ownership rules apply in determining the degree of control.
2. If the rules are not satisfied, the exchange is treated as a taxable dividend to the extent of the corporations' E & P.
   a. first reducing the E & P of the acquiring corporation, then, if necessary, the E & P of the issuing corporation.
   b. the acquiring corporation treats the stock received as a contribution to capital, having the same basis as the transferring shareholder had.
   c. the individual's basis in the stock of the acquiring corporation is increased by his basis in the stock surrendered.
3. If the rules are satisfied, the sale is recast as a redemption of the stock of the acquiring corporation.

IV. DISTRIBUTION OF STOCK AND SECURITIES OF A CONTROLLED CORPORATION

A. Stock in an existing subsidiary corporation can be distributed to the shareholders of the parent tax-free, if the requirements of Section 355 are met.

B. §355 applies only:
1. To distributions which involve at least 80% of the stock of the subsidiary.
2. When, following the distribution, both the parent and the subsidiary are engaged in a trade or business in which they had been so engaged for at least 5 years prior to the distribution, and
3. When the parent has held stock in the subsidiary for at least 5 years prior to the distribution.

C.   The distribution must be motivated by a sound business purpose.

D.   The distribution can be in the form of:
1.   Spin-off: distribution of subsidiary stock to parent shareholders, giving control of the subsidiary to those shareholders.
2.   Split-off: distribution of subsidiary stock in exchange for some parent corporation stock.
3.   Split-up: stock of two subsidiary corporations is distributed to parent shareholders and the parent corporation is liquidated.

E.   Tax Consequences of a §355 Distribution at the Shareholder Level
1.   A shareholder can receive only stock or securities tax-free.
2.   If the principal amount of securities received is greater than the principal amount of the securities surrendered, or if no securities were given up, the securities received are treated and taxed as boot.
3.   The basis of stock held before the exchange is allocated among all stocks held immediately after the transaction in proportion to their relative fair market values.

V.   LIQUIDATIONS

A.   A corporate liquidation occurs, for tax purposes, when a corporation ceases to be a going concern.

B.   Legal dissolution under state law is not required for Federal tax purposes.

VI.   LIQUIDATIONS - EFFECT ON THE DISTRIBUTING CORPORATION

A.   A liquidating corporation recognizes gain and/or loss on the distribution of property.
1.   The property distributed is treated as if sold at its fair market value.
2.   If subject to a liability, the fair market value cannot be less than that liability.

B.   Two exceptions prohibit loss recognition when either of the following situations exist:
1.   Related-party, 50% shareholder ownership, and
a.   the distribution is not pro rata, or
b.   the property distributed is disqualified property.
2.   Built-in loss property distributions

        a.   for property held for 2 years or less, it is assumed that the property was contributed to the corporation for the purpose of providing a loss.

        b.   the restriction applies only to the amount of the built-in loss.

    3.   Disqualified property is property acquired by the corporation as a capital contribution or §351 exchange during the five year period before the liquidating distribution.

VII.   LIQUIDATIONS - EFFECT ON THE SHAREHOLDER

A.   Generally, gain or loss is recognized as though the shareholder sold his stock.

B.   The shareholder's gain recognition on the receipt of notes from corporate installment sales of capital assets may be deferred and recognized as received.

VIII.   LIQUIDATIONS - PARENT SUBSIDIARY SITUATIONS

A.   If a parent corporation liquidates a subsidiary, under §332, no gain or loss is recognized by the parent or by the subsidiary for property distributed to the parent. §332 requires:

    1.   The parent must own at least 80% of the voting stock and 80% of the total value of all subsidiary stock on the date the plan of liquidation is adopted and thereafter until all property is distributed.

    2.   The subsidiary must distribute all its property within the taxable year or within 3 years from the close of the tax year when the plan was adopted and the first distribution was made.

    3.   The subsidiary must be solvent.

B.   Tax Treatment When a Minority Interest Exists

    1.   Distributions to minority shareholders cause gain, but not loss, recognition to the distributing corporation.

    2.   The minority shareholder recognizes gain or loss as on a stock sale.

C.   Indebtedness of Subsidiary to Parent

    1.   The subsidiary does not recognize gain or loss on property transferred to the parent in a §332 liquidation.

    2.   Realized gain or loss is recognized by the parent on property received to satisfy a debt of the subsidiary.

D.   Basis of Property Received by the Parent Corporation

    1.   Property received by the parent retains the same basis as it had in hands of the subsidiary. The parent's basis in the subsidiary's stock disappears.

2.   When a parent liquidates a subsidiary shortly after a qualified stock purchase and elects under §338, it will have a basis in subsidiary assets equal to its basis in subsidiary stock.

E.   A §338 election is irrevocable but liquidation of the subsidiary is not required. To qualify:
1.   At least 80% of the voting power and value must be acquired by the purchasing corporation.
2.   Acquisition takes place within a 12 month period beginning with the first purchase of stock.
3.   The stock must be acquired in a taxable transaction.
4.   The election must be made by the 15th day of the 9th month after the month in which the purchase occurred.

F.   Under §338, the acquired corporation is deemed to have sold its assets for the amount of the purchasing corporation's "grossed up" basis in the stock, adjusted for liabilities of the subsidiary.
1.   The grossed up basis is the parent's basis in the subsidiary stock times 1 over the percentage of value held by the purchasing corporation, on the acquisition date.
2.   This basis is allocated among the assets of the subsidiary using the residual method. Purchase price in excess of the total fair market value of identifiable assets is allocated to goodwill or going concern value.
3.   The subsidiary is treated as having sold all assets for their fair market value on the acquisition date and recognizes gain or loss.
4.   The day after acquisition, the subsidiary is treated as a new corporation that purchased all of the assets and, if not liquidated, the holding period begins anew. If the subsidiary is liquidated, the parent's holding period begins on the date the parent acquired the subsidiary's stock.

TEST FOR SELF-EVALUATION

True or False

T   F   1.   Liquidating distributions, sometimes called liquidating dividends, are, at least in part, one form of a return of capital, assuming the distributee has at least some adjusted basis in the stock.   (IRS 91 1A-5)

T   F   2.   A corporation will recognize a gain or loss on the distribution of its property to its noncorporate shareholders in complete liquidation of the corporation, the same as if the corporation had sold the property to its shareholders at fair market value.
                                                                (IRS 90 3A-17)

T   F   3.   A proportionate distribution to a corporate shareholder by a corporation in partial redemption of stock, pursuant to a plan of partial liquidation, is treated as a dividend to the extent of earnings and profits of the distributing corporation.
                                                                (IRS 90 3A-18)

T   F   4.   When a corporation does not cancel redeemed stock but holds the stock in its treasury, the corporation will recognize a gain or loss on its retransfer or redistribution.   (IRS 92 3A-9)

T   F   5.   Corporation W has 2,000 shares of its only class of stock outstanding. Mr. D owns 1,500 shares and his son, Randy, owns 500 shares. W redeemed all 1,500 shares from Mr. D for $45,000. Mr. D kept his position in W as an officer and director. This redemption qualifies for capital gain treatment by Mr. D since all of his ownership in W has been terminated.   (IRS 90 3A-19)

T   F   6.   Corporation K distributed land use in its business to its shareholders in a qualified redemption of stock. At the time of the distribution, the land had an adjusted basis to K of $200,000, and a fair market value of $500,000. Corporation K does not recognize any gain on this distribution.   (IRS 90 3A-20)

T   F   7.   In a complete liquidation of a corporation, the character of a shareholder's gain or loss is generally determined by the character of the asset(s) in the hands of the corporation before distribution to the shareholder.   (IRS 91 3A-18)

T   F   8.   The gain or loss to a shareholder from a distribution in liquidation of a corporation is to be determined by comparing the amount of the distribution with the adjusted basis of the stock regardless of whether the distribution is in partial or complete liquidation of the corporation.   (IRS 91 3A-19)

T F   9.   After a stock redemption, if a shareholder's ownership percentage of all voting stock is less than 80% of his percentage of all voting stock held before the redemption, and the shareholder owns less than 50% of all voting stock of the corporation after the redemption, the redemption is considered substantially disproportionate.   (IRS 91 3A-20)

T F 10.   In May, 1992, Lion Corporation distributed property in proportionate redemption of its stock in partial liquidation. Lion distributed land to Peter, a 50% shareholder. Lion distributed a building to Black Corporation, a 50% shareholder. The distribution was NOT essentially equivalent to a dividend and was made pursuant to a plan adopted in March of 1992. This transaction meets the requirements of Internal Revenue Code Section 302 and would be treated as a distribution of corporate assets in exchange for stock.   (IRS 93 3A-10)

T F 11.   Under the constructive ownership rules that apply to a partial stock redemption, a waiver of family attribution may qualify a redemption for exchange treatment.
(IRS 92 3A-10)

Fill in the Blanks

1.   Generally, in the application of Section 332 to the liquidation of a subsidiary by a parent corporation, the property received by the parent carries the _____ basis in the hands of the parent as it did in the hands of the subsidiary.

2.   Section 332 _____ apply to an insolvent subsidiary.

3.   The effect of Section 338 is to give the assets acquired by a parent corporation in the liquidation of its subsidiary the _____ basis as the stock which the parent held in the subsidiary.

4.   Liquidations and _____ parallel each other concerning their effect on the E & P of the distributing corporation.

5.   Section 306 was enacted to preclude individuals from pulling earnings out of a corporation via the _____.

6.   Stock redemptions which qualify for exchange treatment include distributions that are: _____ to a dividend, _____, in _____ of a shareholder's interest and, to pay _____.

7.   A stock redemption is treated as "substantially disproportionate" if, after the distribution, the shareholder owns less than _____ of his holdings prior to the distribution and less than _____ of the combined voting power of all stock.

8. A subsidiary does not recognize gain or loss on a liquidating distribution to a parent corporation that directly owns _____ of the subsidiary's stock.

Multiple Choice

_____ 1. You may receive a return of capital distribution based on your stock. All of the following are true except: (IRS 96 1B-28)

    a. A return of capital reduces the basis of your stock.
    b. When the basis of your stock has been reduced to zero, report any additional return of capital as a capital loss.
    c. Any liquidating distribution you receive is NOT taxable to you until you have recovered the basis of your stock.
    d. If the total liquidating distributions you receive are less than the basis of your stock, you may have a capital loss.

_____ 2. Ranger Corporation's only class of stock is owned as follows:

Matthew	40%
Darlene, Matthew's sister	25%
Matthew's and Darlene's father	25%
Matthew's and Darlene's grandfather	10%

What is Matthew's percentage of stock ownership under the attribution rules for stock redemptions? (IRS 96 3B-26)

    a. 65%
    b. 75%
    c. 90%
    d. 100%

_____ 3. Heritage Corporation distributed an antique automobile to Rene, its sole shareholder. On the date of the distribution, the automobile had a fair market value of $30,000 and an adjusted basis to Heritage of $22,000. What is the amount of Heritage Corporation's recognized gain on the distribution? (IRS 96 3C-60)

    a. $30,000
    b. $12,000
    c. $8,000
    d. $0

_____ 4.   Ann owned two blocks of Biddle Corporation stock which had the following characteristics:

Block	Shares	Acquired	Basis
1	200	06/01/94	$20,000
2	50	07/01/95	$12,500

Ann's two blocks of stock combined represented 10% of Biddle's only class of stock outstanding. Pursuant to Biddle's complete liquidation, Ann received a $50,000 cash distribution on December 1, 1995 in exchange for her 250 shares. Biddle's earnings and profits balance immediately before any liquidating distribution was $50,000. What is the amount and character of Ann's gain or loss?
(IRS 96 3C-61)

a. $50,000 dividend income
b. $17,50 long-term capital gain
c. $20,000 long-term capital gain and $2,500 short-term capital loss
d. No gain or loss

_____ 5.   Daring Corporation, pursuant to a plan of complete liquidation, distributed land acquired in 1990 to Maria, its sole shareholder. The land had a fair market value of $120,000, an adjusted basis to Daring of $90,000, and was subject to a liability of $125,000 which was assumed by Maria. Maria owned 500 shares of Daring which she had purchased in 1988 for $50,000. Daring does NOT qualify as a small business corporation. What is the character and the amount of the gain or (loss) recognized by Maria and Daring Corporation?   (IRS 96 3C-62)

	Maria	Daring
a.	$50,000 ordinary loss	$30,000 ordinary gain
b.	$50,000 long-term capital loss	$35,000 long-term capital gain
c.	$55,000 long-term capital loss	$30,000 long-term capital gain
d.	$55,000 long-term capital loss	$35,000 long-term capital gain

_____ 6.   Mouse Corporation owns as an investment, 10% of the stock of Salem Corporation with an adjusted basis of $4,000 and a fair market value of $44,000. Mouse uses the Salem stock to redeem approximately 1%, or $10,000 par value, of its own outstanding stock from unrelated, noncorporate shareholders. As a result of this transaction, Mouse must report gain of: (IRS 96 3C-64)

a. $0
b. $2,000
c. $40,000
d. $44,000

_____ 7.   Diana, the sole shareholder of Ancient Corporation's only class of stock, owns 1000 shares which she purchased in 1984. Diana's basis in the stock is $2,000,000. During 1995, Ancient, which had earnings and profits $5,000,000, redeeemed 900 shares for $4,500,000. What is the amount and character of Diana's gain? (IRS 96 3C-65)

    a. $4,500,000 dividend
    b. $4,500,000 capital gain
    c. $2,700,000 dividend
    d. $2,700,000 capital gain

_____ 8.   Select the answer that best describes what happens when shareholders receive a series of distributions, NOT part of an installment obligation, covering two or more consecutive tax years in redemption of ALL of the stock of a corporation pursuant to a plan intended to result in the complete liquidation of the corporation. (IRS 95 3B-30)

    a. The shareholders will be allowed to recover their respective basis in the stock before recognizing any gains.
    b. The shareholders will treat the distributions as dividends to the extent of the corporation's earnings and profits.
    c. The shareholders will recognize a pro-rata portion of the gain in each of the years that distributions are received.
    d. NO losses from the transactions will be deductible.

_____ 9.   Turbo Corporation distributed land to shareholder Lea in partial liquidation of her interest. At the time of the distribution, the land had an adjusted basis of $80,000 and a fair market value of $125,000. Lea exchanged 90 of 100 shares of Turbo stock for the land. At the time of the partial liquidation, Lea's adjusted basis in the 90 shares was $60,000. Other unrelated shareholders of Turbo own a combined 150 shares outstanding. Just prior to the distribution, Turbo had earnings and profits of $150,000. What are the amounts and character of income that Turbo Corporation and Lea must recognize on the partial liquidation? (IRS 95 3C-69)

	Turbo	Lea
a.	$0	$65,000 capital gain
b.	$0	$65,000 dividend
c.	$45,000 capital gain	$65,000 capital gain
d.	$45,000 capital gain	$125,000 dividend

_____ 10. Two unrelated individuals, Ward and June, own all the stock of Beaver Corporation, which has earnings and profits of $300,000. Because of his inactivity in the business for the last several years, Ward has decided to retire from the business completely and move to Oregon. Accordingly, Beaver Corporation will redeem all the stock owned by Ward and, in return, Ward will receive a distribution of $450,000. Ward's adjusted basis in the stock is $250,000. What will be the tax effect to Ward?   (IRS 95 3C-70)

   a. $150,000 capital gain
   b. $300,000 dividend
   c. $400,000 dividend
   d. $200,000 capital gain

_____ 11. All of the following are requirements for a distribution to be treated as a partial liquidation of a corporation except: (IRS 94 3B-29)

   a. The distribution is NOT essentially equivalent to a dividend which is determined at the shareholder level rather than the corporate level.
   b. The distribution is attributable to the distributing corporation's ceasing to conduct a qualifying trade or business which was actively conducted throughout the 5-year period ending on the date of the redemption.
   c. The distribution is pursuant to a plan and occurs within the taxable year in which the plan is adopted or within the succeeding taxable year.
   d. ALL of the above would be treated as a distribution in partial liquidation of a corporation.

_____ 12. With respect to the redemption of stock, each of the following tests establishes that the redemption can be treated as an exchange of stock rather than as a dividend except: (IRS 94 3B-31)

   a. The redemption is substantially disproportionate with respect to the shareholder's constructive holdings.
   b. The redemption is NOT substantially equivalent to a dividend.
   c. The redemption terminates the shareholder's entire interest in the corporation.
   d. The redemption is of stock held by a corporate shareholder and is made in partial liquidation of the redeeming corporation.

SOLUTIONS

True or False

1. T (p. 5-22)
2. T (p. 5-24)
3. T (p. 5-11; sale or exchange treatment in partial liquidations apply only to noncorporate shareholders)
4. F (p. 5-15; capital transaction)
5. F (p. 5-10; no interest other than as a creditor)
6. F (p. 5-15; FMV - adjusted basis)
7. F (p. 5-29; in the hands of the shareholder)
8. T (p. 5-4, 29)
9. T (p. 5-8)
10. F (p. 5-11; only noncorporate shareholders)
11. T (p. 5-6; attribution waived only for complete termination redemptions)

Fill in the Blanks

1. same (p. 5-35)
2. doesn't (p. 5-30)
3. same (p. 5-35)
4. stock redemptions (p. 5-23)
5. preferred stock bail-out approach (p. 5-16)
6. not essentially equivalent; substantially disproportionate; termination; shareholder's death taxes (p. 5-6)
7. 80%; 50% (p. 5-8)
8. 80% or more (p. 5-30)

Multiple Choice

1. b (additional return of capital would be capital gain)
2. a (spouse, children, grandchildren and parents, not sibling or grandparent)
3. c (30,000 - 22,000)
4. c (distribution @ $200 per share, 200 shares @ $100 per share, long-term, 50 shares @ $250, short-term)
5. d (Maria,: 120,000 FMV-50,000 basis = 70,000 gain - 125,000 liability = 55,000 loss Daring: 125,000 liability - 90,000 basis)
6. c (FMV - basis)
7. a (no reduction in proportionate ownership and adequate E & P)
8. a (p. 5-29)
9. c (Turbo: 125,000 FMV - 80,000 basis, Lea: 125,000 FMV - 60,000 basis)
10. d (p. 5-10)
11. a (not essentially equivalent to a dividend is determined at the corporate level)
12. d (only noncorporate shareholders)

CHAPTER 6

ALTERNATIVE MINIMUM TAX AND CERTAIN PENALTY TAXES IMPOSED ON CORPORATIONS

LEARNING OBJECTIVES

After completing Chapter 6, you should be able to:

1. Explain the reason for the alternative minimum tax.

2. Calculate the alternative minimum tax applicable to corporation.

3. Understand the function of adjusted current earnings (ACE).

4. Appreciate the purpose of the accumulated earnings tax.

5. Determine the reasonable needs of the business.

6. Compute the accumulated earnings tax.

7. Discuss the reason for the personal holding company tax.

8. Recognize the requirements for personal holding company status.

9. Compute the personal holding company tax.

10. Compare the accumulated earnings and personal holding company taxes.

KEY TERMS

Accumulated earnings credit	Consent dividend	Personal holding company
Accumulated earnings tax (AET)	Deficiency dividend	(PHC)
Adjusted current earnings (ACE)	Dividends paid deduction	Reasonable needs of the
Adjusted ordinary gross income (AOGI)	Minimum credit (AET)	business
Alternative minimum tax (AMT)	Minimum tax credit (AMT)	Tax preference items
Alternative minimum taxable income (AMTI)	Ordinary gross income (OGI)	

OUTLINE

I.   ALTERNATIVE MINIMUM TAX

    A.   C corporations are subject to an alternative minimum tax (AMT).
        1.   Qualified 'small corporations' having average gross receipts of $5 million or less, in the preceding 3 years, are not subject to the AMT for tax years beginning after December 31, 1997.
        2.   If the corporation did not exist for three years, the gross receipts test is applied on the basis of the period during which it did exist.
        3.   A corporation that passes the $5 million average gross receipts test will continue to qualify as a small corporation as long as average gross receipts for three years preceding the tax year do not exceed 7.5 million.

    B.   AMT calculation:
        Regular Taxable Income Before NOL Deduction

        +/- Adjustments
        1.   Depreciation of property placed in service after 1986 and before 1999:
            a.   real property - the excess of regular tax depreciation over straight-line, 40 year life, mid-month convention.
            b.   personal property - the excess of accelerated depreciation over the amount determined using 150% DB, ADS class life, same convention as for regular tax.
        2.   After 1998, the depreciation adjustment for real estate is eliminated and the adjustment for personal property is applied to the difference between DDB and 150% DB over the property's MACRS recovery period.
        3.   Amortization of mining and exploration costs - the difference between the costs incurred and what would have resulted if the costs were capitalized and amortized over 10 years.
        4.   Adjusted gain or loss - the difference between AMT and regular tax gain or loss on asset dispositions.
        5.   Long-term contracts for AMT purposes are determined under the percentage of completion method for contracts entered into after March 1, 1986.
        6.   Passive activities losses of certain closely held and personal service corporations.

        + Preferences
        1.   Amortization claimed on certified pollution control facilities.
        2.   Accelerated depreciation on real property in excess of straight line for property placed in service before 1987.
        3.   Tax-exempt interest from specified private activity bonds.
        4.   Percentage depletion claimed in excess of the adjusted basis of property.

= Unadjusted AMTI

+/- ACE adjustments
1.   ACE depreciation for property placed in service prior to 1994.
2.   Inclusion in ACE of items included in E & P, net of related expenses
   a.   tax-exempt interest income
   b.   death benefits from life insurance contracts
   c.   tax benefit exclusions.
3.   Disallowance of items not deductible from E & P: 70% dividends received deduction from a less than 20% owned corporation.
4.   Other adjustments based on rules for determining E & P
   a.   intangible drilling costs
   b.   circulation expenditures
   c.   amortization of organizational expenditures
   d.   LIFO inventory adjustments
   e.   installment sales

- AMT NOL (not more than 90% of AMTI)

= AMTI

C.   Generally the AMT is 20% of alternative minimum taxable income (AMTI) which exceeds the exemption amount of $40,000. The exemption is reduced by 25% of AMTI in excess of $150,000.

D.   Minimum Tax Credit
   1.   AMT paid in one tax year may be carried forward indefinitely and used as a credit against regular tax liability that exceeds its tentative minimum tax.
   2.   Minimum tax credit may not be carried back and may not be offset against any future minimum tax liability.

II.   PENALTY TAX ON UNREASONABLE ACCUMULATIONS

A.   The tax law is designed to discourage the retention of earnings in a corporation beyond the normal business needs. A penalty tax is imposed on corporations that retain a surplus amount of earnings which, had they been distributed to the shareholder, would have been taxed, §531.

B.   The Element of Intent
   1.   Application of the penalty tax is triggered when a group of shareholders control corporate policy and withhold dividends with the INTENT to avoid personal, ordinary income taxes.

2. Tax avoidance need not be the controlling reason for retaining earnings in the corporation; it just has to be a contributing reason to result in the application of the accumulated earnings tax.

C. Imposition of the Tax and the Accumulated Earnings Credit
1. The AET is in addition to the regular corporate tax and the alternative minimum tax.
2. It is 39.6% of the current year's addition to the corporate accumulated earnings balance not needed for a reasonable business purpose.
3. The accumulated earnings credit is the greater of:
   a. current E & P for the tax year needed to meet the reasonable needs of the business less net long-term capital gains for the year.
   b. The minimum credit: the difference between $250,000 ($150,000 for certain personal service corporations) and accumulated E & P at the close of the previous year.

D. Reasonable Needs of the Business
1. Must be specific, definite and feasible, anticipated needs for
   a. working capital and
   b. noncurrent expenditures, i.e. capital expenditures and extraordinary expenses.
2. The "Bardahl" formula is the standard method used to determine the working capital needs of an inventory corporation.

   Inventory Cycle

   \+   Accounts Receivable Cycle

   \-   Accounts Payable Cycle

   x   Operating expenses other than accrued Federal income tax, depreciation, profit sharing and charitable contributions.

   =   Working Capital Needs

3. A formula to develop the working capital needs required in a noninventory corporation has not been resolved as of yet. It is assumed it will follow the Bardahl formula using a human resource accounting approach.

E. Mechanics of the Penalty Tax
1. The accumulated earnings tax is applied against accumulated taxable income
2. Accumulated taxable income equals:
   a. Taxable Income
   b. +/- Certain Adjustments

      c.   - Dividends Paid Deduction

      d.   - Accumulated Earnings Credit

3.   The certain adjustments which are deducted are:

      a.   Corporate income tax accrued.

      b.   Excess charitable contributions

      c.   Capital loss adjustment.

      d.   Excess of net long-term capital gain over net short-term capital loss, minus the capital gain tax and net capital losses from prior years.

4.   The certain adjustments, which are added are:

      a.   Capital loss carryovers and carrybacks

      b.   Net operating loss deductions.

      c.   The dividends received deduction.

III.   PERSONAL HOLDING COMPANY PENALTY TAX

A.   The Personal Holding Company Penalty Tax, §541, was imposed to discourage the sheltering of passive income in a personal holding company, PHC.

B.   The PHC penalty tax is in addition to the regular corporate tax and is 39.6% of undistributed personal holding company income.

C.   Definition

1.   For a company to be classified as a PHC, that company must meet both of the following tests:

      a.   More than 50% of the value of the outstanding stock of the corporation must have been owned by five or fewer individuals at any time during the last half of the taxable year.

      b.   Sixty percent or more of the corporation's adjusted ordinary gross income must be composed of passive types of incomes: dividends, interest, rents, royalties or certain personal service income.

2.   For the 50% test for stock ownership, very broad rules of constructive ownership apply, §544:

      a.   stock owned by a corporation, partnership, trust, or estate is considered to be owned proportionately by its stockholders, partners, or beneficiaries.

      b.   stock owned by members of an individual's family or by his or her partner is considered to be owned by the individual.

      c.   A stock option is regarded as stock.

      d.   A convertible security is considered stock.

3.   For the gross income test adjusted ordinary gross income (AOGI) is gross income, less gains from the sale or disposition of capital assets, and expenditures attributable to income from rents and mineral royalties.

D.   Rental income is normally classified as PHC income. However, it may be excluded if:
1.   50% or more of the corporation's AOGI is "adjusted income from rents," and
2.   the dividends paid during the year are equal to or greater than the amount by which the nonrent PHC income exceeds 10% of ordinary gross income.

E.   Adjusted income from mineral, oil, and gas royalties may be excluded from PHC income classification if the following three tests are met:
1.   50% or more of AOGI must constitute income from royalties;
2.   nonroyalty PHC income may not exceed 10% of OGI; and
3.   Section 162 business expenses, other than compensation paid to stockholders, must be at least 15% of AOGI.

F.   Income from personal service contracts is PHC income only if:
1.   the individual who is to perform the service is designated by someone other than the corporation and
2.   the person designated to perform owns 25% or more of the corporation directly or indirectly at some time during the year.

G.   Calculation of the PHC Tax
1.   The PHC tax is applied against undistributed PHC income.
2.   Undistributed PHC income is:
   a.   Taxable income
   b.   Plus:
      1.   Dividends received deductions.
      2.   A net operating loss, other than from the preceding year
      3.   The excess of business expenses and depreciation over the income from nonbusiness property owned by the corporation.
   c.   Minus:
      1.   Federal income tax accrued.
      2.   Excess charitable contributions
      3.   The excess of long-term capital gain over short-term capital loss (net of tax).
   d.   Equals: Adjusted taxable income
   e.   Minus: Dividends paid deduction
   f.   Equals: Undistributed personal holding company income (UPHCI)

H.   Dividends include the total of dividends paid during the year, dividends considered as paid on the last day of the tax year, and consent dividends.

IV.   A COMPARISON OF ACCUMULATED EARNINGS AND PHC TAXES

    A.   The imposition of §541 does not require intent.

    B.   §541 is applied to newly formed as well as older corporations.

    C.   The stock ownership test of §542(a)(2) is very explicit with regard to the PHC penalty tax. § 531, AET, is subjective.

    D.   Sufficient dividend distributions can eliminate either tax.
       1.   The dividends include actual dividends, consent dividends, and distributions made during the grace period.
       2.   In the case of a PHC, a deficiency dividend procedure can be used.

    E.   §541 is a self-assessed tax; §531 is assessed by the IRS.

V.   TAX PLANNING

    A.   A corporation cannot be subjected to Sections 531 and 541 taxes simultaneously.

    B.   To avoid the accumulated earnings tax:
       1.   justification of earnings accumulated should be:
          a.   documented during the period of accumulation,
          b.   sincere, and
          c.   pursued to the extent feasible
       2.   avoid the argument that loans to shareholders have no bona fide business purpose.
       3.   payments of dividends demonstrate good faith and the lack of tax avoidance motivation.

    C.   An S corporation election will circumvent the application of §531 tax. The election is prospective in nature and may not be applied retroactively.

    D.   Avoiding the PHC tax may be accomplished by:
       1.   failing either test to avoid PHC classification
          a.   dispersion of stock ownership, or
          b.   decreasing the percentage relationship of PHCI to AOGI (reduce PHCI or increase AOGI)
       2.   where rents or royalties are involved, consider maximizing the adjusted income to exempt it from PHC treatment.
       3.   properly timing dividend distributions.

TEST FOR SELF-EVALUATION

True or False

T F 1. A business that is a mere holding or investment company is of no consideration for the intent of tax avoidance.

T F 2. A corporation may have to pay the alternative minimum tax if taxable income for regular income tax purposes, when combined with certain adjustments and preference items that apply in computing the alternative minimum tax, total more than $40,000.   (IRS 90 3A-10)

T F 3. The reasonable business needs of a corporation are precisely outlined by the IRS.

T F 4. If a corporation paid an alternative minimum tax in 1988 because of adjustments or preference items that defer its tax liability rather than cause a permanent avoidance of the tax, the corporation's 1988 alternative minimum tax is available to be claimed as credit against its regular income for 1989 and later years.
                                                              (IRS 90 3A-11)

T F 5. The Bardahl Manufacturing Corporation formula is used to determine the reasonable needs of the business to the exclusion of other significant data.

T F 6. Long-term capital gains can be accumulated by a corporation without any penalty tax.

T F 7. Accumulation of income for exotic ventures into areas not related to the business are acceptable as long as the company stays under the $250,000 accumulated earnings credit.

T F 8. Assuming a company is close to being classified as a personal holding company, due to its proximity to the 60% PHC income rule, it would be wise for the company to hold growth stocks, as opposed to high yield stocks; this is because the high growth stocks will not enter into the PHC income calculation until they are sold and consequently taxed at a capital gains rate.

T F 9. For tax years beginning after 1989, the alternative minimum tax rules require that the 150% declining balance method of depreciation be used for property placed in service after 1989.   (IRS 91 3A-12)

T F 10. In determining working capital needs, it has been firmly established that all assets should be evaluated at their fair market values.

T   F   11.   Corporation X carries its net operating loss for 1986 back to 1983 for which X incurred a minimum tax liability. Corporation X must recompute its minimum tax liability for 1983.   (IRS 87 3A-17)

Fill in the Blanks

1.   The penalty tax on unreasonable accumulation of income is known as the _____ tax.

2.   The tax rate on the excess accumulated income in excess of the $250,000 credit is _____%.

3.   The justifiable needs of a business may be classified into two categories: _____ and _____ expenditures.

4.   Average inventory, divided by the cost of goods sold, equals the _____.

5.   The _____ of the marketable securities should be used in determining whether a corporation has excess accumulated earnings.

6.   Accumulated taxable income (ATI) is the result of taxable income, plus or minus certain adjustments, minus the dividend paid deduction and the _____.

7.   The payment of dividends _____ the amount of accumulated earnings subject to the accumulated earnings tax.

8.   A personal holding company (PHC) is defined as a corporation which meets _____ of the following tests:

9.   More than _____% of the value of the outstanding stock must be owned by _____ or fewer individuals at any time during the _____ of the taxable year.

10. A substantial proportion, _____%, of the corporate income (AOGI) must be composed of passive type income.

Multiple Choice

_____ 1.   XYZ Corporation has the following items of income and expense during the year:

Dividend income	$ 30,000
Rent income	120,000
Depreciation expense	30,000
Mortgage interest	25,000
Real estate taxes	25,000

Salaries	15,000
Dividends paid (4 shareholders)	18,000
Corporate income tax liability ?	

From the above data, AOGI would be:

a. $150,000
b. $132,000
c. $ 70,000
d. $ 55,000
e. None of the above

_____ 2.   From the above data, the corporate income tax liability is:

a. 4,855
b. 4,560
c. 5,100
d. 3,750
e. None of the above

_____ 3.   To meet the ten percent rental income test, XYZ Corporation must pay out how much in dividends?

a. $30,000
b. $15,000
c. $18,000
d. -0-
e. None of the above

_____ 4.   Assume 1997 taxable income is $41,500, of which $1,500 is dividend income, after the dividend exclusion. The Section 11 tax is $6,225 and dividends paid are $2,000. The PHC tax liability would be:

a. $8,338
b. $14,563
c. $14,421
d. $15,821
e. None of the above

_____ 5.   Given the following data, determine the accumulated taxable income of Z Corporation for 1997:

Tax liability	116,630
Excess charitable contributions	15,000
Long-term capital gain, adjusted	20,000
Dividends received	80,000
Dividends paid this year	30,000
Accumulated earnings (1/1/97)	110,000
Taxable income	342,000

a. $ 76,370
b. $104,370
c. $ 84,730
d. $ 67,930
e. None of the above

_____ 6.   Assume the accumulated taxable income of the Z Corporation in Question 5 was $110,500. The accumulated earnings tax would be:

a. $43,758
b. $41,580
c. $31,542
d. $40,387
e. None of the above

_____ 7.   To avoid the classification of rental income as PHC income, adjusted income from rents must be 50% or more of AOGI. In the following problem, what is that percentage?

Interest on mortgage	$ 3,000
Real estate property taxes	2,000
Depreciation	1,500
Salaries	5,000
Rental income	14,000
AOGI	18,000

a. 61%
b. 19%
c. 42%
d. 25%
e. None of the above

_____ 8.   Given the following data:

Annual revenues	$800,000
Average annual accounts receivable	80,000
Yearly expenses	700,000
Average accounts payable	60,000

the operating capital needed for one business cycle would be:

a. $10,010
b. $80,000
c. $60,000
d. $70,000
e.   None of the above

_____ 9.   The accumulated earnings tax does not apply to corporations that:

a.   Are personal service corporations
b.   Are personal holding companies
c.   Are members of an affiliated group

_____ 10.   The personal holding company tax

a.   Is imposed on corporations having 15 or more equal stockholders
b.   Applies regardless of the extent of dividend distributions
c.   Is self-assessed
d.   May apply if the minimum credit of $150,000 is exceeded

_____ 11.   The accumulated earnings tax can be imposed

a.   Regardless of the number of stockholders of a corporation
b.   On personal holding companies
c.   On companies that make distributions in excess of accumulated earnings
d.   Only on conglomerates

_____ 12.   Ray Holding Corp. has 18 unrelated equal stockholders. For the year ended December 31, 1997, Ray's income was from the following:

Interest Income	$ 25,000
Merchandising Operations	$ 40,000
Dividends from taxable domestic corporations	$125,000

Deductible expenses for 1997 totaled $20,000. Ray paid no dividends for the past three years. Ray's liability for personal holding company tax for 1997 will be based on

a. $102,500
b. $ 12,500
c. $ 90,000
d. $ -0-

_____ 13. If a corporation's tentative minimum tax exceeds the regular tax, the excess amount is: (IRS 95 3B-28)

a.   payable in addition to the regular tax.
b.   carried back to the third preceding tax year.
c.   carried back to the first preceding tax year.
d.   subtracted from the regular tax.

_____ 14. Given the following facts, what is the amount of Wood Corporation's alternative minimum tax?   (IRS 95 3C-59)

Taxable income before net operating loss deductions	$85,000
Total adjustments to taxable income	(2,000)
Total tax preference items	45,000
Regular income tax	17,150

a. $1,250
b. $850
c. $450
d. $-0-

_____ 15. Barrett Corporation's 1994 alternative minimum taxable income was $200,000. The exempt portion of Barrett's 1994 alternative minimum taxable income was:
                                                       (IRS 95 3C-60)

a. $0
b. $12,500
c. $27,500
d. $40,000

SOLUTIONS

True or False

1. F (p. 6-12)
2. T (p. 6-9)
3. F (p. 6-14)
4. T (p. 6-10)
5. F (p. 6-14)
6. T (p. 6-19)
7. T (p. 6-12)
8. T (p. 6-27)
9. F (p. 6-4)
10. F (p. 6-18)
11. T (p. 6-4; AMT NOL cannot exceed 90% of AMTI)

Fill in the Blanks

1. accumulated earnings (p. 6-12)
2. 39.6% (p. 6-12)
3. working capital; extraordinary (p. 6-14)
4. inventory cycle (p. 6-15)
5. fair market value (p. 6-18)
6. accumulated earnings credit (p. 6-18)
7. reduces (p. 6-19)
8. both (p. 6-20)
9. 50%; five; last half (p. 6-21)
10. 60% (p. 6-21)

Multiple Choice

1. c ($30,000 + 120,000) - ($30,000 + $25,000 + $25,000) = $70,000

2. c

Dividend income	$ 30,000	
Rental income	120,000	$150,000
Less:		
Depreciation expense	$ 30,000	
Mortgage expense	25,000	
Real estate taxes	25,000	
Salaries	15,000	$ 95,000
		55,000
Less dividend received deduction		21,000
Taxable income		34,000
Tax: 15%(34,000)		5,100

3.	b	Nonrental PHC income	$ 30,000
		Less 10% of OGI	15,000
			$ 15,000
4.	b	Taxable income	$ 41,500
		Plus dividend received deduction	
		($1,500/.30) - ($1,500)	3,500
			45,000
		Less Section 11 tax	6,225
		Less dividends paid	2,000
			36,775
			x 39.6%
		PHC tax liability	14,563
5.	a	Taxable income	342,000
		Plus 70% dividend deduction	56,000
			398,000
		Less:	
		Tax liability	116,630
		Excess charitable contributions	15,000
		Net long-term capital gain	20,000
		Dividends paid	30,000
		Accumulated earnings credit carryover	140,000
		Accumulated taxable income	76,370

6.   a   39.6% (110,500)

7.   c $14,000 - ($3,000 + $2,000 + 1,500) = $7,500 adjusted income from rents. $7,500/$18,000 = 42%

8.   a   (($80,000/$800,000)-($60,000/$700,000))x$700,000 = (.1-.0857) x $700,000 = $10,010

9.   b   (p. 6-20)

10.   c   (p. 6-32)

11.   a   (p. 6-11)

12.   d   (p. 6-21; definition, 5 or fewer owning 50% or more)

13.   a   (p. 6-2)

14. c   Taxable income before NOL   85,000
         Minus adjustments   2,000
         Plus preferences   45,000
         Minus exemption   40,000
         AMTI   88,000
         Times 20%   17,600
         Less Regular tax   17,150

15. c   (p. 6- 9; $40,000 reduced by 25% of AMTI in excess of $150,000; 40,000 - 25%(50,000))

CHAPTER 7

CORPORATIONS: REORGANIZATIONS

LEARNING OBJECTIVES

After completing Chapter 7, you should be able to:

1. Gain a general understanding of corporate reorganizations.

2. Identify and apply the tax consequences of a corporate reorganization.

3. Identify the statutory requirements for the different types of reorganizations.

4. Recognize the judicial and administrative conditions that complement the statutory requirements for a nontaxable corporate reorganization.

5. Use the rules applicable to the carryover of tax attributes in a corporate reorganization.

6. Structure corporate reorganizations to obtain favorable tax consequences.

KEY TERMS

Business purpose
Consolidation
Continuity of business enterprise
Continuity of interest test

Equity structure shift
Long-term tax-exempt rate
Merger
Owner shift

Recapitalization
Reorganization
Step transaction

OUTLINE

I.   GENERAL CONSIDERATIONS

    A.   Summary of the Different Types of Reorganizations
        1.   Type A: a statutory merger or consolidation;
        2.   Type B: an exchange of stock for voting stock;
        3.   Type C: an exchange of assets for voting stock;
        4.   Type D: a divisive reorganization
        5.   Type E: a recapitalization;
        6.   Type F: a change in identity, form, or place of organization;
        7.   Type G: an insolvent corporation

    B.   Summary of Tax Consequences in a Tax-Free Reorganization
        1.   Gain or Loss
            a.   generally, no gain or loss is recognized unless consideration other than stock or securities is received.
            b.   gain is recognized on securities received if the principal amount received is more than the principal amount of the securities surrendered.
            c.   if consideration other than stock or securities is received, the recognized gain is limited to the cash and fair market value of other property received.
            d.   if no stock is surrendered, the consideration received is treated as a dividend to the extent of the shareholder's pro rata share of the corporations E & P.
            e.   losses are not recognized.
        2.   Basis
            a.   the basis of property received by the acquiring corporation is the same basis as in the hands of the target increased by the amount of gain recognized by the target on the transfer.
            b.   the basis of stock and securities surrendered carries over to the stock and securities received, decreased by the amount of boot received, and increased by the amount of gain and dividend income recognized, if any.

II.   TYPES OF TAX-FREE REORGANIZATIONS

    A.   Type A
        1.   Type A reorganizations include statutory mergers and consolidations.
        2.   Advantages

a. Type A reorganizations permit the greatest flexibility of any of the tax-free organizations, because the use of voting stock is not required.

b. The use of money or property will constitute "boot," which may require the recognition of a gain. However, this will not destroy the tax-free treatment if the continuity of interest test is satisfied: at least 50% of the consideration must be stock.

3. Disadvantages

a. Statutory compliance usually requires a majority approval of all shareholders; dissenting shareholders have the right to have their shares appraised and bought.

b. The acquiring corporation must assume all liabilities of the acquired corporation.

c. The use of a subsidiary to acquire the stock of the target company may reduce these problems,

1. because the parent corporation is the majority stockholder, only the board of directors' approval is required.

2. the parent's asset will be protected from target's creditors.

B. Type B

1. Type B reorganizations require the exchange of stock for voting stock.

a. the acquiring corporation must give up only voting stock, and

b. after the exchange must own at least 80% of all classes of the target corporation's stock.

2. Voting stock must be the sole consideration; this requirement is strictly construed.

C. Type C

1. Type C reorganizations require the exchange of substantially all the assets of the target corporation for the voting stock of the acquiring corporation.

2. The acquired corporation must distribute the stock, securities, and other properties it receives in the reorganization, as well as its own properties to its shareholders. It then, generally, is liquidated.

3. The "voting stock" requirement for a C reorganization is less strict than it is for a B reorganization.

D. Type D

1. Acquisitive D reorganization

a. the acquiring corporation transfers assets to the target corporation in exchange for control, 50%, of the target.

b. all stock and property received by the acquiring corporation must be distributed to the acquiring corporation's shareholders.

2. Divisive D reorganization
   a. the acquiring corporation transfers assets to the target corporation in exchange for control, 80%, of the target.
   b. all stock received by the acquiring corporation must be distributed to the acquiring corporation's shareholders as:
      1. a spin-off - the shareholders do not give up any stock in the distributing corporation.
      2. a split-off - the shareholders exchange stock in the distributing corporation for stock in the new corporation.
   c. in a split-up, the assets of one corporation are transferred to two or more new corporations
      1. the stock of the new corporations is distributed to the transferor corporation's shareholders.
      2. the transferor corporation is liquidated.

E. Type E
   1. E reorganizations are recapitalizations, an exchange of:
      a. bonds for stock
      b. stock for stock
      c. bonds for bonds
   2. Potential tax consequences affect the shareholders who exchange stock or securities, not the corporation.

F. Type F
   1. F reorganizations merely change the identity, form or place of organization.
   2. Because the surviving corporation is the same corporation as its predecessor, tax attributes carry over.
   3. F reorganizations are restricted to single operating corporations.
   4. An F reorganization does not jeopardize a valid S election or §1244 stock status.

G Type G
   1. All or part of the assets of a debtor corporation are transferred to an acquiring corporation in a bankruptcy proceeding.
   2. Debtor corporation creditors must receive voting stock of the acquiring corporation for debt representing 80% or more of the fair market value of the debt of the debtor corporation.

III. JUDICIAL CONDITIONS

A. Five judicially-created doctrines have become the basic requirements for a tax-free corporate reorganization. They are:
   1. Sound business purpose,

2.   Continuity of interest,

3.   Continuity of business enterprise,

4.   Step transaction, and

5.   Plan of reorganization.

B.   Continuity of Interest

1.   The seller must acquire an equity interest in the purchasing corporation.

2.   Generally, this test is met if the shareholders of the target corporation receive stock in the purchasing corporation equal in value to at least 50% of all formerly outstanding stock of the target corporation.

C.   Continuity of Business Enterprise

1.   The acquiring corporation continues the historic business of the transferor corporation, or

2.   The acquiring corporation uses a significant portion of the assets of the transferor in its business.

IV.   CARRYOVER OF CORPORATE TAX ATTRIBUTES

A   Allowance of Carryovers

1.   Section 381(c) lists specific tax attributes of an acquired corporation which can be carried over to a successor corporation.

2.   Only the A, C, acquisitive D, F, and G reorganizations are subject to the rules.

B.   Loss Carryovers

1.   An NOL or capital loss carryover is permitted as a deduction of the successor corporation but, may be limited.

2.   The amount of loss, in the year of transfer, is limited to the taxable income or capital gain of the acquiring corporation multiplied by a percentage representing the days remaining in that tax year.

3.   An owner shift or equity structure shift causes imposition of a §382 limitation. This section limits the amount of an NOL carryover which can be used on an annual basis.

C.   Earnings and Profits

1.   E & P of a predecessor corporation carries over to the successor corporation as of the date of the transfer.

2.   A deficit can only offset E & P accumulated after the date of the transfer.

TEST FOR SELF-EVALUATION

True or False

T F 1.   Generally, if a reorganization consists of only stocks and/or securities, there will no tax consequences to the security holders.

T F 2.   The recognition of gain on a Section 368 reorganization is limited to the amount of cash received and the fair market value of other property.

T F 3.   Even though a corporation distributes all the cash and securities it receives to its shareholders in a tax-free reorganization, it still must pay a tax to the Federal government.

T F 4.   The Type B reorganization is restricted to the exchange of stock for assets.

T F 5.   The effective control level which must be reached by the acquiring corporation in a Type B reorganization is at least 80% of the total combined voting power of all classes of stock entitled to vote, and at least 80% of the total number of shares of all other classes of stock of the corporation.

T F 6.   A Type D reorganization is a mechanism through which a corporation can divide itself--that is, effect a spin-off, split-off, or split-up.

T F 7.   The Type E reorganization is of significance to the shareholders only, and is of no consequence to the corporation.

T F 8.   The IRS has ruled that if a reorganization qualifies as an A, C, or D reorganization, and at the same time as an F reorganization, Type F will prevail.

T F 9.   A split-up involves three corporations, none of which are liquidated.

T F 10. In a Type B reorganization, the assumption of a liability will not violate the "solely for voting stock" requirement.

Fill in the Blanks

1.   Section 382 limitations on NOL carryovers are triggered only if there is an _____ or _____ .

2.   The 382 limitations apply if there has been a change of more than _____% in the ownership of the loss corporation.

3.   Earnings and profits and deficits carry over, but deficits reduce E & P only after _____ .

4. In order to substantiate a reorganization as having a bona fide business purpose, it is practically mandatory to have a _____ of _____.

5. In an A-type reorganization, the use of a subsidiary to acquire another corporation requires compliance with _____.

Multiple Choice

_____ 1.   Green Corporation exchanges voting stock in Blue Corporation, its parent, for 91% of the stock in Yellow Corporation. This is an example of which type of reorganization?

    a. Type A
    b. Type B
    c. Type C
    d. Type D
    e. None of the above

_____ 2.   Jots Corporation is acquired in a merger with Tons Corporation. Tons, the surviving corporation, has a $40,000 deficit in E & P, while Jots has a $150,000 positive E & P. After the merger, Tons distributes $75,000 to its shareholders. The distribution will be treated as:

    a. $35,000 ordinary dividend
    b. $75,000 ordinary dividend
    c. $35,000 ordinary income and $40,000 long-term capital gain
    d. $75,000 long-term capital gain
    e. None of the above

_____ 3.   Taos Corporation, a Texas corporation, organizes Chilton Corporation in Oklahoma. It transfers all of its assets to Chilton and distributes the Chilton stock to its shareholders, who turn in their Taos stock. Consequently, Taos is liquidated. This is an example of which type of reorganization?

    a. Type A
    b. Type C
    c. Type D
    d. Type F
    e. None of the above

_____ 4.   Which one of the following is not a corporate reorganization as defined in Section 368?

    a.   Stock redemption
    b.   Recapitalization
    c.   Change in identity
    d.   Split off

_____ 5.   Thomas and Bond each own a 50% interest in TomBoy Corporation. TomBoy is merged into Gunnison Corporation. Thomas receives cash for his stock, while Bond receives stock in Gunnison. As a result:

    a.   Both Thomas and Bond are not taxed
    b.   Thomas is taxed but Bond is not
    c.   Bond is taxed but Thor~ ~s is not
    d.   Both Thomas and Bor~ ~e taxed
    e.   None of the above

_____ 6.   The above is an example of:

    a.   "Continuity of business purpose"
    b.   A step transaction
    c.   "Continuity of interest"
    d.   All of the above
    e.   None of the above

_____ 7.   In order to have the full tax advantage of a net operating loss carry-over between two corporations, one of which is the acquired corporation, the change in ownership of the acquired corporation cannot exceed:

    a.   40%
    b.   33 - 1/3%
    c.   60%
    d.   50%
    e.   None of the above

_____ 8.   Carter Corporation merges with Dutch Corporation, which has a $140,000 net operating loss. Carter acquires Dutch in order to obtain the $140,000 loss. Carter had a profit of $200,000 for the year, and they acquired Dutch Corporation on September 1, 1993. Carter will get a tax write-off for Dutch's loss of:

    a.   -0-
    b. $66,667
    c. $46,667
    d. $140,000
    e. $200,000

____ 9.   Would you answer to Question 8 by any different if both firms had other business reasons for the merger?

    a. Yes
    b. No

____ 10.   Tums Corporation has been engaged in two businesses over the last 12 years. It decides to transfer the assets from one of its businesses to a new corporation, and distributes the stock to the shareholders of Tums. This is an example of a:

    a. Spin-off
    b. Split-off
    c. Split-up
    d. Type A reorganization
    e. None of the above

____ 11.   Following a plan of corporate reorganization Mike exchanged 5,000 shares of Cable Corporation common stock for 900 shares of Wire Corporation common stock. Mike had paid $18,750 for the Cable stock. The fair market value of the Wire stock was $21,500 on the date of the exchange. How much was Mike's recognized gain?

    a. $2,050
    b. $4,100
    c. $2,750
    d. $-0-

____ 12.   With regard to corporate reorganizations, which one of the following statements is not correct?

    a. A mere change in identity, form, or place of organization of one corporation qualifies as reorganization.
    b. The reorganization provisions can be used to provide tax-free treatment for corporate transactions.
    c. A plan of reorganization is not required.
    d. A Letter Ruling should be requested when planning a corporate reorganization.

____ 13.   Following a plan of corporate reorganization adopted in February 1995, Lori exchanged 10 shares of Green Corp. common stock that she had purchased in March 1988 at a cost of $1,000 for 15 shares of Brown Corp. common stock having a fair market value of $1,200. Lori's recognized gain on this exchange was:

a. $-0-
b. $200 ordinary income
c. $200 short-term capital gain
d. $200 long-term capital gain

SOLUTIONS

True or False

1. T (p. 7-6)
2. T (p. 7-6)
3. F (p. 7-17)
4. F (p. 7-12)
5. T (p. 7-12)
6. T (p. 7-17)
7. T (p. 7-20)
8. T (p. 7-20)
9. F (p. 7-17)
10. F (p. 7-14)

Fill in the Blanks

1. (p. 7-24; owner shift or an equity structure shift)
2. (p. 7-25; 50%)
3. (p. 7-26; the date of transfer)
4. (p. 7-3; written plan of reorganization)
5. (p. 7-9; state law)

Multiple Choice

1. b (Figure 7-4)
2. b (Positive E & P of $150,000 cannot offset deficit)
3. d (Figure 7-8)
4. a (p. 7-4)
5. b (p. 7-22)
6. c (p. 7-22)
7. d (p. 7-24)
8. a (p. 7-27; tax avoidance scheme)
9. a
10. a (Figure 7-7)
11. d (no consideration other than stock was received)
12. c (p. 7-3, 4)
13. a (no consideration other than stock was received)

CHAPTER 8

CONSOLIDATED
TAX RETURNS

LEARNING OBJECTIVES

After completing Chapter 8, you should be able to:

1. Apply the fundamental concepts of consolidated tax returns.

2. Identify the sources of the rules for consolidated taxable income.

3. Recognize the major advantages and disadvantages of filing consolidated tax returns.

4. Describe the corporations that are eligible to file on a consolidated basis.

5. Explain the compliance aspects of consolidated returns.

6. Compute a parent's investment basis in a subsidiary.

7. Account for intercompany transactions of a consolidated group.

8. Identify limitations that restrict the use of losses and credits of group members derived in separate return years.

9. Derive deductions and credits on a consolidated basis.

10. Demonstrate tax planning opportunities available to consolidated groups.

KEY TERMS

Consolidated return	Restoration event	Separate return limitation year
Excess loss account		(SLRY)

OUTLINE

I.   CONTEXT OF THE CONSOLIDATED RETURN RULES

    A.   Motivations to Consolidate
       1.   A desire to isolate assets of other group members from the liabilities of specific operating divisions.
       2.   A need to carry out specific planning objectives.
       3.   An opportunity to manage the combined tax liability of the group's members.

    B.   Philosophy of Consolidated Return Rules
       1.   The underlying purpose of the consolidated return rules is one of organizational neutrality.
       2.   A group of closely related corporations should have neither a tax advantage nor a disadvantage compared to taxpayers who file separate corporate returns.

II. ASSESSING CONSOLIDATED RETURN STATUS

    A.   Potential Advantages
       1.   Operating and capital loss carryovers of one group member may be used to shelter income of other group members.
       2.   Deferral of gain recognition on some intercompany transactions.
       3.   Optimization of certain deductions and credits by using consolidated amounts to compute pertinent limitations.

    B.   Potential Disadvantages
       1.   The consolidated return election is binding on all subsequent years until an eligible group no longer exists or the IRS consents to revocation of the election.
       2.   Capital and operating loss carryover to separate return year(s) may provide a greater tax benefit than applying the loss to consolidated income.
       3.   Deferral of loss recognition on some intercompany transactions.
       4.   Income bunching and creating short tax years for subsidiaries required to adopt the parent's tax year.
       5.   Incurring additional administrative costs to comply with consolidated return regulations.

III. ELECTING CONSOLIDATED RETURN STATUS

    A.   All members of a corporate group must meet three requirements:

1. The stock ownership criteria of an affiliated group,
   a. the identifiable parent must own 80% of the voting power and 80% of the value of the subsidiary.
   b. this ownership test must be satisfied on every day of the tax year.
2. Be statutorily eligible to make the consolidated election,
   a. noncorporate entities such as partnerships, trusts and estates are ineligible.
   b. foreign corporations, tax-exempt charitable corporations and insurance companies may be statutorily ineligible.
3. Satisfy the compliance requirements in making and maintaining the election.
   a. initially the election is made on Form 1122 attached to the first, consolidated Form 1120 tax return.
   b. subsequent consolidated returns must include Form 851, Affiliations Schedule.
   c. the group continues filing consolidated returns until an eligible group no longer exists, or, the parent applies for and is granted permission to terminate the consolidated election.

B. Liability for consolidated taxes is born by the members, individually and jointly.

C. Tax Accounting Periods and Methods
   1. All consolidated group members must use the same tax year as the parent.
   2. Consolidated group members need not adopt the tax accounting method, cash or accrual, of the parent. However, a cash-basis corporation may need to change to accrual basis reporting because the $5 million gross receipts test is applied to consolidated gross receipts.

IV. STOCK BASIS OF SUBSIDIARY

A. Upon acquisition of a subsidiary, the parent's basis is the acquisition price. At each consolidated year-end, stock basis adjustments are required to prevent double recording of gains and losses.
   1. Positive adjustments include:
      a. an allocable share of consolidated taxable income for the year.
      b. an allocable share of consolidated operating or capital loss of a subsidiary that could not use the loss through a carryback.
   2. Negative adjustments include:
      a. an allocable share of consolidated taxable loss for the year.
      b. an allocable share of any carryover operating or capital loss deducted on the consolidated return and not previously a reduction in stock basis.
      c. dividends paid by the subsidiary to the parent out of E & P.

B.   An "excess loss account" is created when accumulated post-acquisition taxable losses of the subsidiary exceed the acquisition price.
1.   The losses of the subsidiary are recognized in the current year's consolidated return.
2.   The stock basis account is not negative.
3.   If the parent disposes of the subsidiary's stock, this account represents capital gain on disposition.

C.   In a chain of subsidiaries, computation of stock basis begins with the lowest level subsidiary and proceeds up to the parent.

D.   Consolidated tax liability is allocated in proportion to each group members' contribution to consolidated taxable income unless an election to use some other allocation method is made.

V.   COMPUTING CONSOLIDATED TAXABLE INCOME

A.   Computational Procedure
1.   Each group member first computes its taxable income as though a separate entity.
2.   This income is then split to eliminate some intercompany items, to remove transactions which must be accounted for as a group and to recognize certain transactions which receive deferral treatment.
3.   Consolidated taxable income is a combination of the revised separate taxable incomes and the resulting income/loss from group items and deferral/restoration events.

B.   Typical Intercompany Transactions
1.   Transactions which generate income to one member and a deductible expense to another member are left in consolidated income as direct offsets.
2.   Adjustments may be required if all members do not use the same accounting method.
3.   Dividends received from other group members are removed from separate taxable incomes, these dividends cannot be considered for any dividends received deduction.

C.   Computation of Group Items
1.   Transactions which are statutorily limited must be computed as though the consolidated entity is one corporation. Such items are:
a.   net capital gain/loss
b.   §1231 gain/loss
c.   casualty/theft gain/loss

        d.   charitable contributions

        e.   dividends received deduction

        f.   net operating loss

        g.   the general business and research credits

        h.   any recapture of those credits

        i.   the foreign tax credit

        j.   the percentage depletion deduction

        k.   alternative minimum tax elements

    2.   The limitations are applied to consolidated taxable income after adjusting for intercompany transactions.

  D.   Deferral and Restoration Events

    1.   Gain or loss on intercompany sales of assets is deferred until control of the asset leaves the group.

    2.   The entire deferred gain or loss is restored to consolidated income when the asset is transferred outside the group, the transferor leaves the group or the consolidation election is terminated.

    3.   An election may be made to include or deduct all intercompany gain or loss immediately; this election remains in effect until IRS permission for revocation is received.

VI.   TAX PLANNING CONSIDERATIONS

  A.   Optimize overall tax benefits when choosing consolidated partners:

    1.   Loss and credit carryovers

    2.   Passive activity income, loss, or credits

    3.   Gains that can be deferred through intercompany sales

    4.   Contributions to consolidated ACE adjustments

    5.   Excess limitation amounts

    6.   Section 1231 gains, losses, and look-back profiles.

  B.   100% Dividends Received Deduction is an alternative to filing consolidated returns.

TEST FOR SELF-EVALUATION

True or False

T F 1.   The Code describes the various elements of consolidated tax return rules.

T F 2.   All members of the consolidated group must have the same tax year.

T F 3.   All members of the consolidated group must use the same accounting method.

T F 4.   Financial accounting consolidated income is the same as tax-basis consolidated income.

T F 5.   The most commonly encountered intercompany transactions are removed from member's separate taxable incomes for consolidated tax purposes.

T F 6.   Members of an affiliated group must file consolidated income tax returns.

T F 7.   Only the parent corporation is responsible for consolidated tax liabilities.

Fill in the Blanks

1.   The general function of the consolidated return rules is _____.

2.   Controlled groups of corporations include _____ and _____ groups.

3.   An _____ group requires an identifiable parent having control of _____% of the voting stock _____% of the value of the subsidiary.

4.   The three basic requirements for consolidated return rules are: _____, _____, _____.

5.   To qualify as a parent-subsidiary controlled group, the parent must own _____% of the voting stock _____% of the value of the subsidiary.

6.   Upon acquiring a subsidiary, the parent corporation records a stock basis on its tax balance sheet equal to _____.

7.   Adjustments to the parent's stock basis in the subsidiary are made on _____ of the consolidated return year, or _____.

8.   An _____ is created when accumulated deficits in the subsidiary's post-acquisition E & P exceed the acquisition price.

Multiple Choice

_____ 1.   Sub sold a building to Parent for $400,000. Sub had originally paid $300,000 for the building and had accumulated depreciation of $100,000. Parent, after six years, sold the building to an unrelated third party for $500,000. Sub's realized gain on the sale to parent was:

   a. $100,000
   b. $200,000
   c. $300,000
   d. $400,000

_____ 2.   Sub's recognized gain on the sale to parent was:

   a. $-0-
   b. $100,000
   c. $200,000
   d. $300,000

_____ 3.   Parent's realized gain on the sale to the third party was:

   a. $-0-
   b. $100,000
   c. $100,000 plus accumulated depreciation
   d. $100,000 minus accumulated depreciation

_____ 4.   Parent Corporation acquired 100% of the stock of Sub Corporation on July 5, 1996. Both corporations intend to file a consolidated return immediately upon acquisition. Parent's tax year ends March 31; Sub's tax year ends July 30. The first consolidated return is due:

   a.   October 15
   b.   September 15
   c.   June 15
   d.   March 15

_____ 5.   A parent corporation's adjustments to its stock basis in a consolidated subsidiary includes:

   a.   an allocable share of the subsidiary's E & P
   b.   dividends paid by the subsidiary
   c.   both a and b
   d.   neither a nor b

_____ 6.   In the current year Parent Corporation provided services to its 100% owned subsidiary valued at $75,000. Sub will pay Parent next year. Sub uses the cash method of accounting, Parent uses the accrual method. Is any adjustment required in computing consolidated taxable income?

   a.   No
   b.   Yes

_____ 7.   The filing of consolidated tax returns is available only to:

   a.   parent-subsidiary controlled groups
   b.   brother-sister controlled groups
   c.   affiliated groups
   d.   all of the above

_____ 8.   With regard to a controlled corporate group, all of the following statements are correct except: (IRS 94 3B-26)

   a.   The controlled group is allowed only ONE set of graduated income tax brackets.
   b.   Controlled groups are allowed ONE $80,000 exemption amount for alternative minimum tax purposes.
   c.   The controlled group is allowed ONE $250,000 accumulated earnings credit.
   d.   The tax benefits of the graduated rate schedule are to be allocated equally among the members of the group unless they all consent to a different apportionment.

SOLUTIONS

True or False

1. F (p. 8-5)
2. T (p. 8-15)
3. F (p. 8-15)
4. F (p. 8-6)
5. F (p. 8-19)
6. F (p. 8-10)
7. F (p. 8-14)

Fill in the Blanks

1. (p. 8-5; organizational neutrality)
2. (p. 8-9; parent-subsidiary, brother-sister)
3. (p. 8-10; affiliated, 80%, and 80%)
4. (p. 8-6; stock ownership, statutory eligibility and compliance)
5. (p. 8-10; 80%, or 80%)
6. (p. 8-16; the acquisition price)
7. (p. 8-16; last day, date of disposition)
8. (p. 8-16; excess loss account)

Multiple Choice

1. b (p. 8-29; $400,000 sale price - (300,000 - 100,000) basis)
2. a (p. 8-29; deferral event)
3. c (p. 8-29; $500,000 sale price - basis)
4. c (p. 8-15)
5. c (p. 8-16)
6. b (p. 8-19; different methods of accounting requires adjustment)
7. c (p. 8-11)
8. b (the exemption for computing AMTI is $40,000)

CHAPTER 9

TAXATION OF
INTERNATIONAL TRANSACTIONS

LEARNING OBJECTIVES

After completing Chapter 9, you should be able to:

1.　Use the foreign tax credit provisions.

2.　Apply the rules for sourcing income and allocating deductions into U.S. and foreign categories.

3.　Utilize the U.S. tax provisions concerning nonresident alien individuals and foreign corporations.

4.　Appreciate the tax benefits available to certain U.S. individuals working abroad.

5.　Apply the U.S. tax rules for foreign corporations controlled by U.S. persons.

6.　Explain how foreign currency exchange affects the tax consequences of international transactions.

KEY TERMS

Branch profits tax	Foreign earned income exclusion	Nonresident alien
Controlled foreign corporation	Foreign sales corporation	Subpart F
Dividend equivalent amount	Foreign tax credit	Tax haven
Effectively connected income	Functional currency	Tax treaty
FIRPTA	Green card test	Treaty shopping
		U.S. shareholder

OUTLINE

I.   OVERVIEW OF INTERNATIONAL TAXATION

    A.   The United States retains the right to tax its citizens and residents on their worldwide taxable income.

    B.   U.S. persons with international transactions encounter many of the same Federal tax laws as any U.S. taxpayer:
        1.   Income is subject to U.S. taxation.
        2.   Certain expenses and losses are deductible.
        3.   Earnings of domestic corporations face double taxation.

    C.   U.S. taxpayers with international transactions face another set of provisions that apply to international business; these laws:
        1.   are meant to prevent two-country taxation.
        2.   allow the U.S. to remain competitive internationally.
        3.   prevent taxpayers from evading U.S. taxation by moving income-producing activities abroad.

II.   THE FOREIGN TAX CREDIT

    A.   A qualified taxpayer is allowed a credit for foreign income taxes paid.
        1.   The direct credit is available only to the taxpayer who bears the legal incidence of the foreign tax.
        2.   The indirect credit is available to corporate taxpayers who receive dividends from foreign corporations that have paid a foreign tax on earnings.

    B.   FTC Limitations
        1.   The general limitation limits the FTC to:
            a.   the lesser of the actual foreign taxes paid or accrued, or
            b.   U.S. taxes, before the FTC, on foreign-sourced taxable income.
        2.   To prevent cross-crediting, separate limitations apply to certain categories of foreign-source taxable income and the related foreign income taxes.
            a.   a two-year carryback and a five-year carryover of excess foreign taxes are allowed.
            b.   the carryback and carryover provision is available only within the separate baskets.
            c.   refer to the list of categories in Concept Summary 9-1 of text.

    C.   Foreign tax credits are:
        1.   Elective for any particular year.

2.   Applicable only to foreign tax levies which have the predominant character of an income tax in the U.S. sense.

3.   Based on the exchange rate in effect when the foreign tax is paid, if accrued, after 12/31/97, based on average exchange rate for the relevant tax year.

D.   Possessions Corporations

    1.   §936 allows a credit against the U.S. tax attributable to foreign-source taxable income from the active conduct of a trade or business in a U.S. possession.

    2.   Legislation passed in 1996 repeals the credit except for corporations conducting an active trade or business in a possession on October 13, 1995.

    3.   A §936 corporation that adds a new line of business after October 13, 1995 will cease to be eligble.

    4.   The credit will phase out by January 1, 2006.

III.   SOURCING OF INCOME AND ALLOCATION OF DEDUCTIONS

A.   Income sourced within the United States generally includes:

    1.   Interest received from the U.S. government, District of Columbia, noncorporate U.S. residents and domestic corporations.

    2.   Dividends received from domestic corporations.

    3.   Income from personal services performed within the U.S.

    4.   Income from rental of tangible property located within the U.S.

    5.   Income from royalties on intangible property used in the U.S.

    6.   Income from the sale or exchange of real property located in the U.S.

    7.   Income from the sale or exchange of personal property by U.S. residents.

    8.   Income from transportation beginning and ending in the U.S.

    9.   50% of income from transportation beginning or ending in the U.S.

    10.   Space and ocean activities conducted by U.S. residents.

    11.   50% of income from international communications between the U.S. and a foreign country.

B.   Income sourced without the United States is residual income.

C.   Allocation and Apportionment of Deductions

    1.   Deductions directly related to an activity or property are allocated to those classes of income.

    2.   Specific rules apply to the allocation and apportionment of:

        a.   interest expense

        b.   research and development expenditures

        c.   certain stewardship fees

          d.   legal and accounting fees

          e.   income taxes

          f.   losses

     3.   Deductions not definitely related to any class of gross income are ratably allocated to all classes of gross income and apportioned between sources.

IV.   U.S. TAXATION OF NONRESIDENT ALIENS AND FOREIGN CORPORATIONS

A.   NRAs having U.S. source income are taxed at the same rate as U.S. residents on effectively connected income and at a flat, 30%, rate on noneffectively connected income.

    1.   A U.S. trade or business is a prerequisite to having effectively connected income.

    2.   Effectively connected income is determined under the

        a.   asset-use test: derived from assets used in, or held for use in, the trade or business, or

        b.   business-activities test: if the activities of the trade or business were a material factor in the production of the income.

B.   Foreign Corporations

    1.   A foreign corporation is not a domestic corporation; a domestic corporation is created or organized in the U.S.

    2.   U.S. source fixed, determinable, annual or periodic income of foreign corporations is taxed at a flat 30% rate.

    3.   Effectively connected income of foreign corporations conducting a trade or business in the U.S. are subject to the same tax rates as domestic corporations.

    4.   Any U.S. source income attributable to a U.S. office of a foreign corporation is deemed to be effectively connected.

    5.   The branch profits tax may impose a 30% tax on the dividend equivalent amount for the taxable year on any foreign corporation operating through a U.S. subsidiary.

C.   The Foreign Investment in Real Property Tax Act

    1.   Treats gains and losses realized by NRAs and foreign corporations from the sale or disposition of U.S. real property as effectively connected income.

    2.   NRA individuals must pay a tax equal to at least 26, or 28, percent of the lesser of their AMTI, or regular U.S. rates on the net U.S. real property gain for the taxable year.

    3.   Any direct interest in real property located in the U.S. and any equity interest in a domestic corporation are U.S. real property interests.

4.   Anyone acquiring a USRPI from a foreign person must withhold 10% of the amount realized on the disposition and submit it to the IRS within 20 days.

D.   Tax Treaties
1.   Income tax treaties generally provide taxing rights with regard to the taxable income of residents of one treaty country who have income sourced in the other treaty country.
2.   Treaties generally provide for primary taxing rights which require the other treaty partner to allow a credit for the taxes paid on the twice-taxed income.
3.   Primary taxing rights are usually determined by the residence of the taxpayer or the presence of a permanent establishment in a treaty country to which the income is attributable.

V.   U.S. TAXPAYERS ABROAD

A.   Citizens and residents of the U.S. are subject to Federal taxation of their worldwide taxable income.

B.   The Foreign Earned Income Exclusion
1.   Is elective.
2.   Is available to an individual whose tax home is in a foreign country and who is either
    a.   a U.S. citizen and bona fide resident of a foreign country, or
    b.   a citizen or resident of the U.S. who, during any 12 consecutive months, is physically present in a foreign country for at least 330 full days.
3.   The general exclusion is available for foreign earned income and is limited to the lesser of:
    a. $72,000 for 1998
    b.   foreign earned income less the housing cost amount exclusion
        1.   the housing cost amount is equal to the qualified housing expenses of an individual less a base amount
        2.   the base amount is 16% of the salary of an employee of the U.S. government for Step 1 Grade GS-14.
        3.   the housing cost amount exclusion is limited to foreign earned income but can be elected in addition to the foreign earned income exclusion.
    c.   A self-employed individual is not eligible to exclude housing expenses, but may elect to deduct them.

VI.   FOREIGN CORPORATIONS CONTROLLED BY U.S. PERSONS

    A.   Certain types of income generated by controlled foreign corporations must be included in current tax year gross income by U.S. shareholders.

        1.   A U.S. shareholder is a U.S. person who owns, or is considered to own, 10% or more of the total combined voting power of the foreign corporation.

        2.   Stock owned directly, indirectly or constructively is counted.

            a.   indirect ownership is stock held through a foreign corporation, partnership or trust, this stock is considered owned proportionately by the shareholders, partners or beneficiaries.

            b.   constructive ownership rules are modified,

                1.   stock owned by an NRA are not considered

                2.   a partnership, estate, trust or corporation owning, directly or indirectly more than 50% of the voting power of the corporation is deemed to own all of its stock.

                3.   the corporate attribution threshold is 10%.

    B.   A CFC is any foreign corporation in which more than 50% of the combined voting power of all classes of voting stock or the total value of the stock of the corporation is owned by U.S. shareholders on any day during the taxable year.

    C.   For Subpart F to apply, the foreign corporation must have been a CFC for an uninterrupted period of 30 days or more during the taxable year.

    D.   U.S. shareholders must include their pro rata share of Subpart F income in their gross income to the extent of their ownership. Subpart F income consists of:

        1.   Insurance income

        2.   Foreign base company income

            a.   foreign personal holding company income

            b.   foreign base company sales income

            c.   foreign base company service income

            d.   foreign base company shipping income

            e.   foreign base company oil-related income

        3.   International boycott factor income

        4.   Illegal bribes

        5.   Income derived from §901(j) foreign country.

VII. TRANSFERRING OWNERSHIP TO A FOREIGN PERSON

    A.   U.S. persons transferring potential income property to foreign corporations outside the U.S. taxing jurisdiction in the following, domestically tax-free, situations recognize the gain realized at the time of transfer.

1.   property transfers to a controlled foreign corporation, §351
2.   liquidation of a domestic subsidiary into a foreign parent, §332,
3.   acquisition of a domestic corporation by a foreign corporation, B reorganization,
4.   acquisition of a domestic corporation's assets by a foreign corporation, C reorganization.

B.   The character of any gain recognized depends on the character of the property transferred.
    1.   a deemed sale occurs when the following assets are transferred:
        a.   inventory
        b.   accounts receivable and installment obligations
    2.   any recapture potential, depreciation, etc., must be recognized to the extent of the gain realized.

VIII.   FOREIGN CURRENCY TRANSACTIONS

A.   Tax Concepts Dealing with Foreign Exchange
    1.   Foreign currency is treated as property other than money.
    2.   Gain or loss on the exchange of foreign currency is considered separate from the underlying transaction.
    3.   No gain or loss is recognized until a transaction is closed.

B.   Where a QBU, foreign branch, uses foreign currency as its functional currency, profit or loss is computed in the foreign currency and translated using a weighted average exchange rate for the year.

IX.   REPORTING REQUIREMENTS

A.   A domestic corporation that is 25% or more foreign owned must file an informational return and maintain certain records where they will be accessible to the IRS.

B.   Any foreign corporation carrying on a trade or business in the U.S. must file an informational return and maintain certain records where they will be accessible to the IRS.

C.   U.S. partners of a controlled foreign partnership must file an information return.

D.   A foreign partnership with U.S. source or effectively connected with a U.S. trade or business income must file a partnership return.

E.   Changes in 10% or more ownership of interests in a foreign partnership must be reported.

F.   Creation of, or a transfer to, a foreign trust by a U.S. person requires the filing of Form 3520.

G.   Information returns are required in connection with foreign investment in U.S. real property interests.

TEST FOR SELF-EVALUATION

True or False

T F 1. One of the factors that is considered in establishing whether a foreign corporation's fixed or determinable annual or periodic income from U.S. sources is effectively connected with a U.S. trade or business is whether the activities of that trade or business were a material factor in the realization of the income generated.
(IRS 95 3A-19)

T F 2. For a foreign tax levy to qualify for the foreign tax credit, it must resemble U.S. income tax.

T F 3. Unused excess foreign taxes can be carried back 2 years and carried over 5 years subject to limitations in the same basket for the carryover year.

T F 4. One of the factors that is considered in establishing whether a foreign corporation's fixed or determinable annual or periodic income from U.S. sources is effectively connected with a U.S. trade or business is whether the income is from assets used in the conduct of that trade or business.   (IRS 94 3A-18)

T F 5. A purchaser of U.S. real property is required to withhold 10% of the amount realized on purchases from foreign persons.

T F 6. With respect to foreign corporations, one of the factors that can be considered in establishing whether fixed or determinable annual or periodic income and similar amounts from U.S. sources are effectively connected with a U.S. trade or business is whether the business activities were a material factor in the realization of the income.   (IRS 93 3A-19)

T F 7. The Foreign Personal Holding Company Tax is levied on the corporation's U.S. shareholders rather than the corporation.

T F 8. The de minimis rule applies to all Subpart F income.

T F 9. The foreign income exclusion is more beneficial than the foreign tax credit if the foreign country's tax rate is higher than the U.S. income tax rate.

T F 10. Interest expense must always be apportioned and allocated between U.S. and foreign sourced income components.

Fill in the Blanks

1. The Foreign Tax Credit is _____ for any particular year.

2. Issuance of a _____ and physical presence in the U.S. establishes residency for U.S. income taxes.

3. Foreign currency is treated as property other than _____.

4. For FTC purposes, foreign taxes are translated at the exchange rate in effect when _____.

5. Functional currency is translated at _____ exchange rate for the _____.

6. An _____ is an individual who is not a citizen or resident of the U.S.

7. A foreign corporation is a FPHC if _____% or more of gross income is FPHC income and,

8. more than _____% of the total voting power or the total value of the stock is held by _____ or fewer U.S. persons.

Multiple Choice

_____ 1.   Which one of the following factors has to be considered in establishing whether fixed or determinable annual or periodic income and similar amounts from U.S. sources are effectively connected with a U.S. trade or business?

(IRS 92 3B-44)

a. Whether the income is from assets used in, or held for use in, the conduct of that trade or business.
b. Whether the activities in the U.S. were a material factor in the realization of income and whether a certain percent of its employees were U.S. citizens.
c. Whether the trade or business sold a majority of its products to other businesses in the United States.
d. Whether a majority of the principal suppliers to the trade or business were in the United States.

_____ 2.   Foreign tax credits are:

a. elective
b. subject to basket limitations only
c. based on a weighted average exchange rate
d. all of the above
e. none of the above

_____ 3.   Eric, a nonresident alien, employed by a foreign manufacturing company, spent 5 weeks in the U.S. arranging equipment purchases. His salary for the 5 weeks was $4,000.

a.   This will be considered U.S. source income.
b.   This will not be considered U.S. source income.

_____ 4.   Which of the following statements is not correct in respect to withholding on nonresident aliens and foreign corporations?   (IRS 92 3B-45)

a.   Generally, fixed or determinable annual or periodic income from within the United States is subject to withholding unless specifically exempted under the Internal Revenue Code or a tax treaty.
b.   Generally, income is from United States sources if it is paid by any domestic or foreign businesses located in the United States.
c.   Income effectively connected with the conduct of a trade or business in the United States is generally not subject to withholding if certain conditions are met.
d.   Winnings from wagers or blackjack, baccarat, craps, roulette, or big-6 wheel are not subject to income tax withholding or 30 percent withholding tax.

_____ 5.   The foreign earned income exclusion is:

a.   elective
b.   limited in amount
c.   available to self-employed individuals
d.   all of the above
e.   a and b only

_____ 6.   For this year, Bill, a U.S. resident, has worldwide taxable income of $180,000, $150,000 in salary from a U.S. employer and $30,000 from investments in foreign securities. Foreign tax authorities withheld $9,000 of tax on the dividend income. If Bill's U.S. income tax before FTC is $48,540, his FTC is:

a. $9,000
b. $8,090
c. $8,292
d. $7,200

_____ 7.   A, a U.S. corporation, incurred $100,000 of interest expense during the year. None of this interest expense can be attributed to a specific purpose. Based on the following information, how should this interest be allocated and apportioned?

Asset Value:	Fair Market	Tax/Book
U.S. Source Income	$3,500,000	$2,300,000
Foreign Source Income	2,000,000	1,500,000

a. $63,636, U.S. sourced
b. $60,526, foreign sourced
c. $52,632, foreign sourced
d. $41,818, U.S. sourced

_____ 8.   D, a domestic corporation, began operation of a QBU in 1993 with an initial capitalization of 900K, (1K:$1). Determine the income taxed to D in each year based on the following:

Income in Ks		Exchange Rate
1993	200K	1K = $1
1994	200K	1.25K = $1
1995	200K	1.6K = $1

a.   125, 160, 200
b.   200, 160, 125
c.   200, 125, 160
d.   160, 125, 200

_____ 9.   In 1995 the QBU from question 8 above distributes 300 K to D when the exchange rate is 1.6K to $1. Does D have a foreign currency loss and if so, how much?

a.   No, -0-
b.   Yes, $55.50
c.   Yes, $77.50
d.   Yes, $89.50

_____ 10.   Corporation R, a domestic corporation, distributed the following dividends to its shareholders in 1989.

$5,000 to Shareholder A, a foreign partnership
$4,000 to Shareholder B, an unrelated foreign corporation
$3,000 to Shareholder C, a resident alien
$2,000 to Shareholder D, a nonresident alien

All of the income of Corporation R was from sources within the U.S. On what amount of dividends must R withhold tax?   (IRS 90 3B-43)

a. $-0-
b. $7,000
c. $9,000
d. $11,000

_____ 11.   All of the following items of gross income earned by a foreign corporation in the United States are subject to 30% withholding except: (IRS 90 3B-55)

a.   Rents
b.   Sale of real property
c.   Interest
d.   Dividends

SOLUTIONS
True or False

1. T (p. 9-22)
2. T (p. 9-12)
3. T (p. 9-7)
4. T (p. 9-22)
5. F (p. 9-26)
6. T (p. 9-22)
7. T (p. 9-35)
8. F (p. 9-33)
9. F (p. 9-46)
10. F (p. 9-18)

Fill in the Blanks

1. elective (p. 9-12)
2. green card (p. 9-20)
3. money (p. 9-42)
4. foreign taxes are paid (p. 9-44)
5. weighted average; taxable year (p. 9-44)
6. NRA nonresident alien (p. 9-20)
7. 60 (p. 9-35)
8. 50, 5 (p. 9-35)

Multiple Choice

1. a (p. 9-22)
2. a (p. 9-12)
3. a (p. 9-15)
4. b (p. 9-22)
5. d (p. 9-30)
6. b (48540 X 30000/180000)
7. a (using fair market: US = 63636, foreign =36364; using tax book: US = 60526, foreign = 39474)
8. b (p. 9-44)
9. d (equity in K's: 900+200+200+200=1500; basis in $s: 900+200+160+125=1385 distribution 300K of 1500K total equity = 20%; 20% of 1385 basis = 277; 277 - (300K@1.6) or $187.50 = $89.50 loss)
10. d (p. 9-22)
11. b (p. 9-22, 26)

CHAPTER 10

PARTNERSHIPS: FORMATION, OPERATIONS, AND BASIS

LEARNING OBJECTIVES

After completing Chapter 10, you should be able to:

1.   Discuss governing principles and theories of partnership taxation.

2.   Describe the tax effects of forming a partnership with cash and property contributions.

3.   Examine the tax treatment of expenditures of a newly formed partnership and identify elections the partnership should make.

4.   Specify the methods of determining a partnership's tax year.

5.   Calculate partnership taxable income and describe how partnership items affect a partner's income tax return.

6.   Determine a partner's basis in the partnership interest.

7.   Explain how liabilities affect a partner's basis.

8.   Describe the limitations on deducting partnership losses.

9.   Review the treatment of transactions between a partner and the partnership.

10. Provide insights regarding advantageous use of a partnership.

KEY TERMS

Aggregate concept	Entity concept	Outside basis
Basis in partnership interest	General partnership	Precontribution gain or loss
Capital account	Guaranteed payment	Profit and loss sharing ratio
Capital interest	Inside basis	Profits (loss) interest
Capital sharing ratio	Least aggregate deferral rule	Qualified nonrecourse debt
Constructive liquidation scenario	Limited liability company	Recourse debt
Disguised sale	Limited liability partnership	Separately stated items
Economic effect test	Nonrecourse debt	Special allocation
		Syndication costs

OUTLINE

I.   OVERVIEW OF PARTNERSHIP TAXATION

    A.   What is a Partnership?
        1.   A partnership is an association of two or more persons to carry on a trade or business, with each contributing money, property, labor, or skill, and with all expecting to share in profits and losses.
        2.   For Federal tax purposes, a partnership includes a syndicate, group, pool, joint venture, or other unincorporated organization through which any business, financial operation, or venture is carried on, and which is not classified as a corporation, trust, or estate.
        3.   Four types of entities taxed as partnerships are:
            a.   general partnerships
            b.   limited partnerships
            c.   limited liability partnerships
            d.   limited liability companies
        4.   Liability of partners
            a.   general partners are personally liable for partnership debt.
            b.   limited partners are liable for partnership debt only to the extent of their investment in the partnership.
            c.   limited liability partners are not liable for malpractice committed by their partner(s).
            d.   limited liability company members are provided liability protection similar to corporate shareholders.
        5.   Certain unincorporated organizations may elect to be excluded from treatment as partnerships for purposes of Federal income tax. This exclusion applies in situations where:
            a.   the organization's purpose is for investment, rather than the active conduct of a trade or business,
            b.   the organization's purpose is for the joint production, extraction, or use of property, or
            c.   for purposes of underwriting, selling, or distributing a particular security issue.

    B.   Partnership Taxation and Reporting
        1.   Partnership are not taxable entities; the taxable income or loss of the partnership flows through to the partners.
        2.   Each partner reports his allocable share of partnership income or loss on his personal tax return.
        3.   A partnership must report the results of its activities on Form 1065. Each partner receives a Form 1065, Schedule K-1 which shows his share of all partnership items.

C. Partner's Ownership Interest in a Partnership
   1. A capital interest is a partner's percentage ownership of partnership capital usually measured as the percentage of net assets a partner would receive on immediate liquidation of the partnership.
   2. A profits interest is the partner's percentage allocation of current operating results.

D. Conceptual Basis for Partnership Taxation
   1. The conduit concept treats the partnership as a channel through which income, credits and deductions flow to the partners.
   2. The entity concept treats partners and the partnership as distinct, separate units. The nature and amount of gains and losses are determined at the partnership level.

II. FORMATION OF A PARTNERSHIP: TAX EFFECTS

A. Partner's Gain/Loss on Contributions to Entity
   1. The formation of a partnership requires a contribution of assets to the partnership by the partners. Section 721 permits these contributions to, generally, be tax free, gain or loss recognition is deferred.
   2. Exceptions to the nonrecognition provisions occur when:
       a. the transfer consists of appreciated stock or securities and the partnership is an investment partnership.
       b. the transaction is essentially an exchange of properties.
       c. the partner receives his interest in the partnership in exchange for services.

B. Tax Issues Relative to Contributed Property
   1. Basis
       a. the partnership uses a carryover basis, the contributing partner's basis in the property becomes the partnership's basis in that property.
       b. the partner uses a substitute basis, the adjusted basis of the property contributed becomes the basis of that partner's partnership interest.
   2. Holding Period
       a. the holding period of an interest acquired by a cash contribution begins on the day the interest is acquired.
       b. the holding period of an interest acquired by contribution of property that was a §1231 asset or capital asset in the partner's hands carries over to the holding period of the partnership interest.
   3. The transferring partner's method and remaining recovery period of depreciable property contributed to the partnership carries over, the partnership continues the same cost recovery calculations.

C.   Tax Accounting Elections
1.   Most tax elections are made by the partnership, these elections decide how particular transactions and tax attributes will be handled.
2.   Each partner is bound by the elections made by the partnership.
3.   The only elections made by individual partners concern:
   a.   discharge of indebtedness,
   b.   depletion method for oil and gas wells,
   c.   foreign tax deductions and credits.

D.   Initial Costs of a Partnership
1.   Organization costs
   a.   are costs incident to the creation of the partnership.
   b.   may be amortized over 60 months or more.
2.   Start up costs
   a.   are operating costs incurred after formation but before the entity begins business.
   b.   may be amortized over 60 months or more.
3.   Syndication costs
   a.   are costs incurred in promoting and marketing partnership interests.
   b.   are capitalized with no amortization allowed.

E.   Taxable year of the Partnership
1.   A partnership's tax year is, generally, determined in the following order:
   a.   the tax year of the majority partners having the same tax year,
   b.   the tax year of all the principal partners,
   c.   the least aggregate deferral year.
2.   Exceptions are allowed:
   a.   if the existence of a business purpose can be established to IRS satisfaction, i.e., if a partnership recognizes 25% or more of gross receipts in the last two months of a 12 month period.
   b.   taxes are deferred for not more than 3 months from the required year and deposits of estimated deferred taxes are made.

III. OPERATION OF THE PARTNERSHIP

A.   Measuring and Reporting Income
1.   Form 1065 is an informational return which organizes and reports the year's activities.
2.   A partnership must file a return, Form 1065, by the 15th day of the fourth month following the close of the partnership's tax year.
3.   Income measurement:
   a.   First, under the conduit concept, items which affect exclusions, deductions and credits at the partner level are reported separately.

b.   Second, under the entity concept, all items not required to be stated separately are netted at the partnership level to determine the partnership's ordinary income or loss.

B.   Partnership Allocations

1.   The partnership agreement can provide for any partner to share capital, profits and losses in different ratios.

2.   Special allocations must follow the rules and regulations of §704(b). One of these is the Economic Effect Test.

3.   The economic effect test requires that:

a.   income allocations increase a partner's capital account.

b.   deduction or loss allocations decrease a partner's capital account balance.

c.   when a partner's interest is liquidated he must:

1.   receive assets having a FMV equal to his capital account, or

2.   restore his capital account if it is negative.

4.   Precontribution gain or loss

a.   precontribution gain or loss must be allocated among the partners taking into account variations between the basis and the FMV of the property on the contribution date.

b.   built-in gain or loss is allocated to the contributing partner when the partnership disposes of nondepreciable property.

c.   Regulations outline specific calculation for built-in gain or loss on depreciable property.

C.   Basis of Partnership Interest

1.   The original basis of a contributing partner's interest is:

      FMV of any services performed
+   money contributed
+   adjusted basis of property contributed
-     liabilities transferred
+   share of partnership debt

2.   For partnership interests acquired after the partnership has been formed, the method of acquisition determines how the partner's adjusted basis is computed.

a.   purchased from another partner = cost

b.   acquired by gift = donor's basis + some, or all, of the gift tax paid by the donor

c.   acquired by inheritance = FMV on date of partner's death

3.   Basis can never be less than zero.

4.   A partner's basis in the partnership interest is subject to continuous fluctuations. Events and transactions which will have an effect on the partnership interest are:

       a.   Increases:
          1.   additional contributions and debt increases
          2.   taxable income of the partnership, including capital gains
          3.   tax-exempt income of the partnership
       b.   Decreases:
          1.   distribution of partnership property and debt decreases
          2.   partnership expenditures which are not deductible in computing taxable income or loss and which are not capital expenditures
          3.   partnership losses, including capital losses.

5.   Liability sharing
       a.   recourse debt is partnership debt for which the partnership or at least one partner is personally liable.
       b.   nonrecourse debt is debt for which no party is personally liable.
       c.   debts created before January 29, 1989:
          1.   recourse debt is shared according to the partners' loss sharing ratio.
          2.   nonrecourse debt is shared according to the partners' profit sharing ratio.
       d.   debts created after January 29, 1989:
          1.   recourse debt is shared according to "constructive liquidation scenario."
          2.   Nonrecourse debt is allocated in three stages:
             a.   minimum gain
             b.   precontribution gain
             c.   remainder is allocated according to profit sharing or the manner in which nonrecourse deductions are shared.

D.   Loss Limitations
    1.   The overall limitation allows losses only to the extent of the partner's adjusted basis in the partnership interest.
    2.   The "at-risk" limitation allows losses only to the extent of the partner's economic investment basis.
    3.   Passive loss limitations, generally, allow losses only to the extent of passive income.
    4.   These three loss limitations are applied in the order listed: overall, at-risk, passive.

IV. TRANSACTIONS BETWEEN PARTNER AND PARTNERSHIP

A. Fixed or guaranteed payments made by the partnership to a partner as salary or as interest on capital are deducted by the partnership as Section 162 expenses, as long as the payments are not based on the income of the partnership.

B. When a partner engages in certain transaction with the partnership, he or she can be treated as a nonpartner, thus recognizing any gain or loss that might be incurred. Two exceptions to this rule are:

1. Any loss is disallowed on a transaction between a partner and the partnership if the partner has more than a 50% interest in the capital or profits of the partnership.

2. A gain on a sale or exchange of property between a partner and the partnership shall be treated as ordinary income if he/she has more than an 50% interest in the capital or profits of the partnership unless the asset is a capital asset to both the seller and the purchaser.

TEST FOR SELF-EVALUATION

True or False

T F 1.   A partner in a partnership can be an individual, a corporation, an estate, a trust, or another partnership.   (IRS 96 2A-13)

T F 2.   A partnership liability affects a partner's basis in a cash basis partnership if, and to the extent that, the liability increases the partnership's basis in any of its assets.
                                                                              (IRS 96 2A-14)

T F 3.   The partnership agreement can be modified for a particular tax year after the close of the year, but not later than the date for filing the partnership return for that year, NOT including extensions.   (IRS 94 2A-14)

T F 4.   Syndication fees for issuing and marketing interests in the partnership, such as commissions and professional fees, CANNOT be amortized or expensed. They must be capitalized.   (IRS 94 2A-15)

T F 5.   A joint undertaking merely to share expenses or a mere co-ownership of property that is maintained and rented is NOT a partnership. But, if the co-owners provide services to the tenants, a partnership exists.   (IRS 93 2A-16)

T F 6.   A partnership is the relationship between two or more persons who join together to carry on a trade or business. Persons, when used to describe a partner, means only an individual.   (IRS 92 2A-14)

T F 7.   In determining a partner's income tax for the year, a partner must take into account separately his or her distributive share of all of the following partnership items whether or not they are actually distributed.   (IRS 92 3A-15)

1. Net income from rental real estate
2. Charitable contributions
3. Gains and losses from sales or exchanges of capital assets
4. Ordinary income or loss from trade or business activities

T F 8.   On March 10, 1990, Daniel contributed land in exchange for a partnership interest in Parr Company. The fair market value of the land at that time was $40,000 and Daniel's adjusted basis was $25,000. On December 2, 1991, Parr distributed that land to another partner. The fair market value at that time was $40,000. These transactions would not require a gain to be recognized by Daniel.
                                                                              (IRS 92 2A-16)

T F 9.   Mr. Diaz and Mr. Garcia are both dentists who maintain separate practices, but they share the same office space. They equally divide the expenses, such as receptionist salary, rent, and utilities. This arrangement is a partnership for federal income tax purposes.   (IRS 92 2A-13)

T F 10.   The character of partner's distributive share of a partnership item of income, gain, loss, credit or deduction that the partner must take into account separately, is determined as if the partner had realized it directly from the same source or incurred it in the same manner as it was realized or incurred by the partnership.   (IRS 90 2A-23)

Fill in the Blanks

1. Two legal concepts which have had a significant influence on the tax treatment of partners and partnerships are known as the _____ concept and the _____ concept.

2. According to Section 704(a), a partner's share of any partnership item is to be determined by _____.

3. Under Section 707(b) a loss from the sale or exchange of property will be disallowed if the partner has _____ percent interest in the partnership.

4. The measurement of partnership income requires a two step approach: the first step is the _____ and _____ of specific items on the partnership return; the second step is the measurement and reporting of the partnership's _____ income.

5. The partnership return is filed on Form _____.

6. The individual's copy of the partnership return is known as Schedule _____.

7. A partner's share of a distributive loss in the partnership is limited to his _____ in the partnership.

Multiple Choice

_____ 1.   Partnership CDS was formed on September 5, 1995, and elected to use a fiscal year ending November 30. CDS is required to file its partnership return, Form 1065, by which of the following dates?   (IRS 96 2B-21)

    a.   March 15, 1996
    b.   February 15, 1996
    c.   January 15, 1996
    d.   December 31, 1995

_____ 2.   Which of the following statements about partnership agreements and a partner's distributive share of items is incorrect?   (IRS 96 2B-38)

   a.   The partnership agreement generally determines a partner's distributive share of income, gain, loss, deductions, and credits.
   b.   If the partnership agreement provides for a partner with a 50% capital interest to share in 60% of the profits and 90% of the losses, the agreement will be disregarded even though the allocation has substantial economic effect.
   c.   A partner's distributive share is determined by his interest in the partnership if the partnership agreement does NOT provide for the allocation of income, gain, loss, deductions, or credits.
   d.   If the partnership agreement or any modification is silent on any matter, the provisions of local law are treated as part of the agreement.

_____ 3.   Collins Partnership has a December 31 tax year, which is the tax year of all its partners. Collins is NOT a member of a tiered structure, nor has it previously made a section 444 election. If Collins makes a section 444 election, which of the following tax years can it elect?   (IRS 96 2B-39)

   a.   March 31
   b.   June 30
   c.   September 30
   d.   Collins Partnership CANNOT elect any of the above.

_____ 4.   With respect to partnerships, which of the following items is NEVER considered a separately stated item and must be included in the net income from the partnership's business or rental activities?   (IRS 96 2B-40)

   a.   Dividends.
   b.   Charitable contributions.
   c.   Gains or losses from sales or exchanges of capital assets.
   d.   Depreciation expense.

_____ 5.   In computing the ordinary income of a partnership, a deduction is allowed for:
                    (IRS 96 2B-41)
   a.   The net operating loss deduction.
   b.   Guaranteed payments to partners for services or for the use of capital.
   c.   Short-term capital losses.
   d.   Contributions to qualified charities.

_____ 6.   Which of the following choices for partnership items is made by the individual partners and NOT the partnership?   (IRS 96 2B-42)

a. Accounting methods.
b. Amortization of certain organization fees and start-up costs.
c. Treatment of income from cancellation of debt.
d. Method for computing depreciation.

_____ 7. Juan and Adelfo are equal partners in a music store. In 1995, they bought an amplifier for use in the store to demonstrate certain instruments. The amplifier cost $30,000. The partnership's taxable income before the section 179 deduction is $25,000. What amount of section 179 expense can Juan and Adelfo EACH deduct if either has any other section 179 deductions?   (IRS 96 2C-50)

a. $0
b. $8,750
c. $12,500
d. $15,000

_____ 8. During 1995 WHOOS Partnership paid insurance premiums for the following coverage:

Use and occupancy and business interruption insurance	$2,000
Overhead insurance	$ 1,000
Accident and health insurance paid for its partners as guaranteed payments made to the partners	$ 800
Group term life insurance on the lives of all the partners with the partnership as beneficiary	$ 500
Life insurance on the lives of all the partners in order to get or protect a loan	$ 700

What is the amount of WHOOS' deductible insurance expense for 1995?

(IRS 95 2C-50)

a. $5,000
b. $3,800
c. $3,700
d. $3,000

_____ 9. Merlin and Nathan are equal partners in M & N Partnership. The partnership and both partners file their tax returns on a calendar year basis. In 1994, M & N had a $20,000 loss, of which Nathan's share was $10,000. Nathan's adjusted basis in his partnership interest was $4,000 at the beginning of 1994. For 1995, M & N showed a profit of $16,000. Nathan's share was $8,000. If there were NO other adjustments to Nathan's basis in 1994 or 1995, what amounts would Nathan show as his income or (loss) from M & N Partnership in 1994 and 1995?

(IRS 96 2C-67)

	1994	*1995*
a.	($4,000)	$0
b.	($4,000)	$2,000
c.	($10,000)	$8,000
d.	$0	$8,000

_____ 10. Phil and Dean formed a general partnership with cash contributions of $10,000 each. All partnership profits and losses are shared equally as stated in the partnership agreement. During 1995, they borrowed $30,000 to purchase depreciable equipment for use in their shop. Under the terms of the loan, Phil is required to pay the creditor if the partnership defaults. For 1995 the partnership had a loss of $60,000, of which Phil's share was $30,000. What is the amount of partnership loss that Phil can deduct on his 1995 income tax return, assuming NO other transactions occurred?   (IRS 96 2C-68)

a. $0
b. $10,000
c. $30,000
d. $40,000

_____ 11. Mr. Crane acquired a 50% interest in a partnership by contributing a building that had a fair market value of $12,000 and an adjusted basis of $10,000. The building was subject to a liability of $6,000, which the partnership assumed for legitimate business purposes. What is Mr. Crane's adjusted basis in the partnership?
                                                       (IRS 96 2C-69)

a. $12,000
b. $10,000
c. $7,000
d. $4,000

_____ 12. Kathy and Candy form an equal partnership. Kathy contributes $15,000 cash and Candy contributes depreciable office equipment with a fair market value of $15,000 and an adjusted basis of $8,000. What is the partnership's basis in the equipment for purposes of depreciation?   (IRS 96 2C-71)

a. $4,000
b. $7,500
c. $8,000
d. $15,000

_____ 13.   Joy and Ray are partners in JR and Associates. Under the terms of the partnership agreement, Joy is to receive 25% of all partnership income or loss plus a guaranteed payment of $60,000 per year. In 1995, the partnership had $50,000 of ordinary income before any deduction for Joy's guaranteed payment. What is the amount of income or loss Joy would report on her 1995 tax return, assuming she materially participates in partnership activities?   (IRS 96 2C-72)

    a. $15,000 guaranteed payment, $2,500 loss
    b. $57,500 guaranteed payment
    c. $60,000 guaranteed payment
    d. $60,000 guaranteed payment, $2,500 loss

_____ 14.   Andrew invested $10,000 for a 25% interest in CAN Partnership in 1994. In 1995, CAN had taxable income of $20,000 and nontaxable income of $8,000. CAN Partnership also made a cash distribution to Andrew of $12,000. Assuming no other transactions occurred, what is Andrew's basis in the partnership at the end of 1995?   (IRS 96 2C-74)

    a. $ 0
    b. $5,000
    c. $10,000
    d. $17,000

_____ 15.   Roland owns a 55% interest in Kramer Partnership and a 70% interest in Burns Partnership. In February 1994, Kramer sold land to Burns for $70,000. The land had a basis to Kramer of $85,000. In July 1995, Burns sold the land to Wilson, an unrelated individual, for $76,000. How much gain or (loss) must Burns Partnership recognize in 1995?   (IRS 95 2C-71)

    a. $0
    b. $6,000
    c.   ($9,000)
    d.   ($15,000)

SOLUTIONS

True or False

1. T   (p. 10-20)
2. T   (p. 10-27)
3. T   (p. 10-43)
4. T   (p. 10-17)
5. F   (p. 10-5)
6. T   (p. 10-20)
7. F   (p. 10-20)
8. F   (p. 10-10)
9. F   (p. 10-5)
10. T   (P. 10-20)

Fill in the Blanks

1. entity; conduit (p. 10-8)
2. partnership agreement (p. 10-7)
3. more than 50% (p. 10-39)
4. segregation; reporting; ordinary (p. 10-20)
5. 1065 (p. 10-6)
6. K-1 (p. 10-6)
7. adjusted basis (p. 10-32)

Multiple Choice

1. a   (p. 10-20; 15th day of fourth month)
2. b   (p. 10-23; substantial economic effect)
3   d   (p. 10-19; December 31 is required year end)
4. d   (p. 10-20)
5. b   (p. 10-38)
6. c   (p. 10-20)
7. b   (p. 10-20; 50% of 17,500 max. = 8,750)
8. b   (2,000 + 1,000 + 800 guaranteed payments)
9. b   (1994, 4,000 - 10,000 = 6,000 carryforward; 1995, 8,000 profit -6,000 carryover)
10. c   (p. 10-32; basis = 10,000 investment + 30,000 liability)
11. c   (p. 10-27; basis of property 10,000 + 50% of 6,000 liability)
12. c   (p. 10-12)
13. d   (p. 10-38)
14. b   (10,000 + 25%(20,000) + 25%(8,000) - 8,000)
15. a   (p. 10-39)

CHAPTER 11

PARTNERSHIPS: DISTRIBUTIONS, TRANSFER OF INTERESTS, AND TERMINATIONS

LEARNING OBJECTIVES

After completing Chapter 11, you should be able to:

1. Determine the tax treatment of proportionate nonliquidating distributions from a partnership to a partner.

2. Determine the tax treatment of proportionate distributions that liquidate a partnership.

3. Describe the general concepts governing the tax treatment of disproportionate distributions.

4. Determine the tax treatment under §736 of payments from a partnership to a retiring or deceased partner.

5. Calculate the selling partner's amount and character of gain or loss on the sale or exchange of a partnership interest.

6. Calculate the optional adjustments to basis under §754.

7. Outline the methods of terminating a partnership.

8. Describe the special considerations of a family partnership.

9. Describe the application of partnership provisions to limited liability companies (LLCs) and limited liability partnerships (LLPs).

KEY TERMS

Appreciated inventory	Nonliquidating distribution	Section 754 election
Disproportionate distribution	Optional adjustment election	Technical termination of
Hot assets	Proportionate distribution	partnership
Liquidating distribution		Unrealized receivables

OUTLINE

I.   DISTRIBUTIONS FROM A PARTNERSHIP

    A.   Nonliquidating distributions are draws or partial liquidations.
        1.   Draws are distributions of a partner's share of partnership profits that have been taxed to that partner.
        2.   Partial liquidations reduce the partner's interest in partnership capital and are a return OF investment in a partnership interest.

    B.   Generally, no gain or loss is recognized by either the partnership or partner on a nonliquidating distribution.
        1.   The partner takes a carryover basis in the assets distributed.
        2.   The partner's outside basis is reduced by the amount of cash and the adjusted basis of property distributed. The partner's outside basis cannot be reduced below $0.
        3.   If the cash distributed exceeds the partner's outside basis, the partner recognizes gain.
        4.   Losses are not recognized on nonliquidating distributions.
        5.   If the inside basis of the assets distributed exceed the partner's outside basis an ordering of the distribution is required
            a.   first, cash
            b.   second, unrealized receivables and inventory, ordinary income producing property
            c.   third, other property
        6.   If the partner's outside basis cannot absorb the second and/or third order of distributions, his basis, after the cash distribution, is to be allocated pro rata based on the relative inside bases of the assets distributed first within the second class, then, to the other property.

    C.   Liquidating distributions terminate the partner's entire interest in the partnership.

    D.   Partnership Liquidates
        1.   Distributions reduce the partner's outside basis
            a.   cash: dollar for dollar
            b.   unrealized receivables and inventory: partnership (inside) adjusted basis
            c.   other property: inside basis.
        2.   No gain or loss is recognized by the partnership.
        3.   The partner recognizes gain if the cash received exceeds his outside basis.
        4.   The partner recognizes loss if:
            a.   ONLY money, unrealized receivables and inventory are received, and

        b.   the partner's outside basis exceeds the inside basis of the assets distributed.

        c.   if any other property is received, loss recognition is postponed.

E. Precontribution Gain

1. if a partner contributes appreciated property to a partnership, that partner recognizes gain if:

        a.   the contributed property is distributed to another partner within seven years of the contribution date.

        b.   the partnership distributes any property other than cash to that partner within seven years after the partner contributed the appreciated property.

2. the partner's basis in the partnership interest is increased by the amount of gain recognized.

        a.   for property distributed to another partner, the basis of the distributed property is increased by the amount of gain recognized.

        b.   for property other than cash distributed to the contributing partner, the partnership increases its basis in the precontribution gain property remaining in the partnership.

F. Disproportionate Distributions

1. A disproportionate distribution occurs when a partnership makes a distribution that increases or decreases a partner's proportionate interest in certain ordinary income producing property.

2. The transaction is recast so that each partner recognizes and reports his proportionate share of ordinary income based on his proportionate share of the underlying assets of the partnership.

II. LIQUIDATING DISTRIBUTIONS TO RETIRING OR DECEASED PARTNER

A. Payments made by an ongoing partnership in complete liquidation of a retiring partner's or successor of a deceased partner's interest are classified as either property or income payments.

B. Property payments are made in exchange for the partner's pro rata share of each partnership asset, §736(b).

1. In general, §736(b) payments are considered a return of the partner's outside basis in the partnership.

2. Cash payments in excess of that outside basis will be taxed as capital gains.

3. Cash payments insufficient to cover that outside basis will be taxed as capital losses.

C.   Income payments, §736(a), are all payments not classified as §736(b) payments including:

1.   Payments made for a partner's pro rata share of unrealized receivables.

2.   Payments made for the partner's pro rata share of partnership goodwill if such payments are not provided for in the partnership agreement.

3.   Certain annuity and lump sum payments.

4.   Income payments are classified as guaranteed payments or distributive shares.

a.   guaranteed payments are NOT determined by reference to partnership income and are fully deductible by the partnership, taxed as ordinary income to the recipient partner.

b.   distributive share payments are determined by reference to partnership income and retain their character when distributed to the recipient partner.

D.   Series of Payments

1.   If the partners have specifically agreed to the allocation and timing of property and income payments, the agreement normally controls.

2.   If no agreement is made, regulations specify the classification rules for each payment.

III.   SALE OF A PARTNERSHIP INTEREST

A.   As a general rule, capital gain or loss results from the sale or exchange of a partnership interest. The gain or loss recognized is the difference between the amount realized and the partner's adjusted basis, including liability effects.

B.   The partnership's tax year closes as of the date of sale for the partner disposing of his entire interest.

C.   Major exceptions to the general rule arise when a partner sells his or her interest in a partnership and there are unrealized receivables or appreciated inventory. Under Section 751 of the Code, these items, when included in the sale of a partnership interest, generate ordinary income.

1.   "Unrealized receivables" includes:

a.   receivables of a cash basis taxpayer from sales of ordinary income property and rights to receive payments for services.

b.   ordinary income portion of deferred gain on installment sales.

c.   depreciation recapture potential.

2.   "Appreciated inventory" includes essentially all partnership property except money, capital assets and §1231 property. Receivables are included in this definition.

3.   Inventory is appreciated when its aggregate FMV exceeds its adjusted basis to the partnership.

IV.   OTHER TRANSACTIONS WITH PARTNERSHIP INTERESTS

A.   The transfer of a partnership interest to a controlled corporation will be treated as a nontaxable exchange if the conditions of Section 351 are satisfied.

B.   The incorporation method used should be carefully chosen when §1244 stock is to be issued and/or an S corporation election is planned. The partnership should distribute all assets and liabilities to the partners who then transfer their interests to the corporation.

C.   Like-kind exchange rules do not apply to the exchange of different partnerships' interests but, can apply to exchanges of interests in the same partnership.

V.   OPTIONAL ADJUSTMENTS TO PROPERTY BASIS

A.   A partnership may elect to adjust the basis of its property when a partner's interest is sold or exchanged, a partner dies, or an interest is distributed.

B.   The adjustment to the property is the difference between what the transferee paid for the property and his share of the inside basis of the property.

C.   The purpose of this optional adjustment is to equalize the inside and outside bases of the partner's interest.

D.   If a step-up of depreciable property is involved, the optional adjustment is depreciated by the transferee partner, as if a newly acquired asset.

E.   Once made, the election remains in effect until the IRS consents to its revocation.

VI.   TERMINATION OF A PARTNERSHIP

A.   The partnership incorporates.

B.   In a two partner partnership, when one partner buys out the other, creating a sole proprietorship.

C.   The partnership ceases operations and liquidates - a sale or exchange of partnership interest(s) result.

D.   A technical termination occurs if more than 50% of the partnerships' capital and profits are transferred within a 12 month period.

VII.   OTHER ISSUES

A.   Family partnerships require special consideration. Because of the close relationship between family members, there is the possibility of channeling income from high tax-bracket members to low tax-bracket members.

B.   A family member will be recognized as a partner if:
1.   He performs substantial or vital services and capital is not a material consideration in the operation of the business;
2.   The family member acquired his capital interest in a bona fide transaction, actually owns the partnership interest, is vested with control over it, and capital is a material income-producing factor.

C.   When the partner is a child, under 14 years of age, a substantial portion of the child's distributive income may be taxed at the parent/partner's marginal rate. If the minor child is 14 or older, these taxing restrictions might be avoided.

D.   Limited Liability Companies
1.   Generally, none of the owners of a LLC are personally liable for LLC debt.
2.   All owners can participate in management of the LLC.
3.   Transfers of property to the LLC in exchange for an ownership interest are governed by partnership tax provisions.
4.   An owner's basis in an LLC includes the owner's share of the LLC's liabilities under §752; all liabilities are treated as nonrecourse.
5.   Special allocations under §704(b) are permitted.
6.   Optional adjustments to basis election can be made.

E.   Limited Liability Partnerships
1.   Partners in a registered LLP are jointly and severally liable for contractual liability.
2.   Partners are liable for their own malpractice or other torts, but are not liable for their partners' malpractice or torts.

TEST FOR SELF-EVALUATION

True or False

T F 1. During 1995, Sergio contributed property to his partnership. Sergio must recognize gain or loss on the distribution of the property to another partner within 7 years of the contribution.   (IRS 96 2A-15)

T F 2. When there is a sale or liquidation of a partner's interest in a partnership, the adjusted basis of the partner's partnership interest is determined on the date of the sale or liquidation.   (IRS 96 2A-16)

T F 3. Mr. Clysdale is a partner in Clysdale and Associates Partnership. The other two partners are his sister and his 17-year old son, Gregory. The partnership's income consists mostly of of compensation for services performed by Mr. Clysdale and his sister. Gregory is a high school student and acquired his one-third interest by gift. Gregory is recognized as a partner in the firm for tax purposes.   (IRS 95 2A-14)

T F 4. On December 31, 1994, Kay-Ann's adjusted basis in GEM Partnership was zero and her share of partnership liabilities was $30,000. The partnership had no unrealized receivables or substantially appreciated inventory items. Kay-Ann withdrew from the partnership on December 31, 1994, and was relieved of any partnership liabilities. As a result she has a $30,000 capital LOSS.
                    (IRS 95 2A-15)

T F 5. Payments made in liquidation of the interest of a retiring or deceased partner in exchange for his or her interest in partnership property are considered a distribution, not a distributive share or guaranteed payment that could give rise to a deduction (or its equivalent) for the partnership.   (IRS 95 2A-16)

T F 6. Chad's interest in BCD Partnership had an adjusted basis of $80,000. In complete liquidation of his interest, he received $30,000 cash, inventory items having a basis to the partnership of $44,000, and a company automobile having an adjusted basis to the partnership of $12,000. The basis of the automobile in Chad's hands is $12,000.   (IRS 95 2A-17)

T F 7. In a liquidating distribution a loss is recognized if the sum of the cash received plus the basis of distributed unrealized receivables and inventory is less than the adjusted basis of the partner's interest prior to the liquidating distribution and no other property is distributed.

T F 8. Recognition of gain will not occur in the liquidating distribution of property unless cash is received in excess of interest.

T F 9.   The Code permits a partnership to increase or decrease the basis of partnership assets in the event of a death of one of the partners or if a partner's interest is sold or exchanged.

T F 10.   An optional basis adjustment is binding only for the year in which it is made unless consent is received from the IRS to make it continuous.

Fill in the Blanks

1.   Under the general rule of section 741, a partnership interest is a _____ asset, the sale or exchange of which will result in the recognition of _____.

2.   Section 751 provides that amount realized from the sale of a partnership interest which are attributable to _____ or _____ must be treated as the sale of a noncapital asset.

3.   Partnership liabilities forgiven or assumed by another partner are treated as _____ distributions.

Multiple Choice

_____ 1.   Which of the following statements is correct?   (IRS 96 2B-43)

    a.   For property that was an unrealized receivable in the hands of the contributing partner, any gain or loss on a disposition by the partnership is ordinary income or loss.
    b.   An individual cannot acquire an interest in partnership capita as compensation for services performed or to be performed.
    c.   A partner recognizes a gain or loss when the partner contributes to the partnership in exchange for a partnership interest.
    d.   If a partner contributes property to a partnership, the partnership's basis for determining depreciation, depletion, and gain or loss for the property is the fair market value at the time of the contribution.

_____ 2.   Which of the following statements about the sale or exchange of a partner's interest in a partnership is correct?   (IRS 96 2B-44)

    a.   Gain or loss is the difference between the amount realized and the adjusted basis of the partner's interest in the partnership.
    b.   The amount realized by the selling partner does not include any partnership liabilities of which the selling partner is relieved.
    c.   Any amount realized due to substantially appreciated inventory items held by the partnership results in capital gain or loss.
    d.   The exchange of a limited partnership interest for a limited interest in another partnership is a nontaxable exchange of like-kind property.

_____ 3.   Which of the following statements about the liquidation of a partner's interest is correct?   (IRS 96 2B-45)

    a.   A retiring partner is treated as a partner until his or her interest in the partnership has been completely liquidated.

    b.   The remaining partners' distributive shares of partnership income are reduced by payments in exchange for a retiring partner's interest in partnership property.

    c.   The retiring partner will recognize a gain on a liquidating distribution to the extent that any money distributed is MORE than the partner's adjusted basis in the partnership.

    d.   Payments in liquidation of an interest that are NOT made in exchange for the interest in partnership property are reported as ordinary income by the recipient.

_____ 4.   On April 10, 1993, Reuben contributed land in exchange for a 25% partnership interest in Larson Partners. The fair market value of the land at that time was $60,000 and Reuben's adjusted basis was $25,000. On November 1, 1995, Larson distributed that land to another partner. The fair market value at that time was $65,000. What is the amount of Reuben's recognized gain from the transfer of the land by Larson to another partner?   (IRS 96 2C-73)

    a. $5,000
    b. $10,000
    c. $35,000
    d. $40,000

_____ 5.   On December 31, 1995, Rita's adjusted basis in Diamond Partnership was $40,000, which included her $30,000 share of partnership liabilities. The partnership had no unrealized receivables or substantially appreciated inventory. Rita sold her interest for $20,000 cash and was relieved of any partnership liabilities. What is the amount and character of Rita's gain or (loss)?
                                                                    (IRS 2C-75)

    a. $0
    b. $10,000 ordinary income
    c. $10,000 capital gain
    d.   ($40,000) capital loss

_____ 6.   The adjusted basis of Dave's partnership interest in CDS Partnership is $60,000. In a complete liquidation of his interest, Dave received the following:

	Basis to CDS	Fair Market Value
Cash	$20,000	$20,000
Inventory items	15,000	20,000
Land	24,000	40,000
Building	8.000	10,000

What is Dave's basis in the land and in the building?   (IRS 96 2C-76)

	Land	Building
a.	$18,750	$6,250
b.	$24,000	$8,000
c.	$40,000	$10,000
d.	$56,000	$14,000

_____ 7.   The adjusted basis of Danielle's interest in LaSalle Partnership at the end of 1995, after allocation of her share of partnership income, was $35,000. This included her $19,000 share of partnership liabiilities. The partnership had no unrealized receivables or substantially appreciated inventory items. On December 31, 1995, Danielle sold her interest in LaSalle Partnership for $16,000. What is the amount of Danielle's capital gain or (loss)?   (IRS 96 2C-77)

a. $1,000
b. $16,000
c. $0
d.   ($19,000)

_____ 8.   On September 30, 1994, Robert retired from his partnership. At that time, his adjusted basis in the partnership was $40,000, which included his $15,000 share of the partnership's liabilities. In liquidation of Robert's interest in partnership property, he was relieved of his share of the partnership liabilities and received cash retirement payments of $2,500 per month for 15 months, beginning October 1, 1994. Both Robert and the partnership use a calendar tax year. How much must Robert report as capital gain in 1994 and 1995?   (IRS 96 2C-78)

	1994	1995
a.	$18,750	$18,750
b.	$6,250	$6,250
c.	$12,500	$0
d.	$0	$12,500

_____ 9.   Simon is a partner in SG Partnership. The adjusted basis of his partnership interest is $38,000, which includes his $30,000 share of partnership liabilities. Simon's share of unrealized receivables in the partnership is $12,000. Simon sold his partnership interest for $45,000 cash. What is the amount and character of Simon's gain?   (IRS 96 2C-79)

a. $12,000 ordinary gain; $25,000 capital gain
b. $25,000 ordinary gain; $12,000 capital gain
c. $7,000 capital gain
d. $37,000 capital gain

_____ 10.   Bridget and Brenda formed B & B Partnership in 1992 as equal partners. They closed the business during 1994 because it was not profitable. After the partnership closed they had debts to pay. Because Bridget was insolvent, she paid only part of her share of the partnership's debts. Brenda was required to pay ALL of the remaining debts during 1994. Which of the following statements reflects the correct treatment of the debts paid by Brenda on her tax return for 1994?
                                                                                                    (IRS 95 2B-28)

a.   She cannot deduct ANY of the debt she paid.
b.   She can deduct ONLY her payment of her share of the debt as a bad debt.
c.   She can deduct ALL of the debt she paid as a bad debt.
d.   She can deduct ONLY her payment of Bridget's share of debt as a bad debt.

_____ 11.   Members of a family can be partners. Members of a family who must meet special requirements to be recognized as partners include all of the following except:
                                                                                                    (IRS 95 2B-41)

a.   Trusts for the benefits of lineal descendents.
b.   Brothers and sisters
c.   Spouses
d.   Ancestors

SOLUTIONS

True or False

1. T   (p. 11-13)
2. T   (p. 11-22)
3. F   (to be considered a partner, Gregory would need to provide services)
4. F   (debt forgiveness is considered cash, gain results)
5. T   (p. 11-17)
6. F   (Chad's basis in the auto would be 6,000)
7. T   (p. 11-10)
8. T   (p. 11-9)
9. T   (p. 11-32)
10. F   (p. 11-35)

Fill in the Blanks

1. capital; capital gain; loss (p. 11-27)
2. unrealized receivables; appreciated inventory (p. 11-24)
3. cash (p. 11-5)

Multiple Choice

1. a   (p. 11-23)
2. a   (p. 11-22)
3. b   (Concept Summary 11-3)
4. c   (FMV on contribution date - adjusted basis; 60,000 - 25,000)
5. c   (basis 40,000 - 20,000 cash - 30,000 liability = gain)
6. a   (cash and inventory at partnership basis, 35,000, allocate remaining 25,000: land 24/32(25,000) and building 8/32(25,000)
7. c   (basis 35,000 - cash 16,000 - liabilities 19,000)
8. d   (basis 40,000 - liabilities 15,000 = 25,000; -'94, 7,500 = 17,500 - '95, 30,000)
9. a   (basis 38,000 - 30,000 liabilities = 8,000 remaining basis; 45,000 - unrealized receivables (ordinary income) 12,000 - return of capital 8,000 = 25,000 gain)
10. d   (her share is part of her partnership basis, Bridget's share is a bad debt)
11. b   (brothers & sisters because they are not a lineal relationship)

Return Problem 2

Jan and Dee formed a partnership on January 1, 1997. Jan contributed land and a building with an adjusted basis of $180,000, the land was originally valued at $30,000. This property had been used in Jan's sole proprietorship for the past eight years and depreciated using the straight line method over 40 years. The fair market value of the property at the date of formation was $300,000, at which time the land was valued at $50,000. Dee contributed $150,000 cash, which was immediately used to buy new equipment. The equipment had a useful life of six years and zero salvage value. Because of the unequal investment, Jan and Dee agree that Jan should receive a guaranteed payment in the form of salary of $15,000, and all remaining items should be split 60% for Jan and 40% for Dee. Jan and Dee each made a cash withdrawal of $7,500 during the year.

Given the following data, you are to prepare Form 1065, U.S. Partnership Return including Jan's Schedule K-1, plus other related forms as required.

1. Name of partnership: Jan & Dee's
    Employer identification number: 36-1234567
    Address: 951 South Ravine, Chicago, IL 60632
    Method of accounting: Accrual

2. Partners:

Jan Such	Dee Notch
825 North Hopenstead	581 South Marigold
Chicago, IL 60421	Suberian, IL 60600
SSN 362-19-3801	SSN 358-33-0001

3. Revenue: $400,000
    Beginning inventory: -0-
    Purchases   190,000
    Ending inventory at cost: 15,000
    Ending cash balance: 3,000
    Ending accounts receivable: 84,400
    Ending accounts payable: 15,000

Other expenses:
    Wages (not including Jan's) $ 40,000
    Insurance   5,000
    Taxes   3,600
    Advertising   22,000
    Legal and professional   18,000
    Promotion   17,000
    Telephone   2,000

Form **1065**	**U.S. Partnership Return of Income**	OMB No. 1545-0099
Department of the Treasury Internal Revenue Service	For calendar year 1997, or tax year beginning _____ , 1997, and ending _____ , 19 ___ . ▶ See separate instructions.	**1997**

A Principal business activity	Use the IRS label. Other-wise, please print or type.	Name of partnership	D Employer identification number
B Principal product or service		Number, street, and room or suite no. If a P.O. box, see page 10 of the instructions.	E Date business started
C Business code number		City or town, state, and ZIP code	F Total assets (see page 10 of the instructions) $

G Check applicable boxes: (1) ☐ Initial return   (2) ☐ Final return   (3) ☐ Change in address   (4) ☐ Amended return
H Check accounting method: (1) ☐ Cash   (2) ☐ Accrual   (3) ☐ Other (specify) ▶
I Number of Schedules K-1. Attach one for each person who was a partner at any time during the tax year ▶ _____

Caution: *Include only trade or business income and expenses on lines 1a through 22 below. See the instructions for more information.*

Income

1a Gross receipts or sales	1a	
b Less returns and allowances	1b	1c
2 Cost of goods sold (Schedule A, line 8)		2
3 Gross profit. Subtract line 2 from line 1c		3
4 Ordinary income (loss) from other partnerships, estates, and trusts (attach schedule)		4
5 Net farm profit (loss) (attach Schedule F (Form 1040))		5
6 Net gain (loss) from Form 4797, Part II, line 18		6
7 Other income (loss) (attach schedule)		7
8 **Total income (loss).** Combine lines 3 through 7		8

Deductions (see page 11 of the instructions for limitations)

9 Salaries and wages (other than to partners) (less employment credits)		9
10 Guaranteed payments to partners		10
11 Repairs and maintenance		11
12 Bad debts		12
13 Rent		13
14 Taxes and licenses		14
15 Interest		15
16a Depreciation (if required, attach Form 4562)	16a	
b Less depreciation reported on Schedule A and elsewhere on return	16b	16c
17 Depletion (**Do not deduct oil and gas depletion.**)		17
18 Retirement plans, etc.		18
19 Employee benefit programs		19
20 Other deductions (attach schedule)		20
21 **Total deductions.** Add the amounts shown in the far right column for lines 9 through 20		21
22 **Ordinary income (loss)** from trade or business activities. Subtract line 21 from line 8		22

Please Sign Here

Under penalties of perjury, I declare that I have examined this return, including accompanying schedules and statements, and to the best of my knowledge and belief, it is true, correct, and complete. Declaration of preparer (other than general partner or limited liability company member) is based on all information of which preparer has any knowledge.

▶ _____ Signature of general partner or limited liability company member   ▶ _____ Date

Paid Preparer's Use Only

Preparer's signature ▶		Date	Check if self-employed ▶ ☐	Preparer's social security no.
Firm's name (or yours, if self-employed) and address ▶			EIN ▶	
			ZIP code ▶	

For Paperwork Reduction Act Notice, see separate instructions.
ISA
STF FED3361F.1

Form **1065** (1997)

Form 1065 (1997)   Page **2**

Schedule A	Cost of Goods Sold (see page 13 of the instructions)		

1	Inventory at beginning of year	1	
2	Purchases less cost of items withdrawn for personal use	2	
3	Cost of labor.	3	
4	Additional section 263A costs *(attach schedule)*	4	
5	Other costs *(attach schedule)*	5	
6	**Total.** Add lines 1 through 5	6	
7	Inventory at end of year	7	
8	**Cost of goods sold.** Subtract line 7 from line 6. Enter here and on page 1, line 2	8	

9a Check all methods used for valuing closing inventory:

    (i) ☐ Cost as described in Regulations section 1.471-3

    (ii) ☐ Lower of cost or market as described in Regulations section 1.471-4

    (iii) ☐ Other (specify method used and attach explanation) ▶ _____

   b Check this box if there was a writedown of "subnormal" goods as described in Regulations section 1.471-2(c). . . . . ▶ ☐

   c Check this box if the LIFO inventory method was adopted this tax year for any goods *(if checked, attach Form 970)* . ▶ ☐

   d Do the rules of section 263A (for property produced or acquired for resale) apply to the partnership? . . . . ☐ **Yes** ☐ **No**

   e Was there any change in determining quantities, cost, or valuations between opening and closing inventory? . ☐ **Yes** ☐ **No**
     If "Yes," attach explanation.

Schedule B	Other Information		

		Yes	No
1	What type of entity is filing this return? Check the applicable box:		
a	☐ General partnership **b** ☐ Limited partnership **c** ☐ Limited liability company		
d	☐ Other (see page 14 of the instructions) ▶ _____		
2	Are any partners in this partnership also partnerships?		
3	Is this partnership a partner in another partnership?		
4	Is this partnership subject to the consolidated audit procedures of sections 6221 through 6233? If "Yes," see **Designation of Tax Matters Partner** below.		
5	Does this partnership meet **ALL THREE** of the following requirements?		
a	The partnership's total receipts for the tax year were less than $250,000;		
b	The partnership's total assets at the end of the tax year were less than $600,000; **AND**		
c	Schedules K-1 are filed with the return and furnished to the partners on or before the due date (including extensions) for the partnership return.		
	If "Yes," the partnership is not required to complete Schedules L, M-1, and M-2; Item F on page 1 of Form 1065; or Item J on Schedule K-1		
6	Does this partnership have any foreign partners?		
7	Is this partnership a publicly traded partnership as defined in section 469(k)(2)?		
8	Has this partnership filed, or is it required to file, **Form 8264,** Application for Registration of a Tax Shelter?		
9	At any time during calendar year 1997, did the partnership have an interest in or a signature or other authority over a financial account in a foreign country (such as a bank account, securities account, or other financial account)? See page 14 of the instructions for exceptions and filing requirements for Form TD F 90-22.1. If "Yes," enter the name of the foreign country. ▶ _____		
10	During the tax year, did the partnership receive a distribution from, or was it the grantor of, or transferor to, a foreign trust? If "Yes," the partnership may have to file Form 3520 or 926. See page 14 of the instructions		
11	Was there a distribution of property or a transfer (e.g., by sale or death) of a partnership interest during the tax year? If "Yes," you may elect to adjust the basis of the partnership's assets under section 754 by attaching the statement described under **Elections Made By the Partnership** on page 5 of the instructions.		

Designation of Tax Matters Partner (see page 15 of the instructions)

Enter below the general partner designated as the tax matters partner (TMP) for the tax year of this return:

Name of designated TMP	▶	Identifying number of TMP	▶
Address of designated TMP	▶		

STF FED3361F.2

Form 1065 (1997)

Page 3

Schedule K	Partners' Shares of Income, Credits, Deductions, etc.		
	(a) Distributive share items		(b) Total amount
Income (Loss)	**1** Ordinary income (loss) from trade or business activities (page 1, line 22)	1	
	2 Net income (loss) from rental real estate activities *(attach Form 8825)*	2	
	3a Gross income from other rental activities	3a		
	b Expenses from other rental activities *(attach schedule)*	3b		
	c Net income (loss) from other rental activities. Subtract line 3b from line 3a	3c	
	4 Portfolio income (loss):		
	a Interest income	4a	
	b Dividend income	4b	
	c Royalty income	4c	
	d Net short-term capital gain (loss) *(attach Schedule D (Form 1065))*	4d	
	e Net long-term capital gain (loss) *(attach Schedule D (Form 1065))*:		
	(1) 28% rate gain (loss) ▶ _____ **(2)** Total for year . . . . ▶	4e(2)	
	f Other portfolio income (loss) *(attach schedule)*	4f	
	5 Guaranteed payments to partners	5	
	6 Net section 1231 gain (loss) (other than due to casualty or theft) *(attach Form 4797)*:		
	a 28% rate gain (loss) ▶ _____ **b** Total for year . . . . ▶	6b	
	7 Other income (loss) *(attach schedule)*	7	
Deductions	**8** Charitable contributions *(attach schedule)*	8	
	9 Section 179 expense deduction *(attach Form 4562)*	9	
	10 Deductions related to portfolio income (itemize)	10	
	11 Other deductions *(attach schedule)*	11	
Credits	**12a** Low-income housing credit:		
	(1) From partnerships to which section 42(j)(5) applies for property placed in service before 1990	12a(1)	
	(2) Other than on line 12a(1) for property placed in service before 1990	12a(2)	
	(3) From partnerships to which section 42(j)(5) applies for property placed in service after 1989	12a(3)	
	(4) Other than on line 12a(3) for property placed in service after 1989	12a(4)	
	b Qualified rehabilitation expenditures related to rental real estate activities *(attach Form 3468)*	12b	
	c Credits (other than credits shown on lines 12a and 12b) related to rental real estate activities	12c	
	d Credits related to other rental activities	12d	
	13 Other credits	13	
Investment Interest	**14a** Interest expense on investment debts	14a	
	b **(1)** Investment income included on lines 4a, 4b, 4c, and 4f above	14b(1)	
	(2) Investment expenses included on line 10 above	14b(2)	
Self-Employment	**15a** Net earnings (loss) from self-employment	15a	
	b Gross farming or fishing income	15b	
	c Gross nonfarm income	15c	
Adjustments and Tax Preference Items	**16a** Depreciation adjustment on property placed in service after 1986	16a	
	b Adjusted gain or loss	16b	
	c Depletion (other than oil and gas)	16c	
	d **(1)** Gross income from oil, gas, and geothermal properties	16d(1)	
	(2) Deductions allocable to oil, gas, and geothermal properties	16d(2)	
	e Other adjustments and tax preference items *(attach schedule)*	16e	
Foreign Taxes	**17a** Type of income ▶ _____		
	b Name of foreign country or U.S. possession ▶ _____		
	c Total gross income from sources outside the United States *(attach schedule)*	17c	
	d Total applicable deductions and losses *(attach schedule)*	17d	
	e Total foreign taxes (check one): ▶ ☐ Paid ☐ Accrued	17e	
	f Reduction in taxes available for credit *(attach schedule)*	17f	
	g Other foreign tax information *(attach schedule)*	17g	
Other	**18** Section 59(e)(2) expenditures: **a** Type ▶ _____ **b** Amount ▶	18b	
	19 Tax-exempt interest income	19	
	20 Other tax-exempt income	20	
	21 Nondeductible expenses	21	
	22 Distributions of money (cash and marketable securities)	22	
	23 Distributions of property other than money	23	
	24 Other items and amounts required to be reported separately to partners *(attach schedule)* .		

STF FED3361F.3

Form 1065 (1997)   Page **4**

Analysis of Net Income (Loss)

1   Net income (loss). Combine Schedule K, lines 1 through 7 in column (b). From the result, subtract
    the sum of Schedule K, lines 8 through 11, 14a, 17e, and 18b **1**

2 Analysis by partner type:	(i) Corporate	(ii) Individual (active)	(iii) Individual (passive)	(iv) Partnership	(v) Exempt organization	(vi) Nominee/Other
a General partners						
b Limited partners						

Schedule L   Balance Sheets per Books (Not required if Question 5 on Schedule B is answered "Yes.")

	Beginning of tax year		End of tax year	
Assets	(a)	(b)	(c)	(d)
1 Cash				
2a Trade notes and accounts receivable				
b Less allowance for bad debts				
3 Inventories				
4 U.S. government obligations				
5 Tax-exempt securities				
6 Other current assets (attach schedule)				
7 Mortgage and real estate loans				
8 Other investments (attach schedule)				
9a Buildings and other depreciable assets				
b Less accumulated depreciation				
10a Depletable assets				
b Less accumulated depletion				
11 Land (net of any amortization)				
12a Intangible assets (amortizable only)				
b Less accumulated amortization				
13 Other assets (attach schedule)				
14 Total assets				
Liabilities and Capital				
15 Accounts payable				
16 Mortgages, notes, bonds payable in less than 1 year . . .				
17 Other current liabilities (attach schedule)				
18 All nonrecourse loans				
19 Mortgages, notes, bonds payable in 1 year or more				
20 Other liabilities (attach schedule)				
21 Partners' capital accounts				
22 Total liabilities and capital				

Schedule M-1   Reconciliation of Income (Loss) per Books With Income (Loss) per Return
(Not required if Question 5 on Schedule B is answered "Yes." See page 23 of the instructions.)

1   Net income (loss) per books . . . .

2   Income included on Schedule K, lines 1
    through 4, 6, and 7, not recorded on books
    this year (itemize): _____

3   Guaranteed payments (other than health
    insurance) . . . .

4   Expenses recorded on books this year not
    included on Schedule K, lines 1 through
    11, 14a, 17e, and 18b (itemize):

a   Depreciation $ _____

b   Travel and entertainment $ _____

5   Add lines 1 through 4 . . . .

6   Income recorded on books this year not included
    on Schedule K, lines 1 through 7 (itemize):

a   Tax-exempt interest $ _____

7   Deductions included on Schedule K, lines 1
    through 11, 14a, 17e, and 18b, not charged
    against book income this year (itemize):

a   Depreciation $ _____

8   Add lines 6 and 7 . . . .

9   Income (loss) (Analysis of Net Income (Loss), line
    1). Subtract line 8 from line 5 . . . .

Schedule M-2   Analysis of Partners' Capital Accounts (Not required if Question 5 on Schedule B is answered "Yes.")

1   Balance at beginning of year . . . .

2   Capital contributed during year . . . .

3   Net income (loss) per books . . . .

4   Other increases (itemize): _____

5   Add lines 1 through 4 . . . .

6   Distributions: a Cash . . . .
                    b Property . . . .

7   Other decreases (itemize): _____

8   Add lines 6 and 7 . . . .

9   Balance at end of year. Subtract line 8 from line 5 . .

SCHEDULE K-1
(Form 1065)
Department of the Treasury
Internal Revenue Service

Partner's Share of Income, Credits, Deductions, etc.

▶ See separate instructions.

For calendar year 1997 or tax year beginning _____ , 1997, and ending _____ , 19 __

OMB No. 1545-0099

1997

Partner's identifying number ▶ _____

Partnership's identifying number ▶ _____

Partner's name, address, and ZIP code

Partnership's name, address, and ZIP code

A This partner is a ☐ general partner   ☐ limited partner
☐ limited liability company member

B What type of entity is this partner? ▶ _____

C Is this partner a ☐ domestic or a ☐ foreign partner?

D Enter partner's percentage of:

	(i) Before change or termination	(ii) End of year
Profit sharing	_____ %	_____ %
Loss sharing	_____ %	_____ %
Ownership of capital	_____ %	_____ %

E IRS Center where partnership filed return: _____

F Partner's share of liabilities (see instructions):
Nonrecourse . . . . $ _____
Qualified nonrecourse financing . . . . . $ _____
Other . . . . $ _____

G Tax shelter registration number ▶ _____

H Check here if this partnership is a publicly traded partnership as defined in section 469(k)(2) . . . . ☐

I Check applicable boxes: **(1)** ☐ Final K-1 **(2)** ☐ Amended K-1

J Analysis of partner's capital account:

(a) Capital account at beginning of year	(b) Capital contributed during year	(c) Partner's share of lines 3, 4, and 7, Form 1065, Schedule M-2	(d) Withdrawals and distributions	(e) Capital account at end of year (combine columns (a) through (d))
			( )	

(a) Distributive share item			(b) Amount	(c) 1040 filers enter the amount in column (b) on:
1 Ordinary income (loss) from trade or business activities	**1**			See page 6 of Partner's Instructions for Schedule K-1 (Form 1065).
2 Net income (loss) from rental real estate activities	**2**			
3 Net income (loss) from other rental activities	**3**			
4 Portfolio income (loss):				
a Interest	**4a**			
b Dividends	**4b**			Sch. B, Part I, line 1
c Royalties	**4c**			Sch. B, Part II, line 5
d Net short-term capital gain (loss)	**4d**			Sch. E, Part I, line 4
e Net long-term capital gain (loss):				Sch. D, line 5, col. (f)
(1) 28% rate gain (loss)	**e(1)**			
(2) Total for year	**e(2)**			Sch. D, line 12, col. (g)
f Other portfolio income (loss) (attach schedule)	**4f**			Sch. D, line 12, col. (f)
5 Guaranteed payments to partner	**5**			Enter on applicable line of your return.
6 Net section 1231 gain (loss) (other than due to casualty or theft):				See page 6 of Partner's Instructions for Schedule K-1 (Form 1065).
a 28% rate gain (loss)	**6a**			
b Total for year	**6b**			
7 Other income (loss) (attach schedule)	**7**			Enter on applicable line of your return.
8 Charitable contributions (see instructions) (attach schedule) . .	**8**			Sch. A, line 15 or 16
9 Section 179 expense deduction	**9**			See page 7 of Partner's Instructions for Schedule K-1 (Form 1065).
10 Deductions related to portfolio income (attach schedule)	**10**			
11 Other deductions (attach schedule)	**11**			
12a Low-income housing credit:				
(1) From section 42(j)(5) partnerships for property placed in service before 1990	**a(1)**			
(2) Other than on line 12a(1) for property placed in service before 1990 . . .	**a(2)**			
(3) From section 42(j)(5) partnerships for property placed in service after 1989	**a(3)**			Form 8586, line 5
(4) Other than on line 12a(3) for property placed in service after 1989 . . .	**a(4)**			
b Qualified rehabilitation expenditures related to rental real estate activities	**12b**			
c Credits (other than credits shown on lines 12a and 12b) related to rental real estate activities	**12c**			See page 8 of Partner's Instructions for Schedule K-1 (Form 1065).
d Credits related to other rental activities	**12d**			
13 Other credits	**13**			

Income (Loss) — Deductions — Credits

For Paperwork Reduction Act Notice, see Instructions for Form 1065.

ISA
STF FED3405F.1

Schedule K-1 (Form 1065) 1997

Schedule K-1 (Form 1065) 1997   Page **2**

	(a) Distributive share item		(b) Amount	(c) 1040 filers enter the amount in column (b) on:
Investment Interest	**14a** Interest expense on investment debts	14a		Form 4952, line 1
	b (1) Investment income included on lines 4a, 4b, 4c, and 4f . . .	b(1)		See page 8 of Partner's Instructions for Schedule K-1 (Form 1065).
	(2) Investment expenses included on line 10	b(2)		
Self-employment	**15a** Net earnings (loss) from self-employment	15a		Sch. SE, Section A or B
	b Gross farming or fishing income	15b		See page 9 of Partner's Instructions for Schedule K-1 (Form 1065).
	c Gross nonfarm income	15c		
Adjustments and Tax Preference Items	**16a** Depreciation adjustment on property placed in service after 1986	16a		
	b Adjusted gain or loss	16b		See page 9 of Partner's Instructions for Schedule K-1 (Form 1065) and Instructions for Form 6251.
	c Depletion (other than oil and gas)	16c		
	d (1) Gross income from oil, gas, and geothermal properties . . .	d(1)		
	(2) Deductions allocable to oil, gas, and geothermal properties	d(2)		
	e Other adjustments and tax preference items *(attach schedule)*	16e		
Foreign Taxes	**17a** Type of income ▶ _____			Form 1116, check boxes
	b Name of foreign country or possession ▶ _____			
	c Total gross income from sources outside the United States *(attach schedule)*	17c		Form 1116, Part I
	d Total applicable deductions and losses *(attach schedule)*	17d		
	e Total foreign taxes (check one): ▶ ☐ Paid ☐ Accrued . . .	17e		Form 1116, Part II
	f Reduction in taxes available for credit *(attach schedule)*	17f		Form 1116, Part III
	g Other foreign tax information *(attach schedule)*	17g		See Instructions for Form 1116.
Other	**18** Section 59(e)(2) expenditures: **a** Type ▶ _____			See page 9 of Partner's Instructions for Schedule K-1 (Form 1065).
	b Amount	18b		
	19 Tax-exempt interest income	19		Form 1040, line 8b
	20 Other tax-exempt income	20		
	21 Nondeductible expenses	21		See page 9 of Partner's Instructions for Schedule K-1 (Form 1065).
	22 Distributions of money (cash and marketable securities)	22		
	23 Distributions of property other than money	23		
	24 Recapture of low-income housing credit:			
	a From section 42(j)(5) partnerships	24a		Form 8611, line 8
	b Other than on line 24a	24b		

25 Supplemental information required to be reported separately to each partner *(attach additional schedules if more space is needed):*

_____

_____

_____

_____

_____

_____

_____

_____

_____

_____

_____

STF FED3405F.2

Form **4562**	**Depreciation and Amortization**	OMB No. 1545-0172
Department of the Treasury Internal Revenue Service (99)	(Including Information on Listed Property) ▶ See separate instructions. ▶ Attach this form to your return.	**1997** Attachment Sequence No. **67**

Name(s) shown on return	Business or activity to which this form relates	Identifying number

Part I   Election To Expense Certain Tangible Property (Section 179) (Note: *If you have any "listed property," complete Part V before you complete Part I.*)

1	Maximum dollar limitation. If an enterprise zone business, see page 2 of the instructions	**1**	$18,000
2	Total cost of section 179 property placed in service. See page 2 of the instructions	**2**	
3	Threshold cost of section 179 property before reduction in limitation	**3**	$200,000
4	Reduction in limitation. Subtract line 3 from line 2. If zero or less, enter -0-	**4**	
5	Dollar limitation for tax year. Subtract line 4 from line 1. If zero or less, enter -0-. If married filing separately, see page 2 of the instructions	**5**	

(a) Description of property	(b) Cost (business use only)	(c) Elected cost	
6			

7	Listed property. Enter amount from line 27 . . . . **7**		
8	Total elected cost of section 179 property. Add amounts in column (c), lines 6 and 7	**8**	
9	Tentative deduction. Enter the smaller of line 5 or line 8	**9**	
10	Carryover of disallowed deduction from 1996. See page 3 of the instructions	**10**	
11	Business income limitation. Enter the smaller of business income (not less than zero) or line 5 (see instructions) . .	**11**	
12	Section 179 expense deduction. Add lines 9 and 10, but do not enter more than line 11	**12**	
13	Carryover of disallowed deduction to 1998. Add lines 9 and 10, less line 12 . . . . . ▶ **13**		

Note: *Do not use Part II or Part III below for listed property (automobiles, certain other vehicles, cellular telephones, certain computers, or property used for entertainment, recreation, or amusement). Instead, use Part V for listed property.*

Part II   MACRS Depreciation For Assets Placed in Service ONLY During Your 1997 Tax Year (Do Not Include Listed Property.)

Section A — General Asset Account Election

14	If you are making the election under section 168(i)(4) to group any assets placed in service during the tax year into one or more general asset accounts, check this box. See page 3 of the instructions . . . . ▶ ☐

Section B — General Depreciation System (GDS) (See page 3 of the instructions.)

(a) Classification of property	(b) Month and year placed in service	(c) Basis for depreciation (business/investment use only — see instructions)	(d) Recovery period	(e) Convention	(f) Method	(g) Depreciation deduction
15a 3-year property						
b 5-year property						
c 7-year property						
d 10-year property						
e 15-year property						
f 20-year property						
g 25-year property			25 yrs.		S/L	
h Residential rental			27.5 yrs.	MM	S/L	
property			27.5 yrs.	MM	S/L	
i Nonresidential real			39 yrs.	MM	S/L	
property				MM	S/L	

Section C — Alternative Depreciation System (ADS) (See page 6 of the instructions.)

16a Class life					S/L	
b 12-year			12 yrs.		S/L	
c 40-year			40 yrs.	MM	S/L	

Part III   Other Depreciation (Do Not Include Listed Property.) (See page 6 of the instructions.)

17	GDS and ADS deductions for assets placed in service in tax years beginning before 1997	**17**	
18	Property subject to section 168(f)(1) election	**18**	
19	ACRS and other depreciation	**19**	

Part IV   Summary (See page 7 of the instructions.)

20	Listed property. Enter amount from line 26	**20**	
21	**Total.** Add deductions on line 12, lines 15 and 16 in column (g), and lines 17 through 20. Enter here and on the appropriate lines of your return. Partnerships and S corporations — see instructions	**21**	
22	For assets shown above and placed in service during the current year, enter the portion of the basis attributable to section 263A costs **22**		

For Paperwork Reduction Act Notice, see the separate instructions.   ISA   Form **4562** (1997)
STF FED5085F.1

Form 4562 (1997)   Page **2**

Part V	Listed Property — Automobiles, Certain Other Vehicles, Cellular Telephones, Certain Computers, and Property Used for Entertainment, Recreation, or Amusement

Note: *For any vehicle for which you are using the standard mileage rate or deducting lease expense, complete only 23a, 23b, columns (a) through (c) of Section A, all of Section B, and Section C if applicable.*

Section A — Depreciation and Other Information (Caution: *See page 8 of the instructions for limits for passenger automobiles.*)

23a Do you have evidence to support the business/investment use claimed? ☐ Yes ☐ No   23b If "Yes," is the evidence written? ☐ Yes ☐ No

(a) Type of property (list vehicles first)	(b) Date placed in service	(c) Business/ investment use percentage	(d) Cost or other basis	(e) Basis for depreciation (business/investment use only)	(f) Recovery period	(g) Method/ Convention	(h) Depreciation deduction	(i) Elected section 179 cost
24 Property used more than 50% in a qualified business use (See page 7 of the instructions.):								
		%						
		%						
		%						
25 Property used 50% or less in a qualified business use (See page 7 of the instructions.):								
		%			S/L –			
		%			S/L –			
		%			S/L –			

26 Add amounts in column (h). Enter the total here and on line 20, page 1 . . . . | 26 |
27 Add amounts in column (i). Enter the total here and on line 7, page 1 . . . . | 27 |

Section B — Information on Use of Vehicles

Complete this section for vehicles used by a sole proprietor, partner, or other "more than 5% owner," or related person.
If you provided vehicles to your employees, first answer the questions in Section C to see of you meet an exception to completing this section for those vehicles.

	(a) Vehicle 1	(b) Vehicle 2	(c) Vehicle 3	(d) Vehicle 4	(e) Vehicle 5	(f) Vehicle 6
28 Total business/investment miles driven during the year (DO NOT include commuting miles)						
29 Total commuting miles driven during the year						
30 Total other personal (noncommuting) miles driven						
31 Total miles driven during the year. Add lines 28 through 30						

	Yes	No	Yes	No	Yes	No	Yes	No	Yes	No	Yes	No
32 Was the vehicle available for personal use during off-duty hours?												
33 Was the vehicle used primarily by a more than 5% owner or related person?												
34 Is another vehicle available for personal use?												

Section C — Questions for Employers Who Provide Vehicles for Use by Their Employees

*Answer these questions to determine if you meet an exception to completing Section B for vehicles used by employees who **are not** more than 5% owners or related persons.*

	Yes	No
35 Do you maintain a written policy statement that prohibits all personal use of vehicles, including commuting, by your employees?		
36 Do you maintain a written policy statement that prohibits personal use of vehicles, except commuting, by your employees? See page 9 of the instructions for vehicles used by corporate officers, directors, or 1% or more owners		
37 Do you treat all use of vehicles by employees as personal use?		
38 Do you provide more than five vehicles to your employees, obtain information from your employees about the use of the vehicles, and retain the information received?		
39 Do you meet the requirements concerning qualified automobile demonstration use? See page 9 of the instructions.		

Note: *If your answer to 35, 36, 37, 38, or 39 is "Yes," you need not complete Section B of the covered vehicles.*

Part VI	Amortization

(a) Description of costs	(b) Date amortization begins	(c) Amortizable amount	(d) Code section	(e) Amortization period or percentage	(f) Amortization for this year
40 Amortization of costs that begins during your 1997 tax year:					
41 Amortization of costs that began before 1997	41	
42 Total. Enter here and on "Other Deductions" or "Other Expenses" line of your return	42	

STF FED5085F.2

Form **1065**	U.S. Partnership Return of Income	OMB No. 1545-0099
Department of the Treasury Internal Revenue Service	For calendar year 1997, or tax year beginning _____ , 1997, and ending _____ , 19 ___ . ▶ See separate instructions.	**1997**

A Principal business activity	Use the IRS label. Other-wise, please print or type.	Name of partnership **JAN & DEE'S**	D Employer identification number **36-1234567**
B Principal product or service		Number, street, and room or suite no. If a P.O. box, see page 10 of the instructions. **951 SOUTH RAVINE**	E Date business started **01/01/97**
C Business code number		City or town, state, and ZIP code **CHICAGO IL 60632**	F Total assets (see page 10 of the instructions) $ **406,278**

G Check applicable boxes: (1) [X] Initial return (2) [ ] Final return (3) [ ] Change in address (4) [ ] Amended return

H Check accounting method: (1) [ ] Cash (2) [X] Accrual (3) [ ] Other (specify) ▶ _____

I Number of Schedules K-1. Attach one for each person who was a partner at any time during the tax year ▶ 2 _____

Caution: *Include **only** trade or business income and expenses on lines 1a through 22 below. See the instructions for more information.*

Income	1a	Gross receipts or sales	1a	400,000		
	b	Less returns and allowances	1b		1c	400,000
	2	Cost of goods sold (Schedule A, line 8)			2	175,000
	3	Gross profit. Subtract line 2 from line 1c			3	225,000
	4	Ordinary income (loss) from other partnerships, estates, and trusts *(attach schedule)*			4	
	5	Net farm profit (loss) *(attach Schedule F (Form 1040))*			5	
	6	Net gain (loss) from Form 4797, Part II, line 18			6	
	7	Other income (loss) *(attach schedule)*			7	
	8	**Total income (loss).** Combine lines 3 through 7			8	225,000
Deductions (see page 11 of the instructions for limitations)	9	Salaries and wages (other than to partners) (less employment credits)			9	40,000
	10	Guaranteed payments to partners			10	15,000
	11	Repairs and maintenance			11	
	12	Bad debts			12	
	13	Rent			13	
	14	Taxes and licenses			14	3,600
	15	Interest			15	
	16a	Depreciation (if required, attach Form 4562)	16a	26,122		
	b	Less depreciation reported on Schedule A and elsewhere on return	16b		16c	26,122
	17	Depletion **(Do not deduct oil and gas depletion.)**			17	
	18	Retirement plans, etc.			18	
	19	Employee benefit programs			19	
	20	Other deductions *(attach schedule)*			20	64,000
	21	**Total deductions.** Add the amounts shown in the far right column for lines 9 through 20			21	148,722
	22	**Ordinary income (loss)** from trade or business activities. Subtract line 21 from line 8			22	76,278

Please Sign Here

Under penalties of perjury, I declare that I have examined this return, including accompanying schedules and statements, and to the best of my knowledge and belief, it is true, correct, and complete. Declaration of preparer (other than general partner or limited liability company member) is based on all information of which preparer has any knowledge.

▶ _____
Signature of general partner or limited liability company member

▶ _____
Date

Paid Preparer's Use Only

Preparer's signature ▶		Date	Check if self-employed ▶ [ ]	Preparer's social security no.
Firm's name (or yours, if self-employed) and address			EIN ▶	
			ZIP code ▶	

For Paperwork Reduction Act Notice, see separate instructions.

ISA
STF FED3361F.1

Form **1065** (1997)

Form 1065 (1997)   Page **2**

Schedule A	Cost of Goods Sold (see page 13 of the instructions)		

1	Inventory at beginning of year	1	
2	Purchases less cost of items withdrawn for personal use	2	190,000
3	Cost of labor	3	
4	Additional section 263A costs (attach schedule)	4	
5	Other costs (attach schedule)	5	
6	**Total.** Add lines 1 through 5	6	190,000
7	Inventory at end of year	7	15,000
8	**Cost of goods sold.** Subtract line 7 from line 6. Enter here and on page 1, line 2	8	175,000

9a Check all methods used for valuing closing inventory:

    (i) [X] Cost as described in Regulations section 1.471-3

    (ii) [ ] Lower of cost or market as described in Regulations section 1.471-4

    (iii) [ ] Other (specify method used and attach explanation) ▶ _____

  b Check this box if there was a writedown of "subnormal" goods as described in Regulations section 1.471-2(c). ..... ▶ [ ]

  c Check this box if the LIFO inventory method was adopted this tax year for any goods (if checked, attach Form 970) . ▶ [ ]

  d Do the rules of section 263A (for property produced or acquired for resale) apply to the partnership? .... [ ] **Yes** [ ] **No**

  e Was there any change in determining quantities, cost, or valuations between opening and closing inventory? . [ ] **Yes** [ ] **No** If "Yes," attach explanation.

Schedule B	Other Information		

		Yes	No
1	What type of entity is filing this return? Check the applicable box:		
a	[X] General partnership b [ ] Limited partnership c [ ] Limited liability company		
d	[ ] Other (see page 14 of the instructions) ▶ _____		
2	Are any partners in this partnership also partnerships?		X
3	Is this partnership a partner in another partnership?		X
4	Is this partnership subject to the consolidated audit procedures of sections 6221 through 6233? If "Yes," see **Designation of Tax Matters Partner** below		X
5	Does this partnership meet **ALL THREE** of the following requirements?		
a	The partnership's total receipts for the tax year were less than $250,000;		
b	The partnership's total assets at the end of the tax year were less than $600,000; **AND**		
c	Schedules K-1 are filed with the return and furnished to the partners on or before the due date (including extensions) for the partnership return.		
	If "Yes," the partnership is not required to complete Schedules L, M-1, and M-2; Item F on page 1 of Form 1065; or Item J on Schedule K-1		X
6	Does this partnership have any foreign partners?		X
7	Is this partnership a publicly traded partnership as defined in section 469(k)(2)?		X
8	Has this partnership filed, or is it required to file, **Form 8264,** Application for Registration of a Tax Shelter?		X
9	At any time during calendar year 1997, did the partnership have an interest in or a signature or other authority over a financial account in a foreign country (such as a bank account, securities account, or other financial account)? See page 14 of the instructions for exceptions and filing requirements for Form TD F 90-22.1. If "Yes," enter the name of the foreign country. ▶ _____		X
10	During the tax year, did the partnership receive a distribution from, or was it the grantor of, or transferor to, a foreign trust? If "Yes," the partnership may have to file Form 3520 or 926. See page 14 of the instructions		X
11	Was there a distribution of property or a transfer (e.g., by sale or death) of a partnership interest during the tax year? If "Yes," you may elect to adjust the basis of the partnership's assets under section 754 by attaching the statement described under **Elections Made By the Partnership** on page 5 of the instructions		X

Designation of Tax Matters Partner (see page 15 of the instructions)

Enter below the general partner designated as the tax matters partner (TMP) for the tax year of this return:

Name of designated TMP ▶		Identifying number of TMP ▶	
Address of designated TMP ▶			

STF FED3361F.2

Form 1065 (1997)   Page **3**

Schedule K	Partners' Shares of Income, Credits, Deductions, etc.		
	(a) Distributive share items		**(b) Total amount**

Income (Loss)

1	Ordinary income (loss) from trade or business activities (page 1, line 22)	**1**	76,278
2	Net income (loss) from rental real estate activities *(attach Form 8825)*	**2**	
3a	Gross income from other rental activities	**3a**	
b	Expenses from other rental activities *(attach schedule)*	**3b**	
c	Net income (loss) from other rental activities. Subtract line 3b from line 3a	**3c**	
4	Portfolio income (loss):		
a	Interest income	**4a**	
b	Dividend income	**4b**	
c	Royalty income	**4c**	
d	Net short-term capital gain (loss) *(attach Schedule D (Form 1065))*	**4d**	
e	Net long-term capital gain (loss) *(attach Schedule D (Form 1065))*:		
	(1) 28% rate gain (loss) ▶ _____ **(2)** Total for year . . . . ▶	**4e(2)**	
f	Other portfolio income (loss) *(attach schedule)*	**4f**	
5	Guaranteed payments to partners	**5**	15,000
6	Net section 1231 gain (loss) (other than due to casualty or theft) *(attach Form 4797)*:		
a	28% rate gain (loss) ▶ _____ **b** Total for year . . . . ▶	**6b**	
7	Other income (loss) *(attach schedule)*	**7**	

Deductions

8	Charitable contributions *(attach schedule)*	**8**	
9	Section 179 expense deduction *(attach Form 4562)*	**9**	
10	Deductions related to portfolio income (itemize)	**10**	
11	Other deductions *(attach schedule)*	**11**	

Credits

12a	Low-income housing credit:		
	(1) From partnerships to which section 42(j)(5) applies for property placed in service before 1990	**12a(1)**	
	(2) Other than on line 12a(1) for property placed in service before 1990	**12a(2)**	
	(3) From partnerships to which section 42(j)(5) applies for property placed in service after 1989	**12a(3)**	
	(4) Other than on line 12a(3) for property placed in service after 1989	**12a(4)**	
b	Qualified rehabilitation expenditures related to rental real estate activities *(attach Form 3468)*	**12b**	
c	Credits (other than credits shown on lines 12a and 12b) related to rental real estate activities	**12c**	
d	Credits related to other rental activities	**12d**	
13	Other credits	**13**	

Investment Interest

14a	Interest expense on investment debts	**14a**	
b	**(1)** Investment income included on lines 4a, 4b, 4c, and 4f above	**14b(1)**	
	(2) Investment expenses included on line 10 above	**14b(2)**	

Self-Employment

15a	Net earnings (loss) from self-employment	**15a**	91,278
b	Gross farming or fishing income	**15b**	
c	Gross nonfarm income	**15c**	

Adjustments and Tax Preference Items

16a	Depreciation adjustment on property placed in service after 1986	**16a**	12,060
b	Adjusted gain or loss	**16b**	
c	Depletion (other than oil and gas)	**16c**	
d	**(1)** Gross income from oil, gas, and geothermal properties	**16d(1)**	
	(2) Deductions allocable to oil, gas, and geothermal properties	**16d(2)**	
e	Other adjustments and tax preference items *(attach schedule)*	**16e**	

Foreign Taxes

17a	Type of income ▶ _____		
b	Name of foreign country or U.S. possession ▶ _____		
c	Total gross income from sources outside the United States *(attach schedule)*	**17c**	
d	Total applicable deductions and losses *(attach schedule)*	**17d**	
e	Total foreign taxes (check one): ▶ ☐ Paid ☐ Accrued	**17e**	
f	Reduction in taxes available for credit *(attach schedule)*	**17f**	
g	Other foreign tax information *(attach schedule)*	**17g**	

Other

18	Section 59(e)(2) expenditures: **a** Type ▶ _____ **b** Amount ▶	**18b**	
19	Tax-exempt interest income	**19**	
20	Other tax-exempt income	**20**	
21	Nondeductible expenses	**21**	
22	Distributions of money (cash and marketable securities)	**22**	15,000
23	Distributions of property other than money	**23**	
24	Other items and amounts required to be reported separately to partners *(attach schedule)*.		

STF FED3361F.3

Form 1065 (1997)   Page **4**

Analysis of Net Income (Loss)

1	Net income (loss). Combine Schedule K, lines 1 through 7 in column (b). From the result, subtract the sum of Schedule K, lines 8 through 11, 14a, 17e, and 18b				**1**	91,278

2 Analysis by partner type:	(i) Corporate	(ii) Individual (active)	(iii) Individual (passive)	(iv) Partnership	(v) Exempt organization	(vi) Nominee/Other
a General partners		91,278				
b Limited partners						

Schedule L Balance Sheets per Books (Not required if Question 5 on Schedule B is answered "Yes.")

Assets	Beginning of tax year (a)	(b)	End of tax year (c)	(d)
1 Cash				3,000
2a Trade notes and accounts receivable			84,400	
b Less allowance for bad debts				84,400
3 Inventories				15,000
4 U.S. government obligations				
5 Tax-exempt securities.................				
6 Other current assets (attach schedule)				
7 Mortgage and real estate loans				
8 Other investments (attach schedule)				
9a Buildings and other depreciable assets			337,500	
b Less accumulated depreciation			63,622	273,878
10a Depletable assets...................				
b Less accumulated depletion				
11 Land (net of any amortization)				30,000
12a Intangible assets (amortizable only).				
b Less accumulated amortization				
13 Other assets (attach schedule)				
14 Total assets				406,278
Liabilities and Capital				
15 Accounts payable....................				15,000
16 Mortgages, notes, bonds payable in less than 1 year ...				
17 Other current liabilities (attach schedule)				
18 All nonrecourse loans.................				
19 Mortgages, notes, bonds payable in 1 year or more				
20 Other liabilities (attach schedule)				
21 Partners' capital accounts				391,278
22 Total liabilities and capital				406,278

Schedule M-1 Reconciliation of Income (Loss) per Books With Income (Loss) per Return
(Not required if Question 5 on Schedule B is answered "Yes." See page 23 of the instructions.)

1 Net income (loss) per books	76,278	6 Income recorded on books this year not included on Schedule K, lines 1 through 7 (itemize):		
2 Income included on Schedule K, lines 1 through 4, 6, and 7, not recorded on books this year (itemize): _____		a Tax-exempt interest $ _____		
3 Guaranteed payments (other than health insurance)	15,000	7 Deductions included on Schedule K, lines 1 through 11, 14a, 17e, and 18b, not charged against book income this year (itemize):		
4 Expenses recorded on books this year not included on Schedule K, lines 1 through 11, 14a, 17e, and 18b (itemize):		a Depreciation $ _____		
a Depreciation $ _____				
b Travel and entertainment $ _____		8 Add lines 6 and 7		
5 Add lines 1 through 4	91,278	9 Income (loss) (Analysis of Net Income (Loss), line 1). Subtract line 8 from line 5		91,278

Schedule M-2 Analysis of Partners' Capital Accounts (Not required if Question 5 on Schedule B is answered "Yes.")

1 Balance at beginning of year	0	6 Distributions: a Cash..................		15,000
2 Capital contributed during year.........	330,000	b Property		
3 Net income (loss) per books	76,278	7 Other decreases (itemize): _____		
4 Other increases (itemize): _____				
		8 Add lines 6 and 7		15,000
5 Add lines 1 through 4	406,278	9 Balance at end of year. Subtract line 8 from line 5 ..		391,278

STF FED3361F.4

SCHEDULE K-1 (Form 1065) Department of the Treasury Internal Revenue Service	Partner's Share of Income, Credits, Deductions, etc. ▶ See separate instructions. For calendar year 1997 or tax year beginning , 1997, and ending , 19	OMB No. 1545-0099 **1997**

Partner's identifying number ▶ 362-19-3801	Partnership's identifying number ▶ 36-1234567
Partner's name, address, and ZIP code JAN SUCH 825 N. HOPENSTEAD CHICAGO IL 60421	Partnership's name, address, and ZIP code JAN & DEE'S 951 SOUTH RAVINE CHICAGO IL 60632

A This partner is a ☒ general partner ☐ limited partner
☐ limited liability company member
B What type of entity is this partner? ▶ INDIVIDUAL
C Is this partner a ☒ domestic or a ☐ foreign partner?
D Enter partner's percentage of:

	(i) Before change or termination	(ii) End of year
Profit sharing	____ %	60 %
Loss sharing	____ %	60 %
Ownership of capital	____ %	56 %

E IRS Center where partnership filed return: KANSAS CITY

F Partner's share of liabilities (see instructions):
Nonrecourse . . . . $_____
Qualified nonrecourse financing . . . . . $_____
Other . . . . $_____
G Tax shelter registration number ▶ _____
H Check here if this partnership is a publicly traded
partnership as defined in section 469(k)(2) . . . . ☐
I Check applicable boxes: **(1)** ☐ Final K-1 **(2)** ☐ Amended K-1

J Analysis of partner's capital account:

(a) Capital account at beginning of year	(b) Capital contributed during year	(c) Partner's share of lines 3, 4, and 7, Form 1065, Schedule M-2	(d) Withdrawals and distributions	(e) Capital account at end of year (combine columns (a) through (d))
0	180,000	45,767	(7,500)	218,267

	(a) Distributive share item		(b) Amount	(c) 1040 filers enter the amount in column (b) on:
Income (Loss)	1 Ordinary income (loss) from trade or business activities	1	45,767	See page 6 of Partner's Instructions for Schedule K-1 (Form 1065).
	2 Net income (loss) from rental real estate activities	2		
	3 Net income (loss) from other rental activities	3		
	4 Portfolio income (loss):			
	a Interest	4a		Sch. B, Part I, line 1
	b Dividends	4b		Sch. B, Part II, line 5
	c Royalties	4c		Sch. E, Part I, line 4
	d Net short-term capital gain (loss)	4d		Sch. D, line 5, col. (f)
	e Net long-term capital gain (loss):			
	(1) 28% rate gain (loss)	e(1)		Sch. D, line 12, col. (g)
	(2) Total for year	e(2)		Sch. D, line 12, col. (f)
	f Other portfolio income (loss) (attach schedule)	4 f		Enter on applicable line of your return.
	5 Guaranteed payments to partner	5	15,000	See page 6 of Partner's Instructions for Schedule K-1 (Form 1065).
	6 Net section 1231 gain (loss) (other than due to casualty or theft):			
	a 28% rate gain (loss)	6a		
	b Total for year	6b		
	7 Other income (loss) (attach schedule)	7		Enter on applicable line of your return.
Deductions	8 Charitable contributions (see instructions) (attach schedule) . .	8		Sch. A, line 15 or 16
	9 Section 179 expense deduction	9		See page 7 of Partner's Instructions for Schedule K-1 (Form 1065).
	10 Deductions related to portfolio income (attach schedule)	10		
	11 Other deductions (attach schedule)	11		
Credits	12a Low-income housing credit:			
	(1) From section 42(j)(5) partnerships for property placed in service before 1990	a(1)		
	(2) Other than on line 12a(1) for property placed in service before 1990 . . .	a(2)		
	(3) From section 42(j)(5) partnerships for property placed in service after 1989	a(3)		Form 8586, line 5
	(4) Other than on line 12a(3) for property placed in service after 1989	a(4)		
	b Qualified rehabilitation expenditures related to rental real estate activities	12b		
	c Credits (other than credits shown on lines 12a and 12b) related to rental real estate activities	12c		See page 8 of Partner's Instructions for Schedule K-1 (Form 1065).
	d Credits related to other rental activities	12d		
	13 Other credits	13		

For Paperwork Reduction Act Notice, see Instructions for Form 1065.

Schedule K-1 (Form 1065) 1997

ISA
STF FED3405F 1

Page 2

(a) Distributive share item		(b) Amount	(c) 1040 filers enter the amount in column (b) on:
Investment Interest 14a Interest expense on investment debts	14a		Form 4952, line 1
b (1) Investment income included on lines 4a, 4b, 4c, and 4f	b(1)		See page 8 of Partner's Instructions for Schedule K-1 (Form 1065).
(2) Investment expenses included on line 10	b(2)		
Self-employment 15a Net earnings (loss) from self-employment	15a	60,767	Sch. SE, Section A or B
b Gross farming or fishing income	15b		See page 9 of Partner's Instructions for Schedule K-1 (Form 1065).
c Gross nonfarm income	15c		
Adjustments and Tax Preference Items 16a Depreciation adjustment on property placed in service after 1986	16a	7,236	
b Adjusted gain or loss	16b		
c Depletion (other than oil and gas)	16c		See page 9 of Partner's Instructions for Schedule K-1 (Form 1065) and Instructions for Form 6251.
d (1) Gross income from oil, gas, and geothermal properties	d(1)		
(2) Deductions allocable to oil, gas, and geothermal properties	d(2)		
e Other adjustments and tax preference items (attach schedule)	16e		
Foreign Taxes 17a Type of income ▶ _____			Form 1116, check boxes
b Name of foreign country or possession ▶ _____			
c Total gross income from sources outside the United States (attach schedule)	17c		Form 1116, Part I
d Total applicable deductions and losses (attach schedule)	17d		
e Total foreign taxes (check one): ▶ ☐ Paid ☐ Accrued	17e		Form 1116, Part II
f Reduction in taxes available for credit (attach schedule)	17f		Form 1116, Part III
g Other foreign tax information (attach schedule)	17g		See Instructions for Form 1116.
Other 18 Section 59(e)(2) expenditures: a Type ▶ _____			See page 9 of Partner's Instructions for Schedule K-1 (Form 1065).
b Amount	18b		
19 Tax-exempt interest income	19		Form 1040, line 8b
20 Other tax-exempt income	20		
21 Nondeductible expenses	21		See page 9 of Partner's Instructions for Schedule K-1 (Form 1065).
22 Distributions of money (cash and marketable securities)	22	7,500	
23 Distributions of property other than money	23		
24 Recapture of low-income housing credit:			
a From section 42(j)(5) partnerships	24a		Form 8611, line 8
b Other than on line 24a	24b		

Supplemental Information

25 Supplemental information required to be reported separately to each partner (attach additional schedules if more space is needed):

_____

_____

_____

_____

_____

_____

_____

_____

_____

_____

_____

_____

_____

_____

_____

Form **4562**	**Depreciation and Amortization**	OMB No. 1545-0172
Department of the Treasury Internal Revenue Service (99)	(Including Information on Listed Property) ▶ See separate instructions. ▶ Attach this form to your return.	**1997** Attachment Sequence No. **67**

Name(s) shown on return	Business or activity to which this form relates	Identifying number
JAN & DEE'S	FORM 1065	36-1234567

Part I Election To Expense Certain Tangible Property (Section 179) (Note: *If you have any "listed property," complete Part V before you complete Part I.*)

1	Maximum dollar limitation. If an enterprise zone business, see page 2 of the instructions	**1**	$18,000
2	Total cost of section 179 property placed in service. See page 2 of the instructions	**2**	
3	Threshold cost of section 179 property before reduction in limitation	**3**	$200,000
4	Reduction in limitation. Subtract line 3 from line 2. If zero or less, enter -0-	**4**	
5	Dollar limitation for tax year. Subtract line 4 from line 1. If zero or less, enter -0-. If married filing separately, see page 2 of the instructions	**5**	

(a) Description of property	(b) Cost (business use only)	(c) Elected cost	
6			

7	Listed property. Enter amount from line 27	**7**	
8	Total elected cost of section 179 property. Add amounts in column (c), lines 6 and 7	**8**	
9	Tentative deduction. Enter the smaller of line 5 or line 8	**9**	
10	Carryover of disallowed deduction from 1996. See page 3 of the instructions	**10**	
11	Business income limitation. Enter the smaller of business income (not less than zero) or line 5 (see instructions) . .	**11**	
12	Section 179 expense deduction. Add lines 9 and 10, but do not enter more than line 11	**12**	
13	Carryover of disallowed deduction to 1998. Add lines 9 and 10, less line 12 . . . . . . ▶	**13**	

Note: *Do not use Part II or Part III below for listed property (automobiles, certain other vehicles, cellular telephones, certain computers, or property used for entertainment, recreation, or amusement). Instead, use Part V for listed property.*

Part II MACRS Depreciation For Assets Placed in Service ONLY During Your 1997 Tax Year (Do Not Include Listed Property.)

Section A — General Asset Account Election

14	If you are making the election under section 168(i)(4) to group any assets placed in service during the tax year into one or more general asset accounts, check this box. See page 3 of the instructions . . . . ▶ ☐	

Section B — General Depreciation System (GDS) (See page 3 of the instructions.)

(a) Classification of property	(b) Month and year placed in service	(c) Basis for depreciation (business/investment use only — see instructions)	(d) Recovery period	(e) Convention	(f) Method	(g) Depreciation deduction
15a 3-year property						
b 5-year property						
c 7-year property		150,000	7	HY	DDB	21,435
d 10-year property						
e 15-year property						
f 20-year property						
g 25-year property			25 yrs.		S/L	
h Residential rental property			27.5 yrs.	MM	S/L	
			27.5 yrs.	MM	S/L	
i Nonresidential real property			39 yrs.	MM	S/L	
				MM	S/L	

Section C — Alternative Depreciation System (ADS) (See page 6 of the instructions.)

(a) Classification of property						
16a Class life					S/L	
b 12-year			12 yrs.		S/L	
c 40-year			40 yrs.	MM	S/L	

Part III Other Depreciation (Do Not Include Listed Property.) (See page 6 of the instructions.)

17	GDS and ADS deductions for assets placed in service in tax years beginning before 1997	**17**	4,687
18	Property subject to section 168(f)(1) election	**18**	
19	ACRS and other depreciation	**19**	

Part IV Summary (See page 7 of the instructions.)

20	Listed property. Enter amount from line 26	**20**	
21	**Total.** Add deductions on line 12, lines 15 and 16 in column (g), and lines 17 through 20. Enter here and on the appropriate lines of your return. Partnerships and S corporations — see instructions	**21**	26,122
22	For assets shown above and placed in service during the current year, enter the portion of the basis attributable to section 263A costs	**22**	

For Paperwork Reduction Act Notice, see the separate instructions. ISA	Form **4562** (1997)
STF FED5085F.1	

Form 4562 (1997)   Page **2**

| **Part V** | Listed Property — Automobiles, Certain Other Vehicles, Cellular Telephones, Certain Computers, and Property Used for Entertainment, Recreation, or Amusement |

Note: *For any vehicle for which you are using the standard mileage rate or deducting lease expense, complete **only** 23a, 23b, columns (a) through (c) of Section A, all of Section B, and Section C if applicable.*

Section A — Depreciation and Other Information (Caution: *See page 8 of the instructions for limits for passenger automobiles.***)**

23a Do you have evidence to support the business/investment use claimed? ☐ Yes ☐ No   23b If "Yes," is the evidence written? ☐ Yes ☐ No

(a) Type of property (list vehicles first)	(b) Date placed in service	(c) Business/ investment use percentage	(d) Cost or other basis	(e) Basis for depreciation (business/investment use only)	(f) Recovery period	(g) Method/ Convention	(h) Depreciation deduction	(i) Elected section 179 cost
24 Property used more than 50% in a qualified business use (See page 7 of the instructions.):								
		%						
		%						
		%						
25 Property used 50% or less in a qualified business use (See page 7 of the instructions.):								
		%			S/L –			
		%			S/L –			
		%			S/L –			

26 Add amounts in column (h). Enter the total here and on line 20, page 1 . . . . | **26** |
27 Add amounts in column (i). Enter the total here and on line 7, page 1 . . . . | **27** |

Section B — Information on Use of Vehicles

Complete this section for vehicles used by a sole proprietor, partner, or other "more than 5% owner," or related person.
If you provided vehicles to your employees, first answer the questions in Section C to see if you meet an exception to completing this section for those vehicles.

		(a) Vehicle 1		(b) Vehicle 2		(c) Vehicle 3		(d) Vehicle 4		(e) Vehicle 5		(f) Vehicle 6	
28	Total business/investment miles driven during the year (DO NOT include commuting miles)												
29	Total commuting miles driven during the year												
30	Total other personal (noncommuting) miles driven												
31	Total miles driven during the year. Add lines 28 through 30												
		Yes	No	Yes	No	Yes	No	Yes	No	Yes	No	Yes	No
32	Was the vehicle available for personal use during off-duty hours?												
33	Was the vehicle used primarily by a more than 5% owner or related person?												
34	Is another vehicle available for personal use?												

Section C — Questions for Employers Who Provide Vehicles for Use by Their Employees

*Answer these questions to determine if you meet an exception to completing Section B for vehicles used by employees who **are not** more than 5% owners or related persons.*

		Yes	No
35	Do you maintain a written policy statement that prohibits all personal use of vehicles, including commuting, by your employees?		
36	Do you maintain a written policy statement that prohibits personal use of vehicles, except commuting, by your employees? See page 9 of the instructions for vehicles used by corporate officers, directors, or 1% or more owners		
37	Do you treat all use of vehicles by employees as personal use?		
38	Do you provide more than five vehicles to your employees, obtain information from your employees about the use of the vehicles, and retain the information received?		
39	Do you meet the requirements concerning qualified automobile demonstration use? See page 9 of the instructions.		

Note: *If your answer to 35, 36, 37, 38, or 39 is "Yes," you need not complete Section B of the covered vehicles.*

| **Part VI** | Amortization |

(a) Description of costs	(b) Date amortization begins	(c) Amortizable amount	(d) Code section	(e) Amortization period or percentage	(f) Amortization for this year
40 Amortization of costs that begins during your 1997 tax year:					

41 Amortization of costs that began before 1997 . . . . | **41** |
42 **Total.** Enter here and on "Other Deductions" or "Other Expenses" line of your return . . . . | **42** |

STF FED5085F.2

JAN & DEE'S   36-1234567
Form 1065   12/31/97

Page 1, Line 20, Schedule of Other Expenses:

Advertising	$22,000
Insurance	5,000
Legal and professional	18,000
Promotion	17,000
Telephone	2,000
Total	$64,000

CHAPTER 12

S CORPORATIONS

LEARNING OBJECTIVES

After completing Chapter 12, you should be able to:

1. Explain the tax effects associated with S corporation status.

2. Identify corporations that qualify for the S election.

3. Understand how to make an S election.

4. Explain how an S election can be terminated.

5. Compute nonseparately stated income and identify separately stated items.

6. Allocate income, deductions, and credits to shareholders.

7. Understand how distributions to S corporation shareholders are taxed.

8. Calculate a shareholder's basis in S corporation stock.

9. Explain how losses in an S corporation are treated.

10. Compute the built-in gains tax.

11. Compute the passive investment income penalty tax.

KEY TERMS

Accumulated adjustments account	Passive investment income	Small business corporation
Built-in gains tax	S corporation	Subchapter S

OUTLINE

I.   QUALIFYING FOR S CORPORATION STATUS

    A.   Definition of a Small Business Corporation
        1.   For S corporation status, a small business corporation
            a.   is a domestic corporation.
            b.   is an eligible corporation
                1.   certain banks and insurance companies are ineligible.
                2.   Puerto Rico or possessions corporations are ineligible.
                3.   foreign corporations are ineligible.
            c.   issues only one class of stock.
                1.   differences in voting rights are permitted.
                2.   distribution or liquidation rights must be identical.
            d.   has no more than 75 shareholders.
                1.   husband and wife are considered one shareholder.
                2.   widowers or widows and their spouse's estate are considered one shareholder.
            e.   has as its shareholders only individuals, estates, and certain trusts.
            f.   has no nonresident alien shareholder.

    B.   Making the Election
        1.   The S election is made on Form 2553.
        2.   All shareholders must consent to the election in writing.
        3.   The election must be made on or before the 15th day of the 3rd month to be effective for the current year.
        4.   The election may be made at any time during the current year to be effective for the following year.
        5.   No election can be made for a corporation not yet in existence; the first month of a newly created corporation is the earliest of:
            a.   when the corporation has shareholders,
            b.   when the corporation acquires assets,
            c.   when the corporation begins doing business.

    C.   Loss of the Election
        1.   Violation of one of the eligibility rules causes termination as of the date on which the disqualifying event occurred.
            a.   the number of shareholders exceeds the maximum allowed.
            b.   a nonresident alien becomes a shareholder.
            c.   another class of stock is created.
        2.   Voluntary revocation may be made by shareholders owning a majority of shares.
        3.   Failing the passive investment income limitation causes termination as of the beginning of the 4th year. This limitation:

        a.   applies only to S corporations having accumulated E & P from years in which it was a C corporation.

        b.   applies if the corporation has passive income in excess of 25% of its gross receipts for 3 consecutive years.

        c.   passive investment income includes dividends, interest, rents, gains and losses from sale of securities, and royalties.

  D.   Reelection After Termination

      1.   Generally, 5 years must pass before a new election can be made.

      2.   Exceptions may be allowed when:

        a.   there is a more than 50% change in ownership, or

        b.   the event which caused disqualification was not reasonably within the control of the S corporation or its majority shareholders.

II.   **OPERATIONAL RULES**

  A.   Computation of Taxable Income

      1.   Nonseparately computed income or losses are allocated pro rata to each shareholder for each day the stock is owned.

      2.   Each shareholder also receives a pro rata share of separately stated items.

      3.   Separately stated income, losses, deductions, and credits are items which could uniquely affect the tax liability of a shareholder.

      4.   Refer to the text, for a listing of separately stated items.

  B.   Tax Treatment of Distributions to Shareholders

      1.   The amount of any distribution to an S corporation shareholder is the cash plus the fair market value of any other property distributed.

      2.   An S corporation should maintain an accumulated adjustments account.

        a.   AAA is a cumulative total of undistributed net income items.

        b.   AAA is not adjusted for tax-exempt income and related expenses, or for Federal income taxes attributable to C corporation years.

        c.   Distributions cannot make the AAA negative or increase a negative balance.

      3.   A shareholder has a proportionate interest in the AAA.

      4.   For an S corporation having no accumulated E & P from C corporation years, a distribution is not includible in the shareholders' gross income to the extent that it does not exceed the shareholder's adjusted basis in stock.

      5.   For an S corporation with accumulated E & P, a distribution is:

        a.   tax-free up to the amount in AAA, limited to stock basis,

        b.   if cash, tax-free up to the amount of PTI, previously taxed income, pre 1983,

        c.   a taxable dividend to the extent of accumulated E & P,

        d.   return of capital,

        e.   capital gain.

C.   Tax Treatment of Property Distributions by the Corporation
1.   Property is distributed at fair market value.
2.   Gains, not losses, are recognized.

D.   Shareholder's Tax Basis
1.   Initial stock basis is determined similar to that of basis in a C corporation.
2.   Basis is increased by further stock purchases and capital contributions.
3.   Corporate operations during the year increase and decrease stock basis.
4.   Basis is reduced by distributions of AAA or PTI.
5.   Basis can never be negative.
6.   Once stock basis is zero, any additional basis reductions decrease the shareholder's basis in loans made to the S corporation.
7.   The basis for loans is established by actual advances to the corporation, not by indirect loans.

E.   Treatment of Losses
1.   Net operating losses are passed through to the shareholders and are deductible to the extent of stock and loan bases.
2.   An NOL which exceeds the shareholder's basis may be carried forward and deducted by the same shareholder, if and when, basis is restored.
3.   Passively activity losses and credits flow through to shareholders and decrease the shareholders' basis, whether or not deductible under the passive loss limitation rules.

F.   Tax on Preelection Built-In Gains
1.   A C corporation electing S status, after 1986, may incur a corporate level tax on gains attributable to asset appreciation during C corporation years.
2.   The total amount of gain recognized is limited to the aggregate, net built-in gains at the time of conversion to S status.
3.   The tax applies when the S corporation disposes of such an asset, in a taxable disposition, within 10 years of the conversion to S status.
4.   For purposes of the tax on built-in gains, certain C corporation carryovers are allowed as offsets.
a.   Unexpired NOLs or capital losses
b.   AMT credit carryovers and business credit carryovers

G.   Passive Investment Income Penalty Tax
1.   An S corporation having accumulated E & P from C corporation years is taxed on its excess passive income.
2.   Excess Net Passive Income is:

$$\frac{\text{passive investment income - 25\% of gross receipts}}{\text{total passive investment for the year}} * \frac{\text{net passive investment}}{\text{income for the year}}$$

       3.   The amount subject to tax cannot exceed the corporations taxable income for the year.

       4.   The applicable tax rate is the highest corporate tax rate in effect for that year.

   H.   Other Operational Rules

       1.   S corporations must make estimated tax payments for any recognized built-in gain and excess passive investment income.

       2.   An S corporation may own stock in another corporation but, is not eligible for a dividend received deduction.

       3.   An S corporation is not subject to the 10 percent of taxable income limitation applicable to charitable contributions made by a Subchapter C corporation.

       4.   Any family member who renders services or furnishes capital to the electing corporation must be reasonably compensated to avoid adjustments by the IRS to reflect the value of such services or capital.

       6.   A shareholder's portion of S income is not self-employment income. Compensation for services rendered to an S corporation are subject to FICA taxes.

III.   TAX PLANNING CONSIDERATIONS

   A.   In determining when the S election is advisable, it is necessary to consider all of the provisions that will affect the owners.

   B.   Because Subchapter S is an elective provision, strict compliance with the Code is required in making and preserving the election and operating the corporation. Shareholders and management should be made aware of the various transactions that could cause involuntary termination.

Section 1361 - Definition of a Small Business Corporation

Start

Is it a domestic corporation? — NO

YES

Is it an ineligible corporation? — YES

NO

Does it have more than one class of stock? — YES

NO

Does it have a nonresident alien as a shareholder? — YES

NO

Does it have, as shareholders, entities other than individuals, estates and certain trusts? — YES

NO

Does it have more than 75 shareholders? — YES → Is any stock owned by husband and wife?

NO

Does NOT Qualify To Elect S Corporation Status

Treat as one shareholder

NOW does it have more than 75 shareholders? — YES → Does NOT Qualify

NO → Qualifies To Elect S Status

S CORPORATION
DISTRIBUTIONS TO SHAREHOLDERS

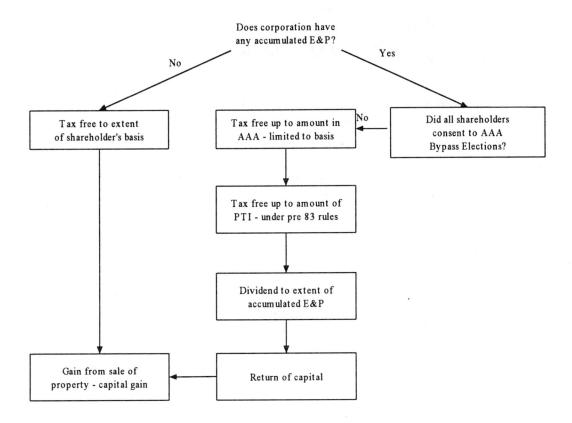

Shareholder's Basis Cannot Be Less Than Zero

TEST FOR SELF-EVALUATION

True or False

T F 1.   A loss on the sale or exchange of property is NOT deductible if the transaction is directly or indirectly between two S corporations and the same persons own more than 50% in value of the outstanding stock of each corporation.
(IRS 96 3A-7)

T F 2.   If an S corporation is subject to the tax on excess net passive investment income, it must reduce the items of passive income passed through to the shareholders.
(IRS 96 3A-10)

T F 3.   If an S corporation's passive investment income is more than 25% of gross receipts for two consecutive tax years and the corporation has pre-S corporation earnings and profits at the end of each of those years, the corporation's S corporation status will be terminated.   (IRS 95 3A-13)

T F 4.   A corporation's election of S status is valid if a majority of its shareholders consent to the election.   (IRS 94 3A-6)

T F 5.   Both separately stated items and the nonseparately stated income or loss are passed through to the shareholders of an S corporation in proportion to their shareholdings.   (IRS 94 3A-7)

T F 6.   Morgan, an S corporation, has no earnings and profits. In 1993, Morgan distributed cash of $40,000 to Sunnie, its sole shareholder, whose basis in Morgan's stock on December 31, 1993 (before considering the distribution), was $35,000. On January 1, 1994, Sunnie's basis in Morgan's stock would be ($5,000).   (IRS 94 3A-8)

T F 7.   Omega Corporation, an S corporation, has 10 shareholders on January 1, 1993. During the year, 8 of the existing shareholders, owning 51% of the stock, sold their interests to one new individual shareholder. Omega will automatically terminate its S corporation status on the day over 50% of Omega's stock was transferred.   (IRS 94 3A-9)

T F 8.   Exodus Corporation, a calendar year corporation, has 35 shareholders on January 1, 1993.   On June 30, 1993, a shareholder sold her stock to Interferon Corporation. On July 1, 1993, Interferon sold the stock to its sole shareholder, Anthony. Exodus Corporation will file TWO short period returns for 1993.
(IRS 94 3A-10)

T F 9.   For any tax year, an S corporation can elect its distributions as coming first from earnings and profits if ALL shareholders who receive a distribution during the tax year consent to the election. This election remains in effect for ALL tax years thereafter.   (IRS 93 3A-12)

T F 10.   For 1991, the books and records of Clover, Inc., a cash basis S corporation, reflected the following: (IRS 92 3A-11)

Salary to Dad Clover, President and 50% shareholder $22,000
Salary to Son Clover, Janitor and 50% shareholder $60,000
Loans to Dad Clover during 1991, no repayments $30,000

Dad Clover worked 40 hour weeks for the entire year but said that the business could not afford to pay him a salary more than $22,000. The IRS could reclassify the $30,000 and/or part of the son's salary to Dad Clover, and assess income tax withholding as well as employment taxes on those amounts.

Fill in the Blanks

1. Generally an S corporation is a tax _____ rather than a tax _____ entity.

2. A distribution by an S corporation having no earnings and profits is _____ in gross income to the extent that it does not exceed the shareholder's adjusted basis in stock.

3. An S corporation's net operating loss pass through cannot exceed a shareholder's adjusted basis in the_____ plus the basis of any _____ made to the corporation.

4. The term "small" for purposes of the S election refers to the _____.

5. The long-term capital gain from the sale of securities would generally be treated as _____ investment income.

6. Distributions that exceed the shareholder's tax basis for the stock are taxable as _____.

7. The _____ of stock in an S corporation is calculated similarly to the basis of stock in a regular corporation.

8. Net operating losses which exceed the shareholder's stock basis are used to reduce _____ the shareholder.

Multiple Choice

_____ 1.   To qualify for S corporation status, a corporation must meet all of the following requirements except: (IRS 96 3B-27)
        a.   Must be a domestic corporation.
        b.   Must have no more than 75 shareholders.

c.   Must have as shareholders only individuals, certain trusts or other corporations.
d.   Must have shareholders who are citizens or residents of the U.S.

_____ 2.   All of the following would reduce the basis of a shareholder's stock in an S corporation except: (IRS 96 3B-28)
a.   A shareholder's pro rata share of nontaxable distributions by the S corporation to its shareholders.
b.   A shareholder's share of all loss and deduction items of the S corporation that are separately stated and passed through to the shareholder.
c.   A shareholder's pro rata share of any nonseparately stated loss of the S corporation.
d.   A shareholder's pro rata share of any nonseparately stated income of the S corporation.

_____ 3.   What is the nonseparately stated income amount of an accrual basis, calendar year S corporation with the following items?   (IRS 3C-66)

Gross receipts	$200,000
Interest income	12,000
Rental income	25,000
Cost of goods sold and commissions	127,000
Net long-term capital gain	17,000
Compensation paid to shareholder	10,000

a. $63,000
b. $73,000
c. $117,000
d. $127,000

_____ 4.   On December 31, 1995, Valor, a calendar year S corporation since 1981, made a $100,000 distribution to its sole shareholder, Bryant. Valor's books and records reflect the following for 1995.

Accumulated adjustments account - 1/1/95	$ 5,000
Ordinary income for 1995	50,000
Previously taxed income account at the time of the distribution	10,000
Accumulated earnings and profits at the time of the distribution	5,000

Bryant's basis in Valor's stock on January 1, 1995 was $40,000. How much income will Bryant report from this S corporation investment in 1995 and what is its character?   (IRS 96 3C-67)

	Ordinary Income	Capital Gain
a.	$50,000	$10,000
b.	$55,000	$5,000
c.	$60,000	$-0-
d.	$50,000	$60,000

_____ 5.   Magnolia Corporation, a calendar year S corporation, was formed on January 1, 1994. Kathy owns 25 percent of Magnolia's outstanding stock which she purchased for $20,000. In 1994, Kathy guaranteed a corporate loan for $40,000. In 1995, Kathy made payments on the loan totaling $10,000. Magnolia had losses of $90,000 and $60,000 in 1994 and 1995 respectively. What is the amount of the unallowed loss that Kathy can carry over to 1996?   (IRS 96 3C-68)

    a. $0
    b. $7,500
    c. $10,000
    d. $17,500

_____ 6.   On January 1, 1995, Mr. Wise purchased 50 percent of S Corporation Cobra's only class of stock outstanding for $150,000. On December 1, 1995, he purchased the other 50% of Cobra's stock for $150,000. For 1995 Cobra incurred a net operating loss of $237,250. How much of the loss can Mr. Wise deduct on his individual income tax return for 1995?   (IRS 96 3C-69)

    a. $118,625
    b. $128,700
    c. $150,000
    d. $237,250

_____ 7.   In 1994, Lisa acquired 100% of the stock of Computers Inc. for $50,000 cash. Computers incurred a loss of $15,600 for 1994. On January 1, 1995, Computers properly elected S corporation status. Its net income for 1995 was $20,000. A dividend of $5,000 was declared and paid in 1995. What is Lisa's basis in Computers Inc. as of December 31, 1995?   (IRS 96 3C-70)

    a. $70,000
    b. $65,000
    c. $51,000
    d. $50,000

_____ 8.   In the context of the tax on excess net passive income paid by S corporations, net passive income does NOT include: (IRS 95 3B-33)

    a.   interest and dividends.

b.   annuities.
c.   net operating losses.
d.   sales or exchanges of stock.

_____ 9.   Mr. Oliver received a distribution from an S corporation that was in excess of the basis of his stock in the corporation. The S corporation had NO earnings and profits. Mr. Oliver should treat the distribution in excess of his basis as

(IRS 95 3B-34)

a.   a return of capital.
b.   previously taxed income.
c.   a capital gain.
d.   a reduction in the basis of his stock.

_____ 10.   With regard to an S corporation and its shareholders, the at-risk rules applicable to losses   (IRS 95 3B-35)

a.   take into consideration the S corporation's ratio of debt to equity.
b.   apply at the shareholder level rather than at the corporate level.
c.   are subject to the elections made by the S corporation's shareholders.
d.   depend on the type of income reported by the S corporation.

_____ 11.   All of the following would reduce the basis of a shareholder's stock in an S corporation except: (IRS 95 3B-36)

a.   A shareholder's pro rata share of any nonseparately stated loss of the S corporation.
b.   A shareholder's share of all loss and deduction items of the S corporation that are separately stated.
c.   A shareholder's pro rata share of any nondeductible expenses of the S corporation that are not properly chargeable to capital account.
d.   A shareholder's pro rata share of any nonseparately stated income of the S corporation.

_____ 12.   Which of the following events would cause an S corporation to cease to qualify as an S corporation: (IRS 95 3B-37)

a.   A 25% shareholder sells her shares to an individual who wants to revoke the S corporation status.
b.   The corporation is liable for tax on excess net passive investment income for two consecutive years.
c.   A shareholder has zero basis in his stock.
d.   The S corporation issues its stock to another corporation.

_____ 13.   The books and records of May Inc., a calendar year S corporation since 1982, reflect the following information for 1994:

Accumulated adjustments account 1/1/94	$ 60,000
Accumulated earnings & profits 1/1/94	150,000
Ordinary income for 1994	204,000

May Inc. has one shareholder, Paula, whose basis in May's stock was $100,000 on January 1, 1994. During 1994, May distributed $300,000 to Paula. What is the amount of the distribution that would be treated as a dividend by Paula?

(IRS 95 3C-73)

a. $0
b. $36,000
c. $264,000
d. $300,000

_____ 14.   On January 1, 1994, Mr. Karl purchased 50% of Olive Inc., an S corporation, for $75,000. At the end of 1994, Olive Inc. incurred an ordinary loss of $160,000. How much of the loss can Mr. Karl deduct on his personal income tax return for 1994?

(IRS 95 3C-74)

a. $160,000
b. $80,000
c. $75,000
d. $37,500

SOLUTIONS

True or False
1. T (related party)
2. T (p. 12-30; passive income reported by each shareholder is reduced by their allocable portion of the tax)
3. F (p. 12-10; three years)
4. F (p. 12-8; all)
5. T (p. 12-14)
6. F (p. 12-18; basis -0-, gain 5,000)
7. F (p. 12-9; only if a voluntary revocation is filed)
8. F (p. 12-10; involuntary termination of S on date event occurred)
9. F (p. 12-18; election is made for a particular distribution)
10. T (p. 12-33)

Fill in the Blanks
1. reporting; paying (p. 12-2)
2. not included (p. 12-16)
3. stock; loans (p. 12-24)
4. number of shareholders (p. 12-6)
5. passive (p. 12-32)
6. capital gains (p. 12-16)
7. initial tax basis (p. 12-21)
8. loans from (p. 12-23)

Multiple Choice
1. c (corporations are ineligible)
2. d (income increases basis)
3. a (200,000 - 127,000 - 10,000)
4. b (50,000 + 5,000 dividend; 100,000 - 5,000 dividend = 95,000 S distribution; 95,000 - 55,000 AAA - 10,000 PTI = 30,000 - basis of 25,000 = 5,000 capital)
5. b ((20,000 - 25%(90,000) + (10,000 - 25%(60,000) = 7,500)
6. b (50%(237,250)(31/365) + 50%(237,250) = 128,700)
7. a (50,000 + 20,000)
8. c (p. 12-32)
9. c (p. 12-16)
10. b (p. 12-28)
11. d (income increases basis)
12. d (p. 12-6)
13. b ($300,000 - 264,000 = 36,000)
14. c (limited to basis)

Return Problem 3

Given the following data, prepare Form 1120S-U.S. Income Tax Return for an S Corporation, other related forms as required and Schedules K-1 for Gerri Glad and Debbie Black.

Name: Glad's Flower Shop, Inc.
E.I.N.: 37-4536271
Address: 311 Main Street, Superior, IL 60654
Business Activity: Selling freshcut flowers and plants

Shareholders:

Gerri Glad, President	Terri Glad, Secretary	Debbie Black
922 Main Street	922 Main Street	38 Madison Street
Superior, IL 60654	Superior, IL 60654	Chicago, IL 60499
354-24-8833	354-42-3257	354-98-7667

The flower shop was formed and incorporated on May 2, 1997. A timely and proper S election was filed and become effective on the same date. Gerri, Terri and Debbie are sisters, each contributed $10,500 to the corporation for a one-third interest. Gerri and Terri received a salary of $8,000 each for operating the flower shop during 1997. The corporation uses the accrual method of accounting and files its returns on the calendar year basis. Balances on the corporation books as of December 31, 1997 were:

Gross Sales	$128,000	Store Equipment & Fixtures	9,750
Returns & Allowances	395	Rent	6,400
Purchases	74,240	Truck	11,250
Delivery Wages	1,200	Interest Income	942
Delivery Truck Expenses	838	Common Stock, $100 par	3,000
Advertising	2,500	Contributions	930
Insurance, Store	800	Taxes, Payroll	2,022
Insurance, Truck	645	Taxes, Sales	7,405
Supplies	3,898	Telephone	4,324
Office Supplies	480	Bank Service Charges	87
Organizational Expense	700	Accounts Payable	2,395
Accounts Receivable	3,790	Cash	12,183
*Land	18,000	Interest Expense	1,000

*The land was purchased as a future building site with a cash down payment of $2,000 and a mortgage of $16,000 on October 31, 1997.

A physical count of inventory, valued at $2,010, was done December 31.

Form **1120S**

Department of the Treasury
Internal Revenue Service

U.S. Income Tax Return for an S Corporation

▶ Do not file this form unless the corporation has timely filed
Form 2553 to elect to be an S corporation.
▶ See separate instructions.

OMB No. 1545-0130

1997

For calendar year 1997, or tax year beginning _____ , 1997, and ending _____ , 19 ___

A Date of election as an S corporation	Use IRS label. Other- wise, please print or type.	Name	C Employer identification number
		Number, street, and room or suite no. (If a P.O. box, see page 9 of the instructions.)	D Date incorporated
B Business code no. (see Specific Instructions)		City or town, state, and ZIP code	E Total assets (see Specific Instructions) $

F Check applicable boxes: (1) ☐ Initial return (2) ☐ Final return (3) ☐ Change in address (4) ☐ Amended return

G Enter number of shareholders in the corporation at end of the tax year . . . . ▶

Caution: *Include* **only** *trade or business income and expenses on lines 1a through 21. See the instructions for more information.*

Income

1a	Gross receipts or sales |_____| b Less returns and allowances |_____| c Bal ▶	**1c**
2	Cost of goods sold (Schedule A, line 8)	**2**
3	Gross profit. Subtract line 2 from line 1c	**3**
4	Net gain (loss) from Form 4797, Part II, line 18 *(attach Form 4797)*	**4**
5	Other income (loss) *(attach schedule)*	**5**
6	**Total income (loss).** Combine lines 3 through 5 . . . . ▶	**6**

Deductions (see page 10 of the instructions for limitations)

7	Compensation of officers	**7**
8	Salaries and wages (less employment credits)	**8**
9	Repairs and maintenance	**9**
10	Bad debts	**10**
11	Rents	**11**
12	Taxes and licenses	**12**
13	Interest	**13**
14a	Depreciation *(if required, attach Form 4562)*	**14a**	
b	Depreciation claimed on Schedule A and elsewhere on return .	**14b**	
c	Subtract line 14b from line 14a	**14c**
15	Depletion **(Do not deduct oil and gas depletion.)**	**15**
16	Advertising	**16**
17	Pension, profit-sharing, etc., plans	**17**
18	Employee benefit programs	**18**
19	Other deductions *(attach schedule)*	**19**
20	**Total deductions.** Add the amounts shown in the far right column for lines 7 through 19 . . ▶	**20**
21	Ordinary income (loss) from trade or business activities. Subtract line 20 from line 6	**21**

Tax and Payments

22	**Tax: a** Excess net passive income tax *(attach schedule)*	**22a**		
b	Tax from Schedule D (Form 1120S)	**22b**		
c	Add lines 22a and 22b (see pages 12 and 13 of the instructions for additional taxes)		**22c**	
23	**Payments: a** 1997 estimated tax payments and amount applied from 1996 return	**23a**		
b	Tax deposited with Form 7004	**23b**		
c	Credit for Federal tax paid on fuels *(attach Form 4136)*	**23c**		
d	Add lines 23a through 23c		**23d**	
24	Estimated tax penalty. Check if Form 2220 is attached . . . . ▶ ☐		**24**	
25	**Tax due.** If the total of lines 22c and 24 is larger than line 23d, enter amount owed. See page 4 of the instructions for depository method of payment . . . . ▶		**25**	
26	**Overpayment.** If line 23d is larger than the total of lines 22c and 24, enter amount overpaid ▶		**26**	
27	Enter amount of line 26 you want: **Credited to 1998 estimated tax** ▶ _____ Refunded ▶		**27**	

Please Sign Here

Under penalties of perjury, I declare that I have examined this return, including accompanying schedules and statements, and to the best of my knowledge and belief, it is true, correct, and complete. Declaration of preparer (other than taxpayer) is based on all information of which preparer has any knowledge.

▶ _____ _____ ▶ _____
   Signature of officer   Date   Title

Paid Preparer's Use Only

Preparer's signature ▶	Date	Check if self- employed ▶ ☐	Preparer's social security number
Firm's name (or yours if self-employed) and address ▶		EIN ▶	
		ZIP code ▶	

For Paperwork Reduction Act Notice, see the separate instructions.

Form **1120S** (1997)

ISA
STF FED4219F.1

Form 1120S (1997)   Page **2**

Schedule A	**Cost of Goods Sold** (see page 13 of the instructions)

1	Inventory at beginning of year	1	
2	Purchases	2	
3	Cost of labor	3	
4	Additional section 263A costs (attach schedule)	4	
5	Other costs (attach schedule)	5	
6	**Total.** Add lines 1 through 5	6	
7	Inventory at end of year	7	
8	**Cost of goods sold.** Subtract line 7 from line 6. Enter here and on page 1, line 2	8	

9a Check all methods used for valuing closing inventory:

    (i) ☐ Cost as described in Regulations section 1.471-3

    (ii) ☐ Lower of cost or market as described in Regulations section 1.471-4

    (iii) ☐ Other (specify method used and attach explanation) ▶ _____

  b Check if there was a writedown of "subnormal" goods as described in Regulations section 1.471-2(c) . . . . ▶ ☐

  c Check if the LIFO inventory method was adopted this tax year for any goods (if checked, attach Form 970) . . . . ▶ ☐

  d If the LIFO inventory method was used for this tax year, enter percentage (or amounts) of closing inventory computed under LIFO . . . . | 9d |

  e Do the rules of section 263A (for property produced or acquired for resale) apply to the corporation? . . . . ☐ Yes ☐ No

  f Was there any change in determining quantities, cost, or valuations between opening and closing inventory? . . ☐ Yes ☐ No
If "Yes," attach explanation.

Schedule B	**Other Information**

		Yes	No

1   Check method of accounting: **(a)** ☐ Cash   **(b)** ☐ Accrual   **(c)** ☐ Other (specify) ▶ _____

2   Refer to the list on page 23 of the instructions and state the corporation's principal:

     (a) Business activity ▶ _____ **(b)** Product or service ▶ _____

3   Did the corporation at the end of the tax year own, directly or indirectly, 50% or more of the voting stock of a domestic corporation? (For rules of attribution, see section 267(c).) If "Yes," attach a schedule showing: **(a)** name, address, and employer identification number and **(b)** percentage owned. . . . .

4   Was the corporation a member of a controlled group subject to the provisions of section 1561? . . . .

5   At any time during calendar year 1997, did the corporation have an interest in or a signature or other authority over a financial account in a foreign country (such as a bank account, securities account, or other financial account)? (See page 14 of the instructions for exceptions and filing requirements for Form TD F 90-22.1.) . . . .

     If "Yes," enter the name of the foreign country ▶ _____

6   During the tax year, did the corporation receive a distribution from, or was it the grantor of, or transferor to, a foreign trust? If "Yes," the corporation may have to file Form 3520 or 926. See page 14 of the instructions . . . .

7   Check this box if the corporation has filed or is required to file **Form 8264,** Application for Registration of a Tax Shelter . . . . ▶ ☐

8   Check this box if the corporation issued publicly offered debt instruments with original issue discount . . . . . ▶ ☐

     If so, the corporation may have to file **Form 8281,** Information Return for Publicly Offered Original Issue Discount Instruments.

9   If the corporation: **(a)** filed its election to be an S corporation after 1986, **(b)** was a C corporation before it elected to be an S corporation **or** the corporation acquired an asset with a basis determined by reference to its basis (or the basis of any other property) in the hands of a C corporation, and **(c)** has net unrealized built-in gain (defined in section 1374(d)(1)) in excess of the net recognized built-in gain from prior years, enter the net unrealized built-in gain reduced by net recognized built-in gain from prior years (see page 14 of the instructions) . . . . ▶ $ _____

10   Check this box if the corporation had accumulated earnings and profits at the close of the tax year (see page 14 of the instructions) . . . . ▶ ☐

Form 1120S (1997) Page **3**

Schedule K	Shareholders' Shares of Income, Credits, Deductions, etc.		
	(a) Pro rata share items		**(b) Total amount**

		(a) Pro rata share items		(b) Total amount
Income (Loss)	1	Ordinary income (loss) from trade or business activities (page 1, line 21)	1	
	2	Net income (loss) from rental real estate activities *(attach Form 8825)*	2	
	3a	Gross income from other rental activities	3a	
	b	Expenses from other rental activities *(attach schedule)*	3b	
	c	Net income (loss) from other rental activities. Subtract line 3b from line 3a	3c	
	4	Portfolio income (loss):		
	a	Interest income	4a	
	b	Dividend income	4b	
	c	Royalty income	4c	
	d	Net short-term capital gain (loss) *(attach Schedule D (Form 1120S))*	4d	
	e	Net long-term capital gain (loss) *(attach Schedule D (Form 1120S))*:		
		(1) 28% rate gain (loss) ▶ _____ (2) Total for year . . ▶	4e(2)	
	f	Other portfolio income (loss) *(attach schedule)*	4 f	
	5	Net section 1231 gain (loss) (other than due to casualty or theft) *(attach Form 4797)*:		
	a	28% rate gain (loss) ▶ _____ b Total for year . . ▶	5b	
	6	Other income (loss) *(attach schedule)*	6	
Deductions	7	Charitable contributions *(attach schedule)*	7	
	8	Section 179 expense deduction *(attach Form 4562)*	8	
	9	Deductions related to portfolio income (loss) (itemize)	9	
	10	Other deductions *(attach schedule)*	10	
Investment Interest	11a	Interest expense on investment debts	11a	
	b	(1) Investment income included on lines 4a, 4b, 4c, and 4f above	11b(1)	
		(2) Investment expenses included on line 9 above	11b(2)	
Credits	12a	Credit for alcohol used as a fuel *(attach Form 6478)*	12a	
	b	Low-income housing credit:		
		(1) From partnerships to which section 42(j)(5) applies for property placed in service before 1990	12b(1)	
		(2) Other than on line 12b(1) for property placed in service before 1990	12b(2)	
		(3) From partnerships to which section 42(j)(5) applies for property placed in service after 1989	12b(3)	
		(4) Other than on line 12b(3) for property placed in service after 1989	12b(4)	
	c	Qualified rehabilitation expenditures related to rental real estate activities *(attach Form 3468)* . . .	12c	
	d	Credits (other than credits shown on lines 12b and 12c) related to rental real estate activities	12d	
	e	Credits related to other rental activities	12e	
	13	Other credits	13	
Adjustments and Tax Preference Items	14a	Depreciation adjustment on property placed in service after 1986	14a	
	b	Adjusted gain or loss	14b	
	c	Depletion (other than oil and gas)	14c	
	d	(1) Gross income from oil, gas, or geothermal properties	14d(1)	
		(2) Deductions allocable to oil, gas, or geothermal properties	14d(2)	
	e	Other adjustments and tax preference items *(attach schedule)*	14e	
Foreign Taxes	15a	Type of income ▶ _____		
	b	Name of foreign country or U.S. possession _____		
	c	Total gross income from sources outside the United States *(attach schedule)*	15c	
	d	Total applicable deductions and losses *(attach schedule)*	15d	
	e	Total foreign taxes (check one): ▶ ☐ Paid ☐ Accrued	15e	
	f	Reduction in taxes available for credit *(attach schedule)*	15 f	
	g	Other foreign tax information *(attach schedule)*	15g	
Other	16	Section 59(e)(2) expenditures: a Type ▶ _____ b Amount ▶	16b	
	17	Tax-exempt interest income	17	
	18	Other tax-exempt income	18	
	19	Nondeductible expenses	19	
	20	Total property distributions (including cash) other than dividends reported on line 22 below	20	
	21	Other items and amounts required to be reported separately to shareholders *(attach schedule)*		
	22	Total dividend distributions paid from accumulated earnings and profits	22	
	23	**Income (loss).** (Required only if Schedule M-1 must be completed.) Combine lines 1 through 6 in column (b). From the result, subtract the sum of lines 7 through 11a, 15e, and 16b	23	

STF FED4219F.3

Form 1120S (1997)   Page **4**

Schedule L	Balance Sheets per Books	Beginning of tax year		End of tax year	
	Assets	**(a)**	**(b)**	**(c)**	**(d)**
1	Cash				
2a	Trade notes and accounts receivable				
b	Less allowance for bad debts				
3	Inventories				
4	U.S. Government obligations				
5	Tax-exempt securities				
6	Other current assets (attach schedule)				
7	Loans to shareholders				
8	Mortgage and real estate loans				
9	Other investments (attach schedule)				
10a	Buildings and other depreciable assets				
b	Less accumulated depreciation				
11a	Depletable assets				
b	Less accumulated depletion				
12	Land (net of any amortization)				
13a	Intangible assets (amortizable only)				
b	Less accumulated amortization				
14	Other assets (attach schedule)				
15	Total assets				
	Liabilities and Shareholders' Equity				
16	Accounts payable				
17	Mortgages, notes, bonds payable in less than 1 year				
18	Other current liabilities (attach schedule)				
19	Loans from shareholders				
20	Mortgages, notes, bonds payable in 1 year or more				
21	Other liabilities (attach schedule)				
22	Capital stock				
23	Additional paid-in capital				
24	Retained earnings				
25	Adjustments to shareholders' equity (attach schedule)				
26	Less cost of treasury stock		( )		( )
27	Total liabilities and shareholders' equity				

Schedule M-1 Reconciliation of Income (Loss) per Books With Income (Loss) per Return (You are not required to complete this schedule if the total assets on line 15, column (d), of Schedule L are less than $25,000.)

1 Net income (loss) per books
2 Income included on Schedule K, lines 1 through 6, not recorded on books this year (itemize): _____
_____
3 Expenses recorded on books this year not included on Schedule K, lines 1 through 11a, 15e, and 16b (itemize):
a Depreciation $ _____
b Travel and entertainment $ _____
4 Add lines 1 through 3

5 Income recorded on books this year not included on Schedule K, lines 1 through 6 (itemize):
a Tax-exempt interest $ _____
_____
6 Deductions included on Schedule K, lines 1 through 11a, 15e, and 16b, not charged against book income this year (itemize):
a Depreciation $ _____
_____
7 Add lines 5 and 6
8 Income (loss) (Schedule K, line 23). Line 4 less line 7

Schedule M-2 Analysis of Accumulated Adjustments Account, Other Adjustments Account, and Shareholders' Undistributed Taxable Income Previously Taxed (see page 21 of the instructions)

		(a) Accumulated adjustments account	(b) Other adjustments account	(c) Shareholders' undistributed taxable income previously taxed
1	Balance at beginning of tax year			
2	Ordinary income from page 1, line 21			
3	Other additions			
4	Loss from page 1, line 21	( )		
5	Other reductions	( )	( )	
6	Combine lines 1 through 5			
7	Distributions other than dividend distributions			
8	Balance at end of tax year. Subtract line 7 from line 6			

STF FED4219F.4

SCHEDULE K-1 (Form 1120S)	Shareholder's Share of Income, Credits, Deductions, etc.	OMB No. 1545-0130
Department of the Treasury Internal Revenue Service	▶ See separate instructions. For calendar year 1997 or tax year beginning , 1997, and ending , 19	**1997**

Shareholder's identifying number ▶	Corporation's identifying number ▶
Shareholder's name, address, and ZIP code	Corporation's name, address, and ZIP code

A Shareholder's percentage of stock ownership for tax year (see instructions for Schedule K-1) . . . . ▶ _____ %

B Internal Revenue Service Center where corporation filed its return ▶ _____

C Tax shelter registration number (see instructions for Schedule K-1) . . . . ▶ _____

D Check applicable boxes: **(1)** ☐ Final K-1   **(2)** ☐ Amended K-1

		(a) Pro rata share items		(b) Amount	(c) Form 1040 filers enter the amount in column (b) on:
Income (Loss)	1	Ordinary income (loss) from trade or business activities	1		See pages 4 and 5 of the Shareholder's Instructions for Schedule K-1 (Form 1120S).
	2	Net income (loss) from rental real estate activities	2		
	3	Net income (loss) from other rental activities	3		
	4	Portfolio income (loss):			
	a	Interest	4a		Sch. B, Part I, line 1
	b	Dividends	4b		Sch. B, Part II, line 5
	c	Royalties	4c		Sch. E, Part I, line 4
	d	Net short-term capital gain (loss)	4d		Sch. D, line 5, col. (f)
	e	Net long-term capital gain (loss):			
		(1) 28% rate gain (loss)	e(1)		Sch. D, line 12, col. (g)
		(2) Total for year	e(2)		Sch. D, line 12, col. (f)
	f	Other portfolio income (loss) (attach schedule)	4f		(Enter on applicable line of your return.)
	5	Net section 1231 gain (loss) (other than due to casualty or theft):			See Shareholder's Instructions for Schedule K-1 (Form 1120S).
	a	28% rate gain (loss)	5a		
	b	Total for year	5b		
	6	Other income (loss) (attach schedule)	6		(Enter on applicable line of your return.)
Deductions	7	Charitable contributions (attach schedule)	7		Sch. A, line 15 or 16
	8	Section 179 expense deduction	8		See page 6 of the Shareholder's Instructions for Schedule K-1 (Form 1120S).
	9	Deductions related to portfolio income (loss) (attach schedule)	9		
	10	Other deductions (attach schedule)	10		
Investment Interest	11a	Interest expense on investment debts	11a		Form 4952, line 1
	b	(1) Investment income included on lines 4a, 4b, 4c, and 4f above	b(1)		See Shareholder's Instructions for Schedule K-1 (Form 1120S)
		(2) Investment expenses included on line 9 above	b(2)		
Credits	12a	Credit for alcohol used as fuel	12a		Form 6478, line 10
	b	Low-income housing credit:			
		(1) From section 42(j)(5) partnerships for property placed in service before 1990	b(1)		
		(2) Other than on line 12b(1) for property placed in service before 1990	b(2)		
		(3) From section 42(j)(5) partnerships for property placed in service after 1989	b(3)		Form 8586, line 5
		(4) Other than on line 12b(3) for property placed in service after 1989	b(4)		
	c	Qualified rehabilitation expenditures related to rental real estate activities	12c		
	d	Credits (other than credits shown on lines 12b and 12c) related to rental real estate activities	12d		See pages 6 and 7 of the Shareholder's Instructions for Schedule K-1 (Form 1120S).
	e	Credits related to other rental activities	12e		
	13	Other credits	13		

For Paperwork Reduction Act Notice, see the Instructions for Form 1120S.

ISA

Schedule K-1 (Form 1120S) 1997

(a) Pro rata share items		(b) Amount	(c) Form 1040 filers enter the amount in column (b) on:
14a Depreciation adjustment on property placed in service after 1986	14a		See page 7 of the Shareholder's Instructions for Schedule K-1 (Form 1120S) and Instructions for Form 6251.
b Adjusted gain or loss	14b		
c Depletion (other than oil and gas)	14c		
d (1) Gross income from oil, gas, or geothermal properties	d(1)		
(2) Deductions allocable to oil, gas, or geothermal properties	d(2)		
e Other adjustments and tax preference items *(attach schedule)*	14e		
15a Type of income ▶ _____			Form 1116, Check boxes
b Name of foreign country or U.S. possession ▶ _____			
c Total gross income from sources outside the United States *(attach schedule)*	15c		Form 1116, Part I
d Total applicable deductions and losses *(attach schedule)*	15d		
e Total foreign taxes (check one): ▶ ☐ Paid ☐ Accrued ...	15e		Form 1116, Part II
f Reduction in taxes available for credit *(attach schedule)*	15f		Form 1116, Part III
g Other foreign tax information *(attach schedule)*	15g		See Instructions for Form 1116.
16 Section 59(e)(2) expenditures: a Type ▶ _____			See Shareholder's Instructions for Schedule K-1 (Form 1120S).
b Amount	16b		
17 Tax-exempt interest income	17		Form 1040, line 8b
18 Other tax-exempt income	18		
19 Nondeductible expenses	19		See page 7 of the Shareholder's Instructions for Schedule K-1 (Form 1120S).
20 Property distributions (including cash) other than dividend distributions reported to you on Form 1099-DIV	20		
21 Amount of loan repayments for "Loans From Shareholders" ..	21		
22 Recapture of low-income housing credit:			
a From section 42(j)(5) partnerships	22a		Form 8611, line 8
b Other than on line 22a	22b		

23 Supplemental information required to be reported separately to each shareholder *(attach additional schedules if more space is needed)*:

_____

SCHEDULE K-1 (Form 1120S)	Shareholder's Share of Income, Credits, Deductions, etc.	OMB No. 1545-0130
Department of the Treasury Internal Revenue Service	▶ See separate instructions. For calendar year 1997 or tax year beginning , 1997, and ending , 19	1997

Shareholder's identifying number ▶ | Corporation's identifying number ▶

Shareholder's name, address, and ZIP code | Corporation's name, address, and ZIP code

A Shareholder's percentage of stock ownership for tax year (see instructions for Schedule K-1) .... ▶ _____ %

B Internal Revenue Service Center where corporation filed its return ▶ _____

C Tax shelter registration number (see instructions for Schedule K-1) .... ▶ _____

D Check applicable boxes: (1) ☐ Final K-1   (2) ☐ Amended K-1

(a) Pro rata share items		(b) Amount	(c) Form 1040 filers enter the amount in column (b) on:
Income (Loss)			
1 Ordinary income (loss) from trade or business activities	1		See pages 4 and 5 of the Shareholder's Instructions for Schedule K-1 (Form 1120S).
2 Net income (loss) from rental real estate activities	2		
3 Net income (loss) from other rental activities	3		
4 Portfolio income (loss):			
a Interest	4a		Sch. B, Part I, line 1
b Dividends	4b		Sch. B, Part II, line 5
c Royalties	4c		Sch. E, Part I, line 4
d Net short-term capital gain (loss)	4d		Sch. D, line 5, col. (f)
e Net long-term capital gain (loss):			
(1) 28% rate gain (loss)	e(1)		Sch. D, line 12, col. (g)
(2) Total for year	e(2)		Sch. D, line 12, col. (f)
f Other portfolio income (loss) (attach schedule)	4f		(Enter on applicable line of your return.)
5 Net section 1231 gain (loss) (other than due to casualty or theft):			See Shareholder's Instructions for Schedule K-1 (Form 1120S).
a 28% rate gain (loss)	5a		
b Total for year	5b		
6 Other income (loss) (attach schedule)	6		(Enter on applicable line of your return.)
Deductions			
7 Charitable contributions (attach schedule)	7		Sch. A, line 15 or 16
8 Section 179 expense deduction	8		See page 6 of the Shareholder's Instructions for Schedule K-1 (Form 1120S).
9 Deductions related to portfolio income (loss) (attach schedule)	9		
10 Other deductions (attach schedule)	10		
Investment Interest			
11a Interest expense on investment debts	11a		Form 4952, line 1
b (1) Investment income included on lines 4a, 4b, 4c, and 4f above	b(1)		See Shareholder's Instructions for Schedule K-1 (Form 1120S).
(2) Investment expenses included on line 9 above	b(2)		
Credits			
12a Credit for alcohol used as fuel	12a		Form 6478, line 10
b Low-income housing credit:			
(1) From section 42(j)(5) partnerships for property placed in service before 1990	b(1)		
(2) Other than on line 12b(1) for property placed in service before 1990	b(2)		Form 8586, line 5
(3) From section 42(j)(5) partnerships for property placed in service after 1989	b(3)		
(4) Other than on line 12b(3) for property placed in service after 1989	b(4)		
c Qualified rehabilitation expenditures related to rental real estate activities	12c		
d Credits (other than credits shown on lines 12b and 12c) related to rental real estate activities	12d		See pages 6 and 7 of the Shareholder's Instructions for Schedule K-1 (Form 1120S).
e Credits related to other rental activities	12e		
13 Other credits	13		

For Paperwork Reduction Act Notice, see the Instructions for Form 1120S.
ISA

Schedule K-1 (Form 1120S) 1997

STF FED4269F 1

	(a) Pro rata share items		(b) Amount	(c) Form 1040 filers enter the amount in column (b) on:
Adjustments and Tax Preference Items	**14a** Depreciation adjustment on property placed in service after 1986	14a		See page 7 of the Shareholder's Instructions for Schedule K-1 (Form 1120S) and Instructions for Form 6251.
	b Adjusted gain or loss	14b		
	c Depletion (other than oil and gas)	14c		
	d **(1)** Gross income from oil, gas, or geothermal properties	d(1)		
	(2) Deductions allocable to oil, gas, or geothermal properties	d(2)		
	e Other adjustments and tax preference items *(attach schedule)*	14e		
Foreign Taxes	**15a** Type of income ▶ _____			Form 1116, Check boxes
	b Name of foreign country or U.S. possession ▶ _____			
	c Total gross income from sources outside the United States *(attach schedule)*	15c		Form 1116, Part I
	d Total applicable deductions and losses *(attach schedule)*	15d		
	e Total foreign taxes (check one): ▶ ☐ Paid ☐ Accrued . . .	15e		Form 1116, Part II
	f Reduction in taxes available for credit *(attach schedule)*	15f		Form 1116, Part III
	g Other foreign tax information *(attach schedule)*	15g		See Instructions for Form 1116.
Other	**16** Section 59(e)(2) expenditures: **a** Type ▶ _____			See Shareholder's Instructions for Schedule K-1 (Form 1120S).
	b Amount	16b		
	17 Tax-exempt interest income	17		Form 1040, line 8b
	18 Other tax-exempt income	18		See page 7 of the Shareholder's Instructions for Schedule K-1 (Form 1120S).
	19 Nondeductible expenses	19		
	20 Property distributions (including cash) other than dividend distributions reported to you on Form 1099-DIV	20		
	21 Amount of loan repayments for "Loans From Shareholders" . .	21		
	22 Recapture of low-income housing credit:			
	a From section 42(j)(5) partnerships	22a		Form 8611, line 8
	b Other than on line 22a	22b		

Supplemental Information

23 Supplemental information required to be reported separately to each shareholder *(attach additional schedules if more space is needed)*:

_____

_____

_____

_____

_____

_____

_____

_____

_____

_____

_____

_____

_____

_____

_____

_____

_____

Form **4562**	**Depreciation and Amortization**	OMB No. 1545-0172
	(Including Information on Listed Property)	**1997**
Department of the Treasury Internal Revenue Service (99)	▶ See separate instructions. ▶ Attach this form to your return.	Attachment Sequence No. 67

Name(s) shown on return	Business or activity to which this form relates	Identifying number

Part I   Election To Expense Certain Tangible Property (Section 179) (Note: *If you have any "listed property,"
complete Part V before you complete Part I.*)

1	Maximum dollar limitation. If an enterprise zone business, see page 2 of the instructions	1	$18,000
2	Total cost of section 179 property placed in service. See page 2 of the instructions	2	
3	Threshold cost of section 179 property before reduction in limitation	3	$200,000
4	Reduction in limitation. Subtract line 3 from line 2. If zero or less, enter -0-	4	
5	Dollar limitation for tax year. Subtract line 4 from line 1. If zero or less, enter -0-. If married filing separately, see page 2 of the instructions	5	

(a) Description of property	(b) Cost (business use only)	(c) Elected cost	
6			

7	Listed property. Enter amount from line 27	7	
8	Total elected cost of section 179 property. Add amounts in column (c), lines 6 and 7	8	
9	Tentative deduction. Enter the smaller of line 5 or line 8	9	
10	Carryover of disallowed deduction from 1996. See page 3 of the instructions	10	
11	Business income limitation. Enter the smaller of business income (not less than zero) or line 5 (see instructions) . .	11	
12	Section 179 expense deduction. Add lines 9 and 10, but do not enter more than line 11	12	
13	Carryover of disallowed deduction to 1998. Add lines 9 and 10, less line 12 . . . . . . ▶	13	

Note: *Do not use Part II or Part III below for listed property (automobiles, certain other vehicles, cellular telephones, certain
computers, or property used for entertainment, recreation, or amusement). Instead, use Part V for listed property.*

Part II   MACRS Depreciation For Assets Placed in Service ONLY During Your 1997 Tax Year (Do Not Include
Listed Property.)

Section A — General Asset Account Election

14	If you are making the election under section 168(i)(4) to group any assets placed in service during the tax year into one or more general asset accounts, check this box. See page 3 of the instructions . . . . ▶ ☐

Section B — General Depreciation System (GDS) (See page 3 of the instructions.)

(a) Classification of property	(b) Month and year placed in service	(c) Basis for depreciation (business/investment use only — see instructions)	(d) Recovery period	(e) Convention	(f) Method	(g) Depreciation deduction
15a 3-year property						
b 5-year property						
c 7-year property						
d 10-year property						
e 15-year property						
f 20-year property						
g 25-year property			25 yrs.		S/L	
h Residential rental			27.5 yrs.	MM	S/L	
property			27.5 yrs.	MM	S/L	
i Nonresidential real			39 yrs.	MM	S/L	
property				MM	S/L	

Section C — Alternative Depreciation System (ADS) (See page 6 of the instructions.)

16a Class life					S/L	
b 12-year			12 yrs.		S/L	
c 40-year			40 yrs.	MM	S/L	

Part III   Other Depreciation (Do Not Include Listed Property.) (See page 6 of the instructions.)

17	GDS and ADS deductions for assets placed in service in tax years beginning before 1997	17	
18	Property subject to section 168(f)(1) election	18	
19	ACRS and other depreciation	19	

Part IV   Summary (See page 7 of the instructions.)

20	Listed property. Enter amount from line 26	20	
21	**Total.** Add deductions on line 12, lines 15 and 16 in column (g), and lines 17 through 20. Enter here and on the appropriate lines of your return. Partnerships and S corporations — see instructions	21	
22	For assets shown above and placed in service during the current year, enter the portion of the basis attributable to section 263A costs	22	

For Paperwork Reduction Act Notice, see the separate instructions.   ISA

STF FED5085F 1

Form **4562** (1997)

Form 4562 (1997)   Page **2**

Part V | **Listed Property — Automobiles, Certain Other Vehicles, Cellular Telephones, Certain Computers, and Property Used for Entertainment, Recreation, or Amusement**

Note: *For any vehicle for which you are using the standard mileage rate or deducting lease expense, complete **only** 23a, 23b, columns (a) through (c) of Section A, all of Section B, and Section C if applicable.*

Section A — Depreciation and Other Information (Caution: *See page 8 of the instructions for limits for passenger automobiles.*)

23a Do you have evidence to support the business/investment use claimed? ☐ **Yes** ☐ **No** **23b** If "Yes," is the evidence written? ☐ **Yes** ☐ **No**

(a) Type of property (list vehicles first)	(b) Date placed in service	(c) Business/ investment use percentage	(d) Cost or other basis	(e) Basis for depreciation (business/investment use only)	(f) Recovery period	(g) Method/ Convention	(h) Depreciation deduction	(i) Elected section 179 cost
24 Property used more than 50% in a qualified business use (See page 7 of the instructions.):								
		%						
		%						
		%						
25 Property used 50% or less in a qualified business use (See page 7 of the instructions.):								
		%			S/L –			
		%			S/L –			
		%			S/L –			

26 Add amounts in column (h). Enter the total here and on line 20, page 1 . . . . | **26** |
27 Add amounts in column (i). Enter the total here and on line 7, page 1 . . . . | **27** |

Section B — Information on Use of Vehicles

Complete this section for vehicles used by a sole proprietor, partner, or other "more than 5% owner," or related person.
If you provided vehicles to your employees, first answer the questions in Section C to see of you meet an exception to completing this section for those vehicles.

	(a) Vehicle 1		(b) Vehicle 2		(c) Vehicle 3		(d) Vehicle 4		(e) Vehicle 5		(f) Vehicle 6	
28 Total business/investment miles driven during the year (DO NOT include commuting miles)												
29 Total commuting miles driven during the year												
30 Total other personal (noncommuting) miles driven												
31 Total miles driven during the year. Add lines 28 through 30												
	Yes	No	Yes	No	Yes	No	Yes	No	Yes	No	Yes	No
32 Was the vehicle available for personal use during off-duty hours?												
33 Was the vehicle used primarily by a more than 5% owner or related person?												
34 Is another vehicle available for personal use?												

Section C — Questions for Employers Who Provide Vehicles for Use by Their Employees

*Answer these questions to determine if you meet an exception to completing Section B for vehicles used by employees who **are not** more than 5% owners or related persons.*

	Yes	No
35 Do you maintain a written policy statement that prohibits all personal use of vehicles, including commuting, by your employees?		
36 Do you maintain a written policy statement that prohibits personal use of vehicles, except commuting, by your employees? See page 9 of the instructions for vehicles used by corporate officers, directors, or 1% or more owners		
37 Do you treat all use of vehicles by employees as personal use?		
38 Do you provide more than five vehicles to your employees, obtain information from your employees about the use of the vehicles, and retain the information received?		
39 Do you meet the requirements concerning qualified automobile demonstration use? See page 9 of the instructions.		

Note: *If your answer to 35, 36, 37, 38, or 39 is "Yes," you need not complete Section B of the covered vehicles.*

Part VI | **Amortization**

(a) Description of costs	(b) Date amortization begins	(c) Amortizable amount	(d) Code section	(e) Amortization period or percentage	(f) Amortization for this year
40 Amortization of costs that begins during your 1997 tax year:					

41 Amortization of costs that began before 1997 . . . . | **41** |
42 **Total.** Enter here and on "Other Deductions" or "Other Expenses" line of your return . . . . | **42** |

STF FED5085F 2

Form **1120S**	U.S. Income Tax Return for an S Corporation	OMB No. 1545-0130
Department of the Treasury Internal Revenue Service	▶ Do not file this form unless the corporation has timely filed Form 2553 to elect to be an S corporation. ▶ See separate instructions.	**1997**

For calendar year 1997, or tax year beginning **MAY 2, 1997**, 1997, and ending **DECEMBER 31**, 19 **97**

A Date of election as an S corporation 05/02/97	Use IRS label. Other-wise, please print or type.	Name **GLAD'S FLOWER SHOP, INC.**	C Employer identification number **37-4536271**
B Business code no. (see Specific Instructions) **5995**		Number, street, and room or suite no. (If a P.O. box, see page 9 of the instructions.) **311 MAIN STREET**	D Date incorporated **05/02/97**
		City or town, state, and ZIP code **SUPERIOR IL 60654**	E Total assets (see Specific Instructions) $ **55,161**

F Check applicable boxes: (1) [X] Initial return   (2) [ ] Final return   (3) [ ] Change in address   (4) [ ] Amended return

G Enter number of shareholders in the corporation at end of the tax year . . . . ▶   **3**

Caution: *Include only trade or business income and expenses on lines 1a through 21. See the instructions for more information.*

Income

1a	Gross receipts or sales **128,000** b Less returns and allowances **395** c Bal ▶	**1c**	**127,605**
2	Cost of goods sold (Schedule A, line 8)	**2**	**76,128**
3	Gross profit. Subtract line 2 from line 1c	**3**	**51,477**
4	Net gain (loss) from Form 4797, Part II, line 18 *(attach Form 4797)*	**4**	
5	Other income (loss) *(attach schedule)*	**5**	
6	**Total income (loss).** Combine lines 3 through 5 . . . . ▶	**6**	**51,477**

Deductions (see page 10 of the instructions for limitations)

7	Compensation of officers	**7**	**16,000**
8	Salaries and wages (less employment credits)	**8**	**1,200**
9	Repairs and maintenance	**9**	
10	Bad debts	**10**	
11	Rents	**11**	**6,400**
12	Taxes and licenses	**12**	**9,427**
13	Interest	**13**	**1,000**
14a	Depreciation *(if required, attach Form 4562)* **14a** **2,429**		
b	Depreciation claimed on Schedule A and elsewhere on return . . **14b**		
c	Subtract line 14b from line 14a	**14c**	**2,429**
15	Depletion **(Do not deduct oil and gas depletion.)**	**15**	
16	Advertising	**16**	**2,500**
17	Pension, profit-sharing, etc., plans	**17**	
18	Employee benefit programs	**18**	
19	Other deductions *(attach schedule)*	**19**	**7,267**
20	**Total deductions.** Add the amounts shown in the far right column for lines 7 through 19 . . ▶	**20**	**46,223**
21	Ordinary income (loss) from trade or business activities. Subtract line 20 from line 6	**21**	**5,254**

Tax and Payments

22	**Tax: a** Excess net passive income tax *(attach schedule)* **22a**		
b	Tax from Schedule D (Form 1120S) **22b**		
c	Add lines 22a and 22b (see pages 12 and 13 of the instructions for additional taxes)	**22c**	
23	**Payments: a** 1997 estimated tax payments and amount applied from 1996 return **23a**		
b	Tax deposited with Form 7004 . . . . **23b**		
c	Credit for Federal tax paid on fuels *(attach Form 4136)* **23c**		
d	Add lines 23a through 23c	**23d**	
24	Estimated tax penalty. Check if Form 2220 is attached . . . . ▶ [ ]	**24**	
25	Tax due. If the total of lines 22c and 24 is larger than line 23d, enter amount owed. See page 4 of the instructions for depository method of payment . . . . ▶	**25**	
26	Overpayment. If line 23d is larger than the total of lines 22c and 24, enter amount overpaid ▶	**26**	
27	Enter amount of line 26 you want: Credited to 1998 estimated tax ▶ _____ Refunded ▶	**27**	

Please Sign Here

Under penalties of perjury, I declare that I have examined this return, including accompanying schedules and statements, and to the best of my knowledge and belief, it is true, correct, and complete. Declaration of preparer (other than taxpayer) is based on all information of which preparer has any knowledge.

▶ _____   _____   ▶ _____
Signature of officer   Date   Title

Paid Preparer's Use Only

Preparer's signature ▶		Date _____ Check if self-employed ▶ [ ]	Preparer's social security number
Firm's name (or yours if self-employed) and address ▶		EIN ▶	
		ZIP code ▶	

For Paperwork Reduction Act Notice, see the separate instructions.

ISA
STF FED4219F 1

Form **1120S** (1997)

Form 1120S (1997)   Page **2**

Schedule A   Cost of Goods Sold (see page 13 of the instructions)

1	Inventory at beginning of year	1	0
2	Purchases	2	74,240
3	Cost of labor	3	
4	Additional section 263A costs (attach schedule)	4	
5	Other costs (attach schedule)	5	3,898
6	**Total.** Add lines 1 through 5	6	78,138
7	Inventory at end of year	7	2,010
8	**Cost of goods sold.** Subtract line 7 from line 6. Enter here and on page 1, line 2	8	76,128

9a Check all methods used for valuing closing inventory:

   (i) ☐ Cost as described in Regulations section 1.471-3

   (ii) ☐ Lower of cost or market as described in Regulations section 1.471-4

   (iii) ☐ Other (specify method used and attach explanation) ▶ _____

  b Check if there was a writedown of "subnormal" goods as described in Regulations section 1.471-2(c) .... ▶ ☐

  c Check if the LIFO inventory method was adopted this tax year for any goods (if checked, attach Form 970) .... ▶ ☐

  d If the LIFO inventory method was used for this tax year, enter percentage (or amounts) of closing inventory computed under LIFO .... | 9d |

  e Do the rules of section 263A (for property produced or acquired for resale) apply to the corporation? .... ☐ Yes ☒ No

  f Was there any change in determining quantities, cost, or valuations between opening and closing inventory? ... ☐ Yes ☒ No
If "Yes," attach explanation.

Schedule B   Other Information

		Yes	No
1	Check method of accounting: **(a)** ☐ Cash **(b)** ☒ Accrual **(c)** ☐ Other (specify) ▶ _____		
2	Refer to the list on page 23 of the instructions and state the corporation's principal: **(a)** Business activity ▶ Retail Sales **(b)** Product or service ▶ Flowers		
3	Did the corporation at the end of the tax year own, directly or indirectly, 50% or more of the voting stock of a domestic corporation? (For rules of attribution, see section 267(c).) If "Yes," attach a schedule showing: **(a)** name, address, and employer identification number and **(b)** percentage owned.		X
4	Was the corporation a member of a controlled group subject to the provisions of section 1561?		X
5	At any time during calendar year 1997, did the corporation have an interest in or a signature or other authority over a financial account in a foreign country (such as a bank account, securities account, or other financial account)? (See page 14 of the instructions for exceptions and filing requirements for Form TD F 90-22.1.)		X
	If "Yes," enter the name of the foreign country ▶ _____		
6	During the tax year, did the corporation receive a distribution from, or was it the grantor of, or transferor to, a foreign trust? If "Yes," the corporation may have to file Form 3520 or 926. See page 14 of the instructions.		X
7	Check this box if the corporation has filed or is required to file **Form 8264**, Application for Registration of a Tax Shelter .... ▶ ☐		
8	Check this box if the corporation issued publicly offered debt instruments with original issue discount ..... ▶ ☐		
	If so, the corporation may have to file **Form 8281**, Information Return for Publicly Offered Original Issue Discount Instruments.		
9	If the corporation: **(a)** filed its election to be an S corporation after 1986, **(b)** was a C corporation before it elected to be an S corporation **or** the corporation acquired an asset with a basis determined by reference to its basis (or the basis of any other property) in the hands of a C corporation, and **(c)** has net unrealized built-in gain (defined in section 1374(d)(1)) in excess of the net recognized built-in gain from prior years, enter the net unrealized built-in gain reduced by net recognized built-in gain from prior years (see page 14 of the instructions) .... ▶ $ _____		
10	Check this box if the corporation had accumulated earnings and profits at the close of the tax year (see page 14 of the instructions) .... ▶ ☐		

Form 1120S (1997)   Page **3**

Schedule K	Shareholders' Shares of Income, Credits, Deductions, etc.		
	(a) Pro rata share items		**(b) Total amount**
Income (Loss)	**1** Ordinary income (loss) from trade or business activities (page 1, line 21)	**1**	5,254
	2 Net income (loss) from rental real estate activities (attach Form 8825)	**2**	
	3a Gross income from other rental activities 3a		
	b Expenses from other rental activities (attach schedule) ... 3b		
	c Net income (loss) from other rental activities. Subtract line 3b from line 3a	**3c**	
	4 Portfolio income (loss):		
	a Interest income	**4a**	942
	b Dividend income	**4b**	
	c Royalty income	**4c**	
	d Net short-term capital gain (loss) (attach Schedule D (Form 1120S))	**4d**	
	e Net long-term capital gain (loss) (attach Schedule D (Form 1120S)):		
	(1) 28% rate gain (loss) ▶ _____ (2) Total for year .. ▶	**4e(2)**	
	f Other portfolio income (loss) (attach schedule)	**4f**	
	5 Net section 1231 gain (loss) (other than due to casualty or theft) (attach Form 4797):		
	a 28% rate gain (loss) ▶ _____ **b** Total for year .. ▶	**5b**	
	6 Other income (loss) (attach schedule)	**6**	
Deductions	**7** Charitable contributions (attach schedule)	**7**	930
	8 Section 179 expense deduction (attach Form 4562)	**8**	
	9 Deductions related to portfolio income (loss) (itemize)	**9**	
	10 Other deductions (attach schedule)	**10**	
Investment Interest	**11a** Interest expense on investment debts	**11a**	
	b (1) Investment income included on lines 4a, 4b, 4c, and 4f above	**11b(1)**	942
	(2) Investment expenses included on line 9 above	**11b(2)**	
Credits	**12a** Credit for alcohol used as a fuel (attach Form 6478)	**12a**	
	b Low-income housing credit:		
	(1) From partnerships to which section 42(j)(5) applies for property placed in service before 1990	**12b(1)**	
	(2) Other than on line 12b(1) for property placed in service before 1990	**12b(2)**	
	(3) From partnerships to which section 42(j)(5) applies for property placed in service after 1989	**12b(3)**	
	(4) Other than on line 12b(3) for property placed in service after 1989	**12b(4)**	
	c Qualified rehabilitation expenditures related to rental real estate activities (attach Form 3468)	**12c**	
	d Credits (other than credits shown on lines 12b and 12c) related to rental real estate activities	**12d**	
	e Credits related to other rental activities	**12e**	
	13 Other credits	**13**	
Adjustments and Tax Preference Items	**14a** Depreciation adjustment on property placed in service after 1986	**14a**	898
	b Adjusted gain or loss	**14b**	
	c Depletion (other than oil and gas)	**14c**	
	d (1) Gross income from oil, gas, or geothermal properties	**14d(1)**	
	(2) Deductions allocable to oil, gas, or geothermal properties	**14d(2)**	
	e Other adjustments and tax preference items (attach schedule)	**14e**	
Foreign Taxes	**15a** Type of income ▶		
	b Name of foreign country or U.S. possession		
	c Total gross income from sources outside the United States (attach schedule)	**15c**	
	d Total applicable deductions and losses (attach schedule)	**15d**	
	e Total foreign taxes (check one): ▶ ☐ Paid ☐ Accrued	**15e**	
	f Reduction in taxes available for credit (attach schedule)	**15f**	
	g Other foreign tax information (attach schedule)	**15g**	
Other	**16** Section 59(e)(2) expenditures: **a** Type ▶ _____ **b** Amount ▶	**16b**	
	17 Tax-exempt interest income	**17**	
	18 Other tax-exempt income	**18**	
	19 Nondeductible expenses	**19**	
	20 Total property distributions (including cash) other than dividends reported on line 22 below	**20**	
	21 Other items and amounts required to be reported separately to shareholders (attach schedule)		
	22 Total dividend distributions paid from accumulated earnings and profits	**22**	
	23 **Income (loss).** (Required only if Schedule M-1 must be completed.) Combine lines 1 through 6 in column (b). From the result, subtract the sum of lines 7 through 11a, 15e, and 16b	**23**	5,266

STF FED4219F 3

Form 1120S (1997) Page **4**

Schedule L	**Balance Sheets per Books**	Beginning of tax year		End of tax year	
	Assets	**(a)**	**(b)**	**(c)**	**(d)**
1	Cash				12,183
2a	Trade notes and accounts receivable			3,790	
b	Less allowance for bad debts				3,790
3	Inventories				2,010
4	U.S. Government obligations				
5	Tax-exempt securities				
6	Other current assets (attach schedule)				
7	Loans to shareholders				
8	Mortgage and real estate loans				
9	Other investments (attach schedule)				
10a	Buildings and other depreciable assets			21,000	
b	Less accumulated depreciation			2,429	18,571
11a	Depletable assets				
b	Less accumulated depletion				
12	Land (net of any amortization)				18,000
13a	Intangible assets (amortizable only)			700	
b	Less accumulated amortization			93	607
14	Other assets (attach schedule)				
15	Total assets				55,161
	Liabilities and Shareholders' Equity				
16	Accounts payable				2,395
17	Mortgages, notes, bonds payable in less than 1 year				16,000
18	Other current liabilities (attach schedule)				
19	Loans from shareholders				
20	Mortgages, notes, bonds payable in 1 year or more				
21	Other liabilities (attach schedule)				
22	Capital stock				3,000
23	Additional paid-in capital				
24	Retained earnings				28,500
25	Adjustments to shareholders' equity (attach schedule)				5,266
26	Less cost of treasury stock		( )		( )
27	Total liabilities and shareholders' equity				55,161

Schedule M-1	**Reconciliation of Income (Loss) per Books With Income (Loss) per Return** (You are not required to complete this schedule if the total assets on line 15, column (d), of Schedule L are less than $25,000.)			
1	Net income (loss) per books	5,266	5 Income recorded on books this year not included on Schedule K, lines 1 through 6 (itemize):	
2	Income included on Schedule K, lines 1 through 6, not recorded on books this year (itemize): _____		a Tax-exempt interest $ _____	
3	Expenses recorded on books this year not included on Schedule K, lines 1 through 11a, 15e, and 16b (itemize):		6 Deductions included on Schedule K, lines 1 through 11a, 15e, and 16b, not charged against book income this year (itemize):	
a	Depreciation $ _____		a Depreciation $ _____	
b	Travel and entertainment $ _____		7 Add lines 5 and 6	
4	Add lines 1 through 3	5,266	8 Income (loss) (Schedule K, line 23). Line 4 less line 7	5,266

Schedule M-2	**Analysis of Accumulated Adjustments Account, Other Adjustments Account, and Shareholders' Undistributed Taxable Income Previously Taxed** (see page 21 of the instructions)		
		(a) Accumulated adjustments account	**(b) Other adjustments account**	**(c) Shareholders' undistributed taxable income previously taxed**
1	Balance at beginning of tax year	0		
2	Ordinary income from page 1, line 21	5,254		
3	Other additions	942		
4	Loss from page 1, line 21	(0)		
5	Other reductions	(930)	( )	
6	Combine lines 1 through 5	5,266		
7	Distributions other than dividend distributions			
8	Balance at end of tax year. Subtract line 7 from line 6	5,266		

STF FED4219F.4

SCHEDULE K-1 (Form 1120S)	**Shareholder's Share of Income, Credits, Deductions, etc.**	OMB No. 1545-0130
Department of the Treasury Internal Revenue Service	▶ See separate instructions.	**1997**

For calendar year 1997 or tax year beginning May 2, 1997, and ending December 31, 19 97

Shareholder's identifying number ▶ 354-24-8833	Corporation's identifying number ▶ 37-4536271
Shareholder's name, address, and ZIP code GERRI GLAD 922 MAIN STREET SUPERIOR IL 60654	Corporation's name, address, and ZIP code GLAD'S FLOWER SHOP, INC. 311 MAIN STREET SUPERIOR IL 60654

A   Shareholder's percentage of stock ownership for tax year (see instructions for Schedule K-1) . . . . ▶ _____33__ %

B   Internal Revenue Service Center where corporation filed its return ▶ KANSAS CITY_____

C   Tax shelter registration number (see instructions for Schedule K-1) . . . . ▶ _____

D   Check applicable boxes: **(1)** ☐ Final K-1   **(2)** ☐ Amended K-1

	(a) Pro rata share items		(b) Amount	(c) Form 1040 filers enter the amount in column (b) on:
Income (Loss)	**1** Ordinary income (loss) from trade or business activities	1	1,751	See pages 4 and 5 of the Shareholder's Instructions for Schedule K-1 (Form 1120S).
	2 Net income (loss) from rental real estate activities	2	.	
	3 Net income (loss) from other rental activities	3		
	4 Portfolio income (loss):			
	a Interest	4a	314	Sch. B, Part I, line 1
	b Dividends	4b		Sch. B, Part II, line 5
	c Royalties	4c		Sch. E, Part I, line 4
	d Net short-term capital gain (loss)	4d		Sch. D, line 5, col. (f)
	e Net long-term capital gain (loss):			
	(1) 28% rate gain (loss)	e(1)		Sch. D, line 12, col. (g)
	(2) Total for year	e(2)		Sch. D, line 12, col. (f)
	f Other portfolio income (loss) (attach schedule)	4 f		(Enter on applicable line of your return.)
	5 Net section 1231 gain (loss) (other than due to casualty or theft):			See Shareholder's Instructions for Schedule K-1 (Form 1120S).
	a 28% rate gain (loss)	5a		
	b Total for year	5b		
	6 Other income (loss) (attach schedule)	6		(Enter on applicable line of your return.)
Deductions	**7** Charitable contributions (attach schedule)	7	310	Sch. A, line 15 or 16
	8 Section 179 expense deduction	8		See page 6 of the Shareholder's Instructions for Schedule K-1 (Form 1120S).
	9 Deductions related to portfolio income (loss) (attach schedule)	9		
	10 Other deductions (attach schedule)	10		
Investment Interest	**11a** Interest expense on investment debts	11a		Form 4952, line 1
	b (1) Investment income included on lines 4a, 4b, 4c, and 4f above	b(1)	314	See Shareholder's Instructions for Schedule K-1 (Form 1120S).
	(2) Investment expenses included on line 9 above	b(2)		
Credits	**12a** Credit for alcohol used as fuel	12a		Form 6478, line 10
	b Low-income housing credit:			
	(1) From section 42(j)(5) partnerships for property placed in service before 1990	b(1)		
	(2) Other than on line 12b(1) for property placed in service before 1990	b(2)		
	(3) From section 42(j)(5) partnerships for property placed in service after 1989	b(3)		Form 8586, line 5
	(4) Other than on line 12b(3) for property placed in service after 1989	b(4)		
	c Qualified rehabilitation expenditures related to rental real estate activities	12c		
	d Credits (other than credits shown on lines 12b and 12c) related to rental real estate activities	12d		See pages 6 and 7 of the Shareholder's Instructions for Schedule K-1 (Form 1120S).
	e Credits related to other rental activities	12e		
	13 Other credits	13		

For Paperwork Reduction Act Notice, see the Instructions for Form 1120S.

ISA

Schedule K-1 (Form 1120S) 1997

Schedule K-1 (Form 1120S) (1997)

Page **2**

(a) Pro rata share items		(b) Amount	(c) Form 1040 filers enter the amount in column (b) on:
Adjustments and Tax Preference Items	**14a** Depreciation adjustment on property placed in service after 1986	**14a**	299	See page 7 of the Shareholder's Instructions for Schedule K-1 (Form 1120S) and Instructions for Form 6251.
	b Adjusted gain or loss	**14b**		
	c Depletion (other than oil and gas)	**14c**		
	d (1) Gross income from oil, gas, or geothermal properties	**d(1)**		
	(2) Deductions allocable to oil, gas, or geothermal properties	**d(2)**		
	e Other adjustments and tax preference items *(attach schedule)*	**14e**		
Foreign Taxes	**15a** Type of income ▶ _____			Form 1116, Check boxes
	b Name of foreign country or U.S. possession ▶ _____			
	c Total gross income from sources outside the United States *(attach schedule)*	**15c**		Form 1116, Part I
	d Total applicable deductions and losses *(attach schedule)*	**15d**		
	e Total foreign taxes (check one): ▶ ☐ Paid ☐ Accrued . . .	**15e**		Form 1116, Part II
	f Reduction in taxes available for credit *(attach schedule)*	**15 f**		Form 1116, Part III
	g Other foreign tax information *(attach schedule)*	**15g**		See Instructions for Form 1116.
Other	**16** Section 59(e)(2) expenditures: **a** Type ▶ _____			See Shareholder's Instructions for Schedule K-1 (Form 1120S).
	b Amount	**16b**		
	17 Tax-exempt interest income	**17**		Form 1040, line 8b
	18 Other tax-exempt income	**18**		
	19 Nondeductible expenses	**19**		See page 7 of the Shareholder's Instructions for Schedule K-1 (Form 1120S).
	20 Property distributions (including cash) other than dividend distributions reported to you on Form 1099-DIV	**20**		
	21 Amount of loan repayments for "Loans From Shareholders" . .	**21**		
	22 Recapture of low-income housing credit:			
	a From section 42(j)(5) partnerships	**22a**		Form 8611, line 8
	b Other than on line 22a	**22b**		

23 Supplemental information required to be reported separately to each shareholder *(attach additional schedules if more space is needed)*:

_____

_____

_____

_____

_____

_____

_____

_____

_____

_____

_____

_____

_____

_____

_____

_____

_____

STF FED4269F.2

SCHEDULE K-1 (Form 1120S) Department of the Treasury Internal Revenue Service	Shareholder's Share of Income, Credits, Deductions, etc. ▶ See separate instructions. For calendar year 1997 or tax year beginning May 2 , 1997, and ending December 31 , 19 97	OMB No. 1545-0130 **1997**

Shareholder's identifying number ▶ 354-98-7667	Corporation's identifying number ▶ 37-4536271
Shareholder's name, address, and ZIP code DEBBIE BLACK 38 MADISON STREET CHICAGO IL 60499	Corporation's name, address, and ZIP code GLAD'S FLOWER SHOP, INC. 311 MAIN STREET SUPERIOR IL 60654

A   Shareholder's percentage of stock ownership for tax year (see instructions for Schedule K-1) . . . . ▶ _____ 33 %
B   Internal Revenue Service Center where corporation filed its return ▶ KANSAS CITY
C   Tax shelter registration number (see instructions for Schedule K-1) . . . . ▶ _____
D   Check applicable boxes: **(1)** ☐ Final K-1   **(2)** ☐ Amended K-1

		(a) Pro rata share items		(b) Amount	(c) Form 1040 filers enter the amount in column (b) on:
Income (Loss)	1	Ordinary income (loss) from trade or business activities	1	1,751	See pages 4 and 5 of the Shareholder's Instructions for Schedule K-1 (Form 1120S).
	2	Net income (loss) from rental real estate activities	2		
	3	Net income (loss) from other rental activities	3		
	4	Portfolio income (loss):			
	a	Interest	4a	314	Sch. B, Part I, line 1
	b	Dividends	4b		Sch. B, Part II, line 5
	c	Royalties	4c		Sch. E, Part I, line 4
	d	Net short-term capital gain (loss)	4d		Sch. D, line 5, col. (f)
	e	Net long-term capital gain (loss):			
		(1) 28% rate gain (loss)	e(1)		Sch. D, line 12, col. (g)
		(2) Total for year	e(2)		Sch. D, line 12, col. (f)
	f	Other portfolio income (loss) (attach schedule)	4f		(Enter on applicable line of your return.)
	5	Net section 1231 gain (loss) (other than due to casualty or theft):			See Shareholder's Instructions for Schedule K-1 (Form 1120S).
	a	28% rate gain (loss)	5a		
	b	Total for year	5b		
	6	Other income (loss) (attach schedule)	6		(Enter on applicable line of your return.)
Deduc-tions	7	Charitable contributions (attach schedule)	7	310	Sch. A, line 15 or 16
	8	Section 179 expense deduction	8		See page 6 of the Shareholder's Instructions for Schedule K-1 (Form 1120S).
	9	Deductions related to portfolio income (loss) (attach schedule)	9		
	10	Other deductions (attach schedule)	10		
Investment Interest	11a	Interest expense on investment debts	11a		Form 4952, line 1
	b	**(1)** Investment income included on lines 4a, 4b, 4c, and 4f above	b(1)	314	See Shareholder's Instructions for Schedule K-1 (Form 1120S).
		(2) Investment expenses included on line 9 above	b(2)		
Credits	12a	Credit for alcohol used as fuel.	12a		Form 6478, line 10
	b	Low-income housing credit:			
		(1) From section 42(j)(5) partnerships for property placed in service before 1990	b(1)		
		(2) Other than on line 12b(1) for property placed in service before 1990	b(2)		Form 8586, line 5
		(3) From section 42(j)(5) partnerships for property placed in service after 1989	b(3)		
		(4) Other than on line 12b(3) for property placed in service after 1989	b(4)		
	c	Qualified rehabilitation expenditures related to rental real estate activities.	12c		
	d	Credits (other than credits shown on lines 12b and 12c) related to rental real estate activities	12d		See pages 6 and 7 of the Shareholder's Instructions for Schedule K-1 (Form 1120S).
	e	Credits related to other rental activities	12e		
	13	Other credits	13		

For Paperwork Reduction Act Notice, see the Instructions for Form 1120S.
ISA

Schedule K-1 (Form 1120S) 1997

Schedule K-1 (Form 1120S) (1997)   Page **2**

	(a) Pro rata share items		(b) Amount	(c) Form 1040 filers enter the amount in column (b) on:
Adjustments and Tax Preference Items	**14a** Depreciation adjustment on property placed in service after 1986	**14a**	299	See page 7 of the Shareholder's Instructions for Schedule K-1 (Form 1120S) and Instructions for Form 6251.
	b Adjusted gain or loss	**14b**		
	c Depletion (other than oil and gas)	**14c**		
	d (1) Gross income from oil, gas, or geothermal properties	**d(1)**		
	(2) Deductions allocable to oil, gas, or geothermal properties	**d(2)**		
	e Other adjustments and tax preference items *(attach schedule)*	**14e**		
Foreign Taxes	**15a** Type of income ∘ _____			Form 1116, Check boxes
	b Name of foreign country or U.S. possession ∘ _____			
	c Total gross income from sources outside the United States *(attach schedule)*	**15c**		Form 1116, Part I
	d Total applicable deductions and losses *(attach schedule)*	**15d**		
	e Total foreign taxes (check one): ∘ j Paid j Accrued . . .	**15e**		Form 1116, Part II
	f Reduction in taxes available for credit *(attach schedule)*	**15 f**		Form 1116, Part III
	g Other foreign tax information *(attach schedule)*	**15g**		See Instructions for Form 1116.
Other	**16** Section 59(e)(2) expenditures: **a** Type ∘ _____			See Shareholder's Instructions for Schedule K-1 (Form 1120S).
	b Amount	**16b**		
	17 Tax-exempt interest income	**17**		Form 1040, line 8b
	18 Other tax-exempt income	**18**		See page 7 of the Shareholder's Instructions for Schedule K-1 (Form 1120S).
	19 Nondeductible expenses	**19**		
	20 Property distributions (including cash) other than dividend distributions reported to you on Form 1099-DIV	**20**		
	21 Amount of loan repayments for "Loans From Shareholders" . .	**21**		
	22 Recapture of low-income housing credit:			
	a From section 42(j)(5) partnerships	**22a**		Form 8611, line 8
	b Other than on line 22a	**22b**		

23 Supplemental information required to be reported separately to each shareholder *(attach additional schedules if more space is needed)*:

Form **4562**	**Depreciation and Amortization**	OMB No. 1545-0172
Department of the Treasury Internal Revenue Service (99)	(Including Information on Listed Property) ► See separate instructions. ► Attach this form to your return.	**1997** Attachment Sequence No. **67**

Name(s) shown on return	Business or activity to which this form relates	Identifying number
GLAD'S FLOWER SHOP, INC.	FORM 1120S	37-4536271

Part I Election To Expense Certain Tangible Property (Section 179) (Note: *If you have any "listed property," complete Part V before you complete Part I.*)

1	Maximum dollar limitation. If an enterprise zone business, see page 2 of the instructions	1	$18,000
2	Total cost of section 179 property placed in service. See page 2 of the instructions.	2	
3	Threshold cost of section 179 property before reduction in limitation	3	$200,000
4	Reduction in limitation. Subtract line 3 from line 2. If zero or less, enter -0-	4	
5	Dollar limitation for tax year. Subtract line 4 from line 1. If zero or less, enter -0-. If married filing separately, see page 2 of the instructions	5	

(a) Description of property	(b) Cost (business use only)	(c) Elected cost	
6			

7	Listed property. Enter amount from line 27	7	
8	Total elected cost of section 179 property. Add amounts in column (c), lines 6 and 7	8	
9	Tentative deduction. Enter the smaller of line 5 or line 8	9	
10	Carryover of disallowed deduction from 1996. See page 3 of the instructions	10	
11	Business income limitation. Enter the smaller of business income (not less than zero) or line 5 (see instructions) . .	11	
12	Section 179 expense deduction. Add lines 9 and 10, but do not enter more than line 11	12	
13	Carryover of disallowed deduction to 1998. Add lines 9 and 10, less line 12 . . . . . ►	13	

Note: *Do not use Part II or Part III below for listed property (automobiles, certain other vehicles, cellular telephones, certain computers, or property used for entertainment, recreation, or amusement). Instead, use Part V for listed property.*

Part II MACRS Depreciation For Assets Placed in Service ONLY During Your 1997 Tax Year (Do Not Include Listed Property.)

Section A — General Asset Account Election

14	If you are making the election under section 168(i)(4) to group any assets placed in service during the tax year into one or more general asset accounts, check this box. See page 3 of the instructions . . . . ► ☐

Section B — General Depreciation System (GDS) (See page 3 of the instructions.)

(a) Classification of property	(b) Month and year placed in service	(c) Basis for depreciation (business/investment use only — see instructions)	(d) Recovery period	(e) Convention	(f) Method	(g) Depreciation deduction
15a 3-year property						
b 5-year property						
c 7-year property		9,750	7	HY	DDB	929
d 10-year property						
e 15-year property						
f 20-year property						
g 25-year property			25 yrs.		S/L	
h Residential rental property			27.5 yrs.	MM	S/L	
			27.5 yrs.	MM	S/L	
i Nonresidential real property			39 yrs.	MM	S/L	
				MM	S/L	

Section C — Alternative Depreciation System (ADS) (See page 6 of the instructions.)

(a) Classification of property	(b) Month and year placed in service	(c) Basis for depreciation	(d) Recovery period	(e) Convention	(f) Method	(g) Depreciation deduction
16a Class life					S/L	
b 12-year			12 yrs.		S/L	
c 40-year			40 yrs.	MM	S/L	

Part III Other Depreciation (Do Not Include Listed Property.) (See page 6 of the instructions.)

17	GDS and ADS deductions for assets placed in service in tax years beginning before 1997	17	
18	Property subject to section 168(f)(1) election	18	
19	ACRS and other depreciation	19	

Part IV Summary (See page 7 of the instructions.)

20	Listed property. Enter amount from line 26	20	1,500
21	**Total.** Add deductions on line 12, lines 15 and 16 in column (g), and lines 17 through 20. Enter here and on the appropriate lines of your return. Partnerships and S corporations — see instructions	21	2,429
22	For assets shown above and placed in service during the current year, enter the portion of the basis attributable to section 263A costs	22	

For Paperwork Reduction Act Notice, see the separate instructions.   ISA

STF FED5085F.1

Form **4562** (1997)

Form 4562 (1997)   Page **2**

Part V   **Listed Property** — Automobiles, Certain Other Vehicles, Cellular Telephones, Certain Computers, and Property Used for Entertainment, Recreation, or Amusement

Note: *For any vehicle for which you are using the standard mileage rate or deducting lease expense, complete only 23a, 23b, columns (a) through (c) of Section A, all of Section B, and Section C if applicable.*

Section A — Depreciation and Other Information (Caution: See page 8 of the instructions for limits for passenger automobiles.)

23a   Do you have evidence to support the business/investment use claimed? ☐ Yes ☐ No   23b   If "Yes," is the evidence written? ☐ Yes ☐ No

(a) Type of property (list vehicles first)	(b) Date placed in service	(c) Business/ investment use percentage	(d) Cost or other basis	(e) Basis for depreciation (business/investment use only)	(f) Recovery period	(g) Method/ Convention	(h) Depreciation deduction	(i) Elected section 179 cost
24 Property used more than 50% in a qualified business use (See page 7 of the instructions.):								
TRUCK	5/2/97	100 %	11,250	11,250	5	HY/DDB	1,500	
		%						
		%						
25 Property used 50% or less in a qualified business use (See page 7 of the instructions.):								
		%				S/L –		
		%				S/L –		
		%				S/L –		

26 Add amounts in column (h). Enter the total here and on line 20, page 1	**26**	1,500
27 Add amounts in column (i). Enter the total here and on line 7, page 1	**27**	

Section B — Information on Use of Vehicles

Complete this section for vehicles used by a sole proprietor, partner, or other "more than 5% owner," or related person.

If you provided vehicles to your employees, first answer the questions in Section C to see of you meet an exception to completing this section for those vehicles.

	(a) Vehicle 1		(b) Vehicle 2		(c) Vehicle 3		(d) Vehicle 4		(e) Vehicle 5		(f) Vehicle 6	
28 Total business/investment miles driven during the year (DO NOT include commuting miles)												
29 Total commuting miles driven during the year												
30 Total other personal (noncommuting) miles driven												
31 Total miles driven during the year. Add lines 28 through 30												
	Yes	No	Yes	No	Yes	No	Yes	No	Yes	No	Yes	No
32 Was the vehicle available for personal use during off-duty hours?												
33 Was the vehicle used primarily by a more than 5% owner or related person?												
34 Is another vehicle available for personal use?												

Section C — Questions for Employers Who Provide Vehicles for Use by Their Employees

*Answer these questions to determine if you meet an exception to completing Section B for vehicles used by employees who **are not** more than 5% owners or related persons.*

	Yes	No
35 Do you maintain a written policy statement that prohibits all personal use of vehicles, including commuting, by your employees?		
36 Do you maintain a written policy statement that prohibits personal use of vehicles, except commuting, by your employees? See page 9 of the instructions for vehicles used by corporate officers, directors, or 1% or more owners		
37 Do you treat all use of vehicles by employees as personal use?		
38 Do you provide more than five vehicles to your employees, obtain information from your employees about the use of the vehicles, and retain the information received?		
39 Do you meet the requirements concerning qualified automobile demonstration use? See page 9 of the instructions.		

Note: *If your answer to 35, 36, 37, 38, or 39 is "Yes," you need not complete Section B of the covered vehicles.*

Part VI   **Amortization**

(a) Description of costs	(b) Date amortization begins	(c) Amortizable amount	(d) Code section	(e) Amortization period or percentage	(f) Amortization for this year
40 Amortization of costs that begins during your 1997 tax year:					
Organizational Costs	5/2/97	700	248	60	93

41 Amortization of costs that began before 1997	**41**	
42 **Total.** Enter here and on "Other Deductions" or "Other Expenses" line of your return	**42**	93

STF FED5085F.2

GLAD'S FLOWER SHOP, INC.   37-4536271
Form 1120S   12/31/1997

Page 1, Line 19, Schedule of Other Deductions:

Amortization	$ 93
Insurance	1,445
Office Supplies	480
Telephone	4,324
Bank Service Charge	87
Truck Expenses	838
	$7,267

Amortization of Organization Expenditures
Initial Year May 2, 1997 - December 31, 1997

Glad's Flower Shop elects ("has elected," for later years) to amortize its organizational expenses ratably over a 60-month period, under Code Sec. 248. The following information is submitted as required by Regulation 1.248-1(c):

Description of Expense	Date Incurred	Amount
Legal Fees for incorporation	May 2, 1997	$700.00
Month taxpayer began business	May 1997	
Amortization period:	60 months	

CHAPTER 13

COMPARATIVE FORMS
OF DOING BUSINESS

LEARNING OBJECTIVES

After completing Chapter 13, you should be able to:

1.   Identify the principal legal and tax forms for conducting a business.

2.   Appreciate the relative importance of nontax factors in making business decisions.

3.   Distinguish between the forms for conducting a business according to whether they are subject to single taxation or double taxation.

4.   Identify techniques for avoiding double taxation and for controlling the entity tax.

5.   Understand the applicability and the effect of the conduit and entity concepts on contributions to the entity, operations of the entity, entity distributions, passive activity loss and at-risk rules, and special allocations.

6.   Analyze the effect of the disposition of a business on the owners and the entity for each of the forms for conducting a business.

KEY TERMS

Conduit concept   Limited liability company (LLC)   Thin capitalization
Entity concept

OUTLINE

I.   FORMS FOR DOING BUSINESS

    A.   The principal legal forms of conducting a business entity are:
        1.   Sole proprietorship
        2.   Partnership
        3.   Corporation

    B.   Generally, a taxpayer is bound by the legal form of business he chooses, however, the IRS may, in some cases, employ the 'substance over form' concept to reclassify an entity for tax purposes.

II.   NONTAX FACTORS

    A.   Capital Formation
        1.   Sole proprietorships depend upon the funds obtainable by the owner.
        2.   Partnerships pool the resources of the partners.
        3.   Corporations can issue additional stock to raise capital.

    B.   Limited Liability
        1.   Only the corporation has limited liability under state law.
        2.   Statutes do not provide limited liability for the performance of professional services.
        3.   In small corporations, shareholders often guarantee loans to the corporation.

    C.   Other Factors significant in selecting an organizational form include:
        1.   Estimated life of the business.
        2.   Number of owners and their role in the management of the business.
        3.   Freedom of choice in transferring ownership interests.
        4.   Organizational formality and the related cost and extent of government regulation.

III. SINGLE VERSUS DOUBLE TAXATION

    A.   Overall Impact on Entity and Owners
        1.   Sole proprietors and partners are taxed only at the owner level.
        2.   Corporations are taxed on earnings at the corporate level and distributions of corporate earnings are taxed at the shareholder level.
        3.   S corporations generally avoid the corporate level tax and earnings are taxed at the shareholder level.

B.   All forms of business are directly or indirectly subject to the alternative minimum tax.

IV.   CONTROLLING THE ENTITY TAX

A.   Favorable Treatment of Certain Fringe Benefits
   1.   Some fringe benefits are deductible by the entity and excludable from the recipient's gross income.
   2.   Of these excludable fringe benefits, some are available only to employees.
        a.   For an owner to be an employee the entity must be a corporation.
        b.   For an S corporation, a more than 2% shareholder is treated as a partner.
   3.   Pension and profit sharing plans defer taxation for the recipient.

B.   Minimizing Double Taxation, Corporations
   1.   Double taxation occurs when a corporation distributes earnings.
   2.   Deductible distributions include reasonable payments for:
        a.   salary to shareholder-employees
        b.   rent to shareholder-lessors
        c.   interest to shareholder-creditors
   3.   Not making distributions carries the risk that the accumulated earnings tax will eventually apply.
   4.   Electing S status causes the tax to be levied at the shareholder, rather than, the corporate level; all of the qualification/maintenance requirements need to be considered.

V.   CONDUIT VERSUS ENTITY TREATMENT

A.   Effect on Recognition at Time of Contribution to the Entity
   1.   Contributions of personal use assets are valued at the lower of adjusted basis or fair market value.
   2.   Partnerships have a carryover basis for contributed property and the partner has a substitute basis in his partnership interest.
   3.   Corporations must satisfy the §351 control requirements to obtain a carryover/substitute basis, otherwise, the transfer will be a taxable event.
   4.   Special allocation treatment is mandatory for partnerships when the adjusted basis and the fair market value of contributed property is not equal.

B.   Effect on Basis of Ownership Interest
   1.   A partner's basis in a partnership interest recognizes the partnership's profits and losses and includes liability effects.

       2.   A C corporation shareholder's basis is not affected by corporate profit or loss nor liability increases or decreases.

       3.   An S corporation shareholder's basis recognizes the corporation's profits and losses but not corporate liability increases or decreases.

C.   Effect on Results of Operations

       1.   Under the entity concept the earnings components of a C corporation lose their identity when passed through to the shareholder as dividends.

       2.   Under the conduit concept, any item subject to special treatment on the taxpayer-owners' tax return is reported separately to the partner or S corporation shareholder.

       3.   Only the partnership completely applies the conduit concept; an S corporation is subject to taxation at the entity level in some circumstances.

D.   Effect on Passive Activity Losses

       1.   Passive activity loss rules apply to partnerships, S corporations, personal service corporations and closely held corporations.

       2.   To be classified as a personal service corporation

           a.   the principal activity of the corporation is the performance of personal services.

           b.   the services are substantially performed by owner-employees.

           c.   owner-employees own more than 10% in value of the stock of the corporation.

       3.   In a closely held corporation more than 50% of the value of the outstanding stock at any time during the last half of the year is owned by 5 or fewer individuals.

       4.   For personal service corporations, passive activity losses cannot be offset against either active or portfolio income.

       5.   For closely-held corporation, passive activity losses can be offset against active income but not against portfolio income.

       6.   The results of passive activities of a partnership and an S corporation are separately stated and passed through to the partners and shareholders.

VI.   DISPOSITION OF A BUSINESS OR OF AN OWNERSHIP INTEREST

A.   Sole Proprietorship

       1.   The sale of a sole proprietorship is treated as the sale of individual assets.

       2.   Classification as ordinary income or capital gain depends upon the nature and holding period of the individual assets.

       3.   If the amount realized exceeds the FMV of identifiable assets, the excess is identified as goodwill which produces capital gain for the seller.

B.   Partnership
1.   If structured as a sale of assets, the treatment is the same as that of a sole proprietorship.
2.   If structured as a sale of an ownership interest, it is treated as a sale of a capital asset under §741 subject to ordinary income potential under §751. Refer to the description of these Code sections in Chapter 11.

C.   Corporation
1.   A corporation is taxed on a sale of assets whether it actually sells the assets or distributes the assets to shareholders.
2.   In a liquidating distribution, the shareholders, in effect, sell their stock back to the corporation and recognize capital gain or loss.
3.   A sale of stock produces capital gain or loss to the selling shareholders. Because the corporation is not involved, there are no tax consequences at the corporate level.

VII.   OVERALL COMPARISON OF FORMS OF DOING BUSINESS

A.   Overall comparison of forms of doing business. Concept Summary 13-2 of the text provides a detailed comparison of the tax consequences of different forms of business.

B.   Considerations should extend beyond the current tax period and include the following:
1.   Asset contributions
2.   Taxation of results of operations
3.   Distributions to owners
4.   Disposition of ownership interests
5.   Business termination

TEST FOR SELF-EVALUATION

True or False

T   F   1.   The capitalized costs of goodwill or going concern value acquired after August 10, 1993, must be amortized over a 15-year period beginning with the month acquired.
(IRS 95 2A-8)

T   F   2.   S Corporations are never taxed.

T   F   3.   The test in determining if the compensation paid to an officer of a corporation is reasonable is based on the total of salaries paid to all of the officers of that corporation.

T   F   3.   Corporations must comply with state statutes to be allowed limited liability.

T   F   4.   All forms of businesses are subject to AMT.

T   F   5.   Sole proprietors have the advantage over corporations when the alternative minimum tax applies.

T   F   6.   Fringe benefits which are not discriminatory are deductible by S Corporations.

T   F   7.   If a personal use asset is contributed to a corporation, the corporation's basis is the lower of adjusted basis or FMV when contributed.

T   F   8.   Mr. P established a calendar tax year when he filed his first individual income tax return. Mr. P in a later year began business as a sole proprietorship and wished to change his tax year to a fiscal year ending in January. P may change his tax year without securing permission from the Commission of Internal Revenue.
(IRS 90 2A-3)

Fill in the Blanks

1.   _____ rules apply to personal service corporations and closely held corporations.

2.   _____% or more of the stock value must be held by _____ or fewer individuals during the last half of the tax year for a corporation to meet the definition of a closely held corporation.

3.   The At-Risk rules apply to both _____ and _____.

4. Under the _____ the business is an extension of the owners; under the _____ the business is distinct from the owners.

5. The ability to share profits and losses differently from the share in capital is a _____ allowed only to _____.

Multiple Choice

_____ 1. John bought land with a building on it that he planned to use in his business. His costs in connection with this purchase were as follows:

Cash downpayment	$ 40,000
Mortgage on property	300,000
Survey costs	2,000
Transfer taxes	1,800
Charges for installation of gas lines	3,000
Back taxes owed by seller and paid by John	1,200

What is John's basis in the property?   (IRS 95 1C-57)

a. $348,000
b. $346,800
c. $345,000
d. $343,000

_____ 2. In 1994, Robert sold a building used in his business. His books and records reflect the following information:

Original cost of building	$150,000
Improvements made to building	50,000
Broker's commissions paid on sale	10,000
Cash received on sale	100,000
Total property taxes for 1993 paid by Robert	3,000
Portion of property taxes imposed on purchaser and reimbursed in a separate payment to Robert by purchaser under IRC 164(d)	500
Mortgage assumed by buyer	80,000
Accumulated depreciation	70,000
Fair market value of other property received	20,000

What is the amount of gain Robert must RECOGNIZE from the sale of the property?   (IRS 95 1C-61)

a. $60,000
b. $61,000
c. $70,000
d. $71,000

_____ 3. Matt purchased a high-volume dry cleaning store on January 1, 1994, for $960,000. NO liabilities were assumed. The fair market values of the assets at the time of the purchase were as follows:

Cash in banks	$210,100
U. S. government securities	100,200
Building and land	312,200
Accounts receivable	100,000
Fixtures and equipment	202,000

Matt will NOT change the name of the cleaners. What is Matt's basis for goodwill or going concern value?   (IRS 95 2C-46)

a. $0
b. $35,500
c. $91,300
d. $110,560

_____ 4. In a sole proprietorship the liabilities of the business:

a. extend to the owner's personal assets
b. extend only to the assets of the business
c. are limited to negligent acts of the owner personally, not employee actions
d. both b and c

_____ 5. Alisa purchased a day care center on December 10, 1993. The contract showed the following adjusted basis and fair market value of the assets:

	Adjusted Basis	Fair Market Value
Building	$150,000	$300,000
Land	40,000	50,000
Furniture & Fixtures	60,000	50,000

The contract provided that the agreed sale price wad a lump sum $360,000. What is Alisa's basis in the building?   (IRS 94 2C-52)

a. $216,000
b. $250,000
c. $270,000
d. $300,000

SOLUTIONS

True or False

1. T (p. 13-25)
2. F (p. 13-9)
3. F (p. 13-15)
4. F (p. 13-9)
5. T (p. 13-10)
6. F (p. 13-12)
7. F (p. 13-17)
8. F (p. 13-30)

Fill in the Blanks

1. Passive activity loss (p. 13-20)
2. 50; 5 (p. 13-20)
3. partnerships; S Corporations (p. 13-21)
4. conduit concept; entity concept (p. 13-17)
5. special allocation; partnerships (p. 13-23)

Multiple Choice

1. a (40,000 + 300,000 + 2,000 + 1,800 + 3,000 + 1,200)
2. a (Sales Price - Adjusted Basis; (100,000 + 80,000 + 20,000) - (150,000 + 50,000 + 10,000 - 70,000))
3. b (960,000 - (210,100 + 100,200 + 312,200 + 100,000 + 202,000))
4. a (p. 13-7)
5. c (relative fair market value: (360,000/400,000) (300,000))

CHAPTER 14

EXEMPT ENTITIES

LEARNING OBJECTIVES

After completing Chapter 14, you should be able to:

1.   Identify the different types of exempt organizations.

2.   Enumerate the requirements for exempt status.

3.   Know the tax consequences of exempt status, including the different consequences for public charities and private foundations.

4.   Determine which exempt organizations are classified as private foundations.

5.   Recognize the taxes imposed on private foundations and calculate the related initial tax and additional tax amounts.

6.   Determine when an exempt organization is subject to the unrelated business income tax and calculate the amount of the tax.

7.   List the reports exempt organizations must file with the IRS and the related due dates.

8.   Identify tax planning opportunities for exempt organizations.

KEY TERMS

Debt-financed income	Feeder organization	Private foundation
Excess lobbying expenditure	Grass roots expenditure	Unrelated business income
Exempt organization	Lobbying expenditure	Unrelated business income tax

OUTLINE

I.   EXEMPT ORGANIZATIONS

A.   To qualify for exempt status an organization must fit one of the categories provided for in the Code. Exhibit 14-1 of the text contains many examples.

B.   Requirements for Exempt Status
1.   Must serve some type of common good,
2.   Must be a not for profit entity,
3.   Must not allow net earnings to be used for the benefit of any private shareholder or individual, and
4.   Must not exert political influence.

II.   TAX CONSEQUENCES OF EXEMPT STATUS

A.   Though generally exempt, Federal taxes may be imposed on an organization classified as exempt if the organization:
1.   Engages in prohibited transactions,
2.   Is a feeder organization,
3.   Is classified as a private foundation, or
4.   Has unrelated business income.

B.   Prohibited transactions include:
1.   Failure to sustain the initial requirements of exempt status,
2.   Certain lobbying activities.

C.   Disqualified organizations, churches, their integrated auxiliaries and private foundations, violate the qualification/maintenance requirements by participating in lobbying activities.

D.   Qualifying §501(c)(3) organizations may elect to participate in lobbying activities on a limited basis. These organizations may not exceed the ceiling amount statutorily imposed on the lobbying expenditures.

E.   Two ceiling amounts apply. The grass roots ceiling limits the amount of expenditures incurred to influence general public opinion. The lobbying expenditures ceiling amount limits expenditures incurred to influence the formulation of legislation.

F.   Though not in excess of the ceiling amount, excess lobbying expenditures are subject to a 25% tax. The ceiling amounts are 150% of the grass roots or lobbying nontaxable amount; the excess lobbying expenditures are more than 100% of the grass roots or lobbying nontaxable amount. See Figure 14-1 of text for calculations of lobbying nontaxable amount.

G.   Feeder organizations carry on a trade or business activity for profit and pay all profits to one or more exempt organizations. These types of organizations are subject to Federal income tax with three exceptions. Those engaged in activities:
1.   Which generate rental income excluded from the definition of rent for unrelated business income tax purposes,
2.   For which substantially all work is performed by volunteers, and
3.   Which sell merchandise substantially all of which had been received as contributions or gifts.

III.   PRIVATE FOUNDATIONS

A.   Private foundations are so classified because these organizations generally do not have broad public support, they are formed to respond to the private interests of a limited number of persons.

B.   Though generally exempt from Federal income tax, §§4940-4945 impose excise taxes on private foundations for certain actions or failure to act. These taxes are levied only on private foundations:
1.   Tax based on investment income
2.   Tax on self-dealing (engaging in transactions with disqualified persons)
3.   Tax on failure to distribute income (distributions for exempt purposes)
4.   Tax on excess business holdings (controlling unrelated businesses)
5.   Tax on investments that jeopardize charitable purposes (speculative investments)
6.   Tax on taxable expenditures (expenditures that should not be made by private foundations)

C.   See Concept Summary 14-3 of the Text.

IV.   UNRELATED BUSINESS INCOME TAX

A.   An exempt organization may be subject to income tax on unrelated business income if:
1.   The organization conducts a trade or business (statutory exceptions may apply),
2.   The trade or business is not substantially related to the exempt purpose of the organization, and
3.   The trade or business is regularly carried on by the organization.

B.   Statutory exceptions to classification as unrelated trade or business apply even if all the above factors are present if:
1.   All work is performed by volunteers.
2.   Substantially all merchandise being sold was received by gift.
3.   The business is conducted primarily for the convenience of the organization's members.
4.   Gross income from an unrelated trade or business is less than $1,000.

C.   When applicable, the tax on unrelated business income is computed at corporate tax rates.

    Gross unrelated business income
-    Deductions
=   Net unrelated business income
+/- Modifications
=   Unrelated business taxable income

V.   REPORTING REQUIREMENTS

A.   Though only certain types of organizations are required to obtain IRS approval for exempt status, exempt organizations should apply to avoid potential disqualification by the IRS.
1.   Application is made on Form 1023 for §501(c)(3) organizations.
2.   Form 1024 is used for most other types of exempt organizations.

B.   Annual filings of Form 990 are required of exempt organizations other than:
1.   Federal agencies,
2.   Churches,
3.   Organizations having annual gross receipts < $25,000,
4.   Private foundations - private foundations are required to file Form 990-PF.

C.   Form 990 is due on the 15th day of the 5th month after the end of the organization's tax year.

TEST FOR SELF-EVALUATION

True or False

T F 1. Exempt status is automatically lost if an exempt organization has any unrelated business income during the year.

T F 2. The ONLY organizations exempt from federal income taxes are those organized and operated exclusively for religious, charitable, scientific or educational purposes.   (IRS 96 4A-26)

T F 3. Any organization that qualifies for tax exempt status can receive contributions that are fully deductible by the donor.   (IRS 94 4A-24)

T F 4. An organization recognized as a tax exempt organization will NOT pay income tax on any income it earns, but is still responsible for withholding, social security taxes and federal unemployment tax for wage payments.   (IRS 94 4A-26)

T F 5. A partnership may qualify as an organization exempt from federal income tax if it is organized and operated exclusively for one or more of the purposes found in Section 501(c)(3) of the Internal Revenue Code.   (IRS 91 4A-39)

T F 6. An exempt organization with $4,999 gross income from an unrelated business is required to file Form 990-T, Exempt Organization Business Income Tax Return.
                                                              (IRS 91 4A-40)

T F 7. Organizations recognized as tax exempt are not responsible for withholding, depositing, paying and reporting federal income tax, FICA and FUTA wages paid to their employees.   (IRS 91 4A-41)

T F 8. A church, its integrated auxiliaries, or a convention or association of churches is not required to file Form 1023, Application for Recognition of Exemption Under Section 501(c)(3) of the Internal Revenue Code, in order to be tax exempt or to receive tax deductible contributions.   (IRS 91 4A-42)

Fill in the Blanks

1. The underlying rationale for all exempt organizations is to _____.

2. Ceiling amounts on lobbying expenditures for exempt organizations are calculated for _____ expenditures and for _____ expenditures.

3. Failure to continue to qualify as a type of exempt organization is a _____.

4.   A _____ carries on a trade or business for the benefit of an exempt organization.

5.   _____ or _____ includes any activity conducted for the production of income through the sale of merchandise or the performance of services.

Multiple Choice

_____ 1.   If applicable the tax on unrelated business income is:

    a.   computed at corporate tax rates
    b.   computed at trust tax rates
    c.   computed at single individual tax rates
    d.   computed at special exempt organization tax rates

_____ 2.   Private foundation status of an exempt organization terminates if it:

    a.   invests in a functionally related business
    b.   becomes a public charity
    c.   receives less than 1/3 of its support from a governmental unit
    d.   becomes an exempt operating foundation

_____ 3.   To qualify as an exempt organization, an entity:

    a.   can never engage in lobbying activities
    b.   cannot have a nonresident shareholder
    c.   must satisfy one of the categories provided for in the Code
    d.   can be a feeder organization

_____ 4.   Income derived from conducting games of chance will be exempt if:

    a.   allowed by state law only to exempt organizations
    b.   the games are legal under state and local law
    c.   both of the above
    d.   neither of the above

_____ 5.   A private foundation may be subject to taxes imposed on:

    a.   investment income
    b.   self dealing
    c.   undistributed income
    d.   all of the above
    e.   none of the above

_____ 6. In determining whether or not an exempt organization is broadly supported and not classified as a private foundation, two tests must be satisfied:

a. one-third support test
b. not more than one-third support test
c. $5,000 or 1% support, the greater, test
d. a and c
e. a and b

_____ 7. Low cost items distributed incidental to solicitation for charitable contributions are not considered unrelated trade or business when:

a. the item is requested by the recipient
b. the item is returned in lieu of a donation
c. the items cost less than $6.90 each
d. all of the above
e. none of the above

_____ 8. An exempt organization will be subject to the tax on unrelated business income if:

a. the trade or business is not regularly carried on
b. the trade or business is not substantially related to the exempt purpose of the organization
c. the trade or business is substantially related to the exempt purpose of the organization
d. the trade or business is conducted primarily for the convenience of members

_____ 9. Which of the following might be considered an unrelated trade or business for a hospital:

a. cafeteria
b. pharmacy
c. gift shop
d. all of the above
e. none of the above

_____ 10. A tax-exempt organization that is required to file Form 990, Return of Organization Exempt From Income Tax, must do so by what date (do NOT consider any extensions, weekends, or holidays)? (IRS 96 4B-67)

a. The last day of the month following the end of the organization's accounting period.
b. The 15th day of the 3rd month following the end of the organization's accounting period.

     c.   The 15th day of the 4th month following the end of the organization's accounting period.

     d.   The 15th day of the 5th month following the end of the organization's accounting period.

_____ 11.   Which of the following organizations, exempt from federal income tax under Section 501(a) of the Internal Revenue Code (IRC), must file an annual information return on Form 990 or Form 990-PF?   (IRS 94 4B-68)

     a.   A private foundation exempt under Sec. 501(c)(3) of the IRC.

     b.   An organization, other than a private foundation, having gross receipts in each year that normally are NOT more than $5,000.

     c.   A stock bonus, pension, or profit-sharing trust that qualifies under Sec. 401 of the IRC.

     d.   A school BELOW college level, affiliated with a church or operated by a religious order, that is NOT an integrated auxiliary of a church.

_____ 12.   With respect to tax-exempt organizations, all of the following statements are correct except: (IRS 93 4B-66)

     a.   A foundation may qualify for exemption from federal income tax if it is organized for the prevention of cruelty to children.

     b.   An individual may qualify as an organization exempt from federal income tax.

     c.   A corporation organized for the prevention of cruelty to animals may qualify for exemption from federal income tax.

SOLUTIONS

True or False

1. F   (p. 14-15)
2. F   (Exhibit 14-1)
3. F   (p. 14-7)
4. F   (p. 14-6)
5. F   (Exhibit 14-1)
6. T   (p. 14-26)
7. F   (exempt from federal income tax)
8. T   (p. 14-24)

Fill in the Blanks

1. serve some type of common good (p. 14-5)
2. lobbying; grass roots (p. 14-8)
3. prohibited transaction (p. 14-7)
4. feeder organization (p. 14-9)
5. trade or business (p. 14-15)

Multiple Choice

1. a   (p. 14-14)
2. b   (p. 14-12)
3. c   (p. 14-3)
4. c   (p. 14-17)
5. d   (p. 14-12)
6. e   (p. 14-11)
7. c   (p. 14-18)
8. b   (p. 14-15)
9. c   (p. 14-16)
10. d   (p. 14-26)
11. a   (p. 14-26)
12. b   (p. 14-2)

CHAPTER 15

MULTISTATE
CORPORATE TAXATION

LEARNING OBJECTIVES

After completing Chapter 15, you should be able to:

1.   Illustrate the computation of a multistate corporation's state tax liability.

2.   Define nexus and its role in state income taxation.

3.   Distinguish between allocation and apportionment of a multistate corporation's taxable income.

4.   Describe the nature and treatment of business and nonbusiness income.

5.   Discuss the sales, payroll, and property apportionment factors.

6.   Apply the unitary method of state income taxation.

7.   Discuss the states' income tax treatment of S corporations.

8.   Describe other commonly encountered state and local taxes on businesses.

9.   Recognize tax planning opportunities available to minimize a corporation's state and local tax liability.

KEY TERMS

Allocate	Passive investment company	Throwback rule
Apportion	Payroll factor	UDITPA
Dock sales	Property factor	Unitary theory
Multistate Tax Commission	Public Law 86-272	Water's edge election
Nexus	Sales factor	

OUTLINE

I.   OVERVIEW OF CORPORATE STATE INCOME TAXATION

    A.   Currently, forty-six states and the District of Columbia impose a tax based on a corporation's income.

    B.   Generally, states require use of the same accounting periods and methods as those used on the corporation's Federal return.

    C.   In the majority of states, state taxable income is determined by reference to the corporation's Federal return with modification. State modifications:
        1.   Reflect differences between state and Federal statutes.
        2.   Remove income that a state is constitutionally prohibited from taxing.
        3.   Eliminate the recovery of income for which the state did not permit a deduction on an earlier return.

    D.   Jurisdiction to Impose Tax
        1.   The state in which a business is incorporated has taxing jurisdiction.
        2.   For corporations operating in other than their state of incorporation, sufficient nexus must be established.
            a.   nexus describes the degree of business activity that must be present before a tax can be imposed.
            b.   nexus is measured according to state statute, its definition and sufficiency varies among states.

II.   ALLOCATION AND APPORTIONMENT OF INCOME

    A.   Allocation assigns specific components of corporate net income to a certain state.

    B.   Allocable income generally includes:
        1.   Income or loss derived from sale of nonbusiness real or tangible property.
        2.   Income or loss derived from rentals and royalties from nonbusiness real or tangible property.

    C.   Apportionment divides a corporation's business income among the taxing states.

    D.   Business and Nonbusiness Income
        1.   Business income arises from the taxpayer's regular course of business or constitutes an integral part of the taxpayer's regular business.
        2.   Nonbusiness income is "all income other than business income."
        3.   Business income is apportioned; nonbusiness income may be apportioned or allocated to the state in which the property is located.

E.   Apportionment Factors
    1.   Each state chooses the type and number of factors used to establish its apportionment formula.
    2.   Most states use a three-factor appointment formula which assigns equal weight to sales, payroll and property.
    3.   Variations in the state's definition of allocable and apportionable income and in apportionment formulas may cause a corporation to be subject to state income tax on more or less than 100% of its Federal taxable income after modifications.

F.   Sales Factor
    1.   In-state sales/Total sales:
        a.   includes sales that generate business income.
        b.   excludes income on federal obligations.
        c.   sales of capital assets are treated differently by different states.
    2.   Most states apply the ultimate destination concept which assumes a sale takes place at the point of delivery to determine in-state sales.
    3.   If an origination state has adopted a throwback rule, out-of-state sales not subject to tax in the destination state or sales to the U.S. government are treated as sales in the state of origination.

G.   The Payroll Factor
    1.   In-state compensation/Total compensation
        a.   generally includes compensation includible in the employees' Federal gross income.
        b.   in some states, certain fringe benefits excluded from Federal income tax under §401(k) are included.
        c.   payments to non-employee, outside contractors, are not included in most states.
    2.   Compensation of an employee is not, normally, split between states unless the employee is transferred or changes position during the year.
    3.   When services are performed in more than one state, that employee's compensation is allocated to the state in which:
        a.   the services are primarily performed.
        b.   the employee's base of operations is located and in which services are performed.
        c.   the services are directed or controlled and in which services are performed.
        d.   the employee resides.
    4.   Only compensation related to the production of apportionable income is includes in the payroll factor.

H.   The Property Factor
1.   In-state property/Total property
   a.   is based on the average value of the corporation's real and tangible personal property owned or rented and used during the year.
   b.   owned property is usually valued at historic cost plus additions and improvements.
   c.   rented property is usually valued at 8 times its annual rent.
2.   Only property used to produce apportionable income is included in the property factor.

III.   EFFECTS OF THE UNITARY THEORY

A.   The unitary approach, adopted by many states, requires a corporation to file combined or consolidate returns which include the operating results of certain affiliated corporations.

B.   The unitary theory
1.   Ignores the separate legal existence of the entities and focuses on practical business realities:
   a.   unity of ownership
   b.   unity of operations
   c.   unity of use
2.   Treats the separate entities as a single business for state income tax purposes.
3.   Applies the apportionment formula to the combined income of the unitary business.

C.   Water's Edge Election
1.   Permits a multinational corporation to elect to limit a state's taxing jurisdiction over out-of-state affiliates to activities occurring within the U.S.
2.   This election usually cannot be revoked for a number of years without permission.
3.   Corporation's making this election may be subject to an additional tax for the privilege of excluding out-of-state entities from the combined report.

IV.   TAXATION OF S CORPORATIONS

A.   Many of the states that recognize S corporations automatically treat them as such if a valid Federal election is in place. Certain states impose additional eligibility requirements.

B.   Most states that impose corporate income taxes have special provisions for S corporations.

C. When an S corporation has nonresident shareholders:
1. A corporate-level tax might be imposed.
2. The corporation might be required to withhold tax on the nonresidents' portion of the income.
3. The nonresident shareholder may have to agree to pay state taxes.
D. Multistate S corporations must allocate and apportion their income and report the amount of state income passed through to shareholders.

V. OTHER STATE AND LOCAL TAXES

A   State and Local Sales and Use Taxes
1. Sales and use taxes are imposed on the final consumer of the taxable item.
2. The seller of taxable property or services acts as an agent of the state in collecting sales tax.
3. The use tax is designed to prevent consumers from evading sales tax by purchasing goods out-of-state for in-state use.

B. Property Taxes
1. Property taxes are ad valorem taxes because they are based on the value of the property.
2. Property taxes may be assessed on real property and/or personal property.
a. different tax rates and assessment methods apply to the two classes.
b. most states limit personal property taxes to tangible property.

IV. TAX PLANNING CONSIDERATIONS include:

A. Redirection of Corporate Activities within various states

B. Selecting the Optimal State in Which to Operate
1. Disconnect activities from undesirable states.
2. Create nexus in a desirable state.

TEST FOR SELF-EVALUATION

True or False

T   F   1.   Total allocable income is included when a state's apportionment percentage is applied.

T   F   2.   Corporations cannot be subject to tax on more than 100% of their income.

T   F   3.   States uniformly define business income.

T   F   4.   Double weighting the sales factor in a state apportionment formula favors corporations domiciled within the state.

T   F   5.   An employee's salary is always apportioned to his state of residence.

T   F   6.   A unitary business cannot be an independent division.

T   F   7.   Generally, if a greater weight is assigned to the sales factor of an apportionment formula, a greater tax burden is imposed on out-of-state taxpayers.

T   F   8.   States are prohibited from imposing an income tax on U.S. government obligations.

T   F   9.   States generally accept an organization's classifications of income as active or passive to be business or nonbusiness income respectively.

T   F   10.   Sales made to a retailer by a manufacturer are exempt from sales tax.

Fill-in-the-Blanks

1.   _____ describes the degree of business activity that must be present before a tax can be imposed on the corporation's income.

2.   Apportionment formulas are generally based on three factors: _____, _____, and _____.

3.   Under the _____, sales are assumed to take place at point of delivery.

4.   To simplify the filing of tax returns, approximately 40 states _____ onto the Federal income tax base.

5.   _____ divide a corporation's business income among states.

6. _____ directly assigns specific income components to a certain state.

Multiple Choice

Use the following data to answer questions 1-3:

Zack Corporation owns and operates two manufacturing facilities, one in State I and one in State W. Zack had $400,000 of taxable income this year from its manufacturing activities. Zack Corporation had no other income.

	I	W
Sales	$750,000	$500,000
Property	500,000	400,000
Payroll	225,000	150,000

_____ 1.   Assuming both states use an equally weighted three factor apportionment formula, what is Zack's taxable income in State W?

    a. $160,000
    b. $165,926
    c. $234,075
    d. $240,000

_____ 2.   Assuming State W uses a double weighted sales factor in its three factor apportionment formula, what would Zack's taxable income be in State W?

    a. $165,926
    b. $160,000
    c. $164,444
    d. $139,259

_____ 3.   Assume I uses a single-factor sales only formula and W uses an equally weighted three factor formula, what will Zack's total taxable income be?

    a. $400,000
    b. $405,926
    c. $474,075
    d. $440,000

_____ 4.   Generally, sales are allocated to the state

    a.   where the shipment originates
    b.   at point of delivery
    c.   of ultimate destination

_____ 5.   Under UDITPA, compensation is treated as paid in the state if:

       a.   service is performed entirely within the state
       b.   the base of operations is within the state
       c.   neither of the above
       d.   both of the above

_____ 6.   A furniture store purchased 20 desks for $500 each. One desk was taken from the inventory and used by the storekeeper. Assuming a 5% use tax rate, how much tax does the store owe?

       a. $0
       b. $4
       c. $25
       d. $50

Zinc, a multistate S corporation, apportioned its $500,000 of ordinary income 40% to state A and 60% to state B. Zinc is owned equally by Larry and Mike. Larry resides in State A; Mike resides in state B.

_____ 7.   On their resident income tax returns, Larry and Mike will each report income of:

       a. $500,000
       b. $300,000
       c. $250,000
       d. $200,000

_____ 8.   On his state B return, Larry will report income of:

       a. $250,000
       b. $150,000
       c. $125,000
       d. $100,000

_____ 9.   On Mike's state A return, he will report income of:

       a. $250,000
       b. $150,000
       c. $125,000
       d. $100,000

Wren Corporation owns property in States A and B. A values property at its historical cost, B values property at its net book value, both use the average value of assets.

	January 1, 1990		December 31, 1990	
	State A	State B	State A	State B
Inventories	$125,000	$100,000	$150,000	$175,000
Buildings & Machinery	225,000	400,000	225,000	400,000
Accumulated Depreciation	(75,000)	(50,000)	(100,000)	(100,000)
Land	25,000	50,000	25,000	50,000
Totals	$300,000	$500,000	$300,000	$525,000

_____ 10.   Compute the property factor for State A.

_____ 11.   Compute the property factor for State B.

_____ 12.   What is the aggregate of Wren's property factors?

    a.   100%
    b.   98%
    c.   102%

SOLUTIONS

True or False

1. F   (p. 15-11)
2. F   (p. 15-12)
3. F   (p. 15-13)
4. T   (p. 15-15)
5. F   (p. 15-22)
6. T   (p. 15-28)
7. T   (p. 15-16)
8. T   (p. 15-6)
9. F   (p. 15-14)
10. T   (p. 15-34)

Fill-in-the-Blanks

1. Nexus (p. 15-9)
2. property, payroll, sales (p. 15-15)
3. ultimate destination concept (p. 15-19)
4. piggyback (p. 15-6)
5. apportionment formulas (p. 15-11)
6. allocation (p. 15-11)

Multiple Choice

1. b   ((500,000/1250,000) + (400,000/900,000) + (150,000/375,000) /3) times 400,000
2. c   ((500,000/1250,000)2 + (400,000/900,000) + (150,000/375,000) /4) times 400,000
3. b   (750,000/1,250,000(400,000) + 165,926)
4. c   (p. 15-19)
5. a   (p. 15-22)
6. c   ($500 x 5%)
7. c   ($500,000 x 50%)
8. b   ($500,000 x 60% x 50%)
9. d   ($500,000 x 40% x 50%)
10.   39.7436% (Example 19)
11.   63.0769% (Example 19)
12. c   (p. 15-24, 25; Example 19)

CHAPTER 16

TAX ADMINISTRATION AND PRACTICE

LEARNING OBJECTIVES

After completing Chapter 16, you should be able to:

1. Describe the organization and structure of the IRS.

2. Identify the various administrative pronouncements issued by the IRS and explain how they can be used in tax practice.

3. Describe the audit process, including how returns are selected for audit and the various types of audits.

4. Explain the taxpayer appeal process, including various settlement options available.

5. Determine the amount of interest on a deficiency or a refund and when it is due.

6. Discuss the various penalties that can be imposed on acts of noncompliance by taxpayers and return preparers.

7. Understand the rules governing the statute of limitations on assessments and on refunds.

8. Summarize the legal and ethical guidelines that apply to those engaged in tax practice.

KEY TERMS

Accuracy-related penalty	Negligence	Statute of limitations
Closing agreement	Ninety-day letter	Substantial authority
Determination letter	Offer in compromise	Technical advice
Enrolled agent (EA)	Reasonable cause	memorandum
Fraud	Revenue Agent's	Thirty-day letter
Letter ruling	Report (RAR)	

OUTLINE

I.   TAX ADMINISTRATION

    A.   IRS responsibilities include:
        1.   providing adequate information,
        2.   identifying delinquent tax payments,
        3.   carrying out assessment and collection procedures.

    B.   IRS Procedures - Letter Rulings
        1.   Letter Rulings, issued by the National Office, are written statements of the IRS' current position on the tax consequences of a course of action contemplated by a taxpayer.
        2.   Rulings are issued only on uncompleted, actual transactions or transactions which have been completed prior to filing the tax return for the year in question.
        3.   Rulings are not issued:
            a.   in hypothetical situations
            b.   in cases involving a question of fact
        4.   Rulings may be revoked if substantial discrepancies are found between the facts in the ruling request and the actual situation.
        5.   A Ruling may be relied on only by the taxpayer who requested and received it.
        6.   Rulings must be attached to the tax return for the year in question.

    C.   IRS Procedures - Additional Issuances
        1.   Determination Letters are issued by the District Director and cover completed transactions when the issue involved is covered by judicial or statutory authority, Regulations or rulings.
        2.   A Technical Advice Memorandum is issued by the National Office to the District Director and/or Regional Commissioner in response to a specific request from either an agent, an Appellate Conferee or a District Director. Technical advice requests arise from the audit process.

    D.   Administrative Powers of the IRS
        1.   The Code empowers the IRS to:
            a.   Examine the books and records of the taxpayer.
            b.   Assess a deficiency and demand a payment for the tax.
        2.   The files, work papers and other material of a tax practitioner are subject to subpoena. The defense of privileged communication often afforded to lawyers and doctors has not been extended to CPA's.

E.   The Audit Process
  1.   Selection of returns for audit
      a.   A computer-assisted procedure, through the use of mathematical formulas, attempts to select returns likely to contain errors.
      b.   Certain groups, self-employed individuals and cash businesses, are subject to audit more frequently than other taxpayers.
      c.   If corresponding informational returns are not in substantial agreement with the taxpayer's return, the return may be audited.
      d.   Itemized deductions in excess of norms may trigger an audit.
      e.   Certain returns are selected on a random sampling basis.
  2.   An initial review corrects math errors or failures to comply with deduction limitations.   These matters are usually settled through correspondence without a formal audit.
  3.   Office audits usually require substantiation of a particular item on an individual's return having few or no items of business income.
  4.   Field audits generally entail a more complete examination of a taxpayer's transactions. Field audits usually deal with corporate returns and individuals engaged in business or professional activities.
  5.   Taxpayer Rights
      a.   Prior to or at the initial interview, the IRS must provide an explanation of the audit process and describe the taxpayer's rights under that process.
      b.   Upon advance request, the IRS must allow an audio recording of any in-person interview.
  6.   Settlement with the revenue agent
      a.   The IRS agent may accept the return as filed or recommend certain adjustments following an audit.
      b.   Usually, questions of fact can be resolved at the agent level. Agents must adhere strictly to published IRS policy.
      c.   If agreement is reached, Form 870, Waiver of Restrictions on Assessment and Collection of Deficiency in Tax, is signed by the taxpayer. Form 870 generally closes the case; however, the IRS may assess additional deficiencies if deemed necessary.

F.   The Taxpayer Appeal Process
  1.   If agreement cannot be reached at the agent level, the taxpayer receives a copy of the Revenue Agent's Report and a letter which grants the taxpayer 30 days to request an administrative appeal.
  2.   If an appeal is not requested, a statutory notice of deficiency, 90 day letter, will be issued.
  3.   A request for appeal must be made to the Appeals Division and must be accompanied by a written protest unless:
      a.   the proposed tax deficiency does not exceed $10,000 or
      b.   the deficiency resulted from a correspondence or office audit.

4. The Appeals Division of the IRS has authority to settle all tax disputes based on the hazards of litigation: the probability of winning a court case.

5. If agreement is reached, Form 870AD is signed by the taxpayer. This agreement is usually binding upon both parties.

6. If agreement is not reached, the IRS issues a statutory notice of deficiency which gives the taxpayer 90 days to file a petition with the Tax Court or to pay the tax and file a claim for refund.

G. Offers in Compromise and Closing Agreements

1. Offers in Compromise are generally used only in extreme cases where the taxpayer's ability to pay the total amount of tax is doubtful.

2. Closing Agreements are used in situations when disputed issues involve future years. A closing agreement is generally binding on both parties.

H. Interest

1. Interest accrues on tax underpayments and overpayments.

2. Interest usually accrues from the unextended due date of the return until 30 days after the taxpayer agrees to the deficiency by signing Form 870.

3. Quarterly adjustments to the interest rates are based on the average market yield of outstanding U.S. marketable obligations maturing in 3 years or less.

   a. underpayments are subject to this short term rate plus 3%,

   b. overpayments earn 1% less,

      1. if an overpayment is refunded within 45 days no interest is allowed

      2. when a return is filed after the due date, interest accrues from the date of filing.

   c. both are compounded daily.

I. Taxpayer Penalties

1. Penalties are additions to tax liability and are not tax-deductible.

2. "Ad valorem" penalties are

   a. based on a percentage of the tax owed,

   b. subject to the same deficiency procedures that apply to the underlying tax.

3. "Assessable" penalties are typically a flat dollar amount.

4. Failure to file penalty is 5% per month up to 25% of the tax liability, a minimum penalty of $100 may be imposed.

5. Failure to pay penalty is 0.5% per month up to 25% of the tax liability.

6. If both the failure to file and the failure to pay penalties apply in any month, the failure to file penalty is reduced by the failure to pay penalty amount.

7. "Accuracy-related" penalties are applied when the taxpayer fails to show reasonable cause for the underpayment or a good faith effort to comply with the tax law. The penalty is 20% of the underpayment for:
    a. negligence or disregard of rules or regulations
    b. substantial understatement of tax liability
    c. substantial valuation overstatement
    d. substantial valuation understatement
8. Negligence includes any failure to make a reasonable attempt to comply with tax law.
9. Fraud is when the taxpayer had a specific intent to evade a tax
    a. civil fraud must be proved by a preponderance of evidence,
    b. criminal fraud must be proved beyond the shadow of a reasonable doubt,
    c. any underpayment resulting from fraud, 75% of the tax liability.

J. Statute of Limitations
1. Generally, any tax imposed must be assessed within three years of the filing of the return. Exceptions to the above rule are:
    a. If no return was filed, or if a fraudulent return was filed, an assessment may be made at any time.
    b. The statute is increased to six years if the taxpayer omits from gross income an amount in excess of 25% of the gross income as stated on the return.
    c. The statute may be extended by mutual consent of the District Director and the taxpayer.
2. The period of time allowed for the IRS to collect the tax is ten years from the date of the assessment.
3. If after the IRS issues a statutory notice of deficiency, the taxpayer, within the allotted time, files a Tax Court petition, the statute of limitations is suspended on both the assessment and period of collection until 60 days after the court's final decision.
4. A taxpayer who wishes to file a tax refund claim must file the appropriate form within three years of the filing of the original tax return, or within two years following the payment of the tax, whichever is later. Individuals use Form 1040X, and corporations use Form 1120X.

II. TAX PRACTICE

A. While anyone can prepare a tax return or give tax advice, practice before the IRS is usually limited to CPA's, attorneys, and IRS enrollees who have passed an IRS-administered examination.

B.   Rules governing tax practice require the tax preparer:
1.   To make known to a client any error or omission on any return or document submitted to the IRS.
2.   To submit records or information lawfully requested by the IRS.
3.   To exercise due diligence as to accurately preparing and filing returns.

C.   Preparers are also subject to restrictions:
1.   Against unreasonably delaying prompt disposition of any matter before the IRS.
2.   Against charging clients "an unconscionable fee".
3.   Against representing clients with conflicting interests.

D.   Preparer penalties include:
1.   A $250 penalty for the understatement of tax liability due to unrealistic positions.
2.   A $1,000 penalty for willful and reckless conduct.
3.   A $1,000 ($10,000 for corporations) penalty per return or document is imposed against those who aid in the preparation of returns or other documents which they know will result in understatement of tax liability.
4.   A $50 fine is assessed for each of the following:
   a.   failure to sign the return
   b.   failure to furnish preparer's identifying number
   c.   failure to furnish the taxpayer with a copy of the return
5.   A $500 penalty may be assessed if a preparer endorses a check for a tax refund which is issued to the taxpayer.

E.   The AICPA Tax Committee has issued statements to guide CPAs in resolving ethical questions related to tax practice. Some of these statements are summarized below.
1.   Positions Contrary to IRS Interpretations: The CPA must believe the position has a realistic possibility of being accepted if challenged and must advise the client of the risks and penalties if the position is not accepted.
2.   Questions on Returns: Reasonable efforts should be made to provide answers to all questions on a tax return.
3.   Procedural Aspects of Preparing Returns: The CPA must inform the client of any applicable expenditure verification rules and must make reasonable inquiries if client representations appear to be incorrect, incomplete or inconsistent.
4.   Estimates: Estimates may be used in preparing a tax return if reasonable and indicated as such if it is impracticable to obtain exact data.
5.   Recognition of Administrative Proceeding: A CPA is not bound by proceedings involving a prior year but is to use his/her own judgment depending on the facts and circumstances of the particular situation.

6. Knowledge of Error: The CPA should promptly advise the client and recommend corrective measures of any errors or omissions on returns.

7. Form and Content of Advice to Clients: The CPA must use judgment in advising clients. His advice should be professionally competent and appropriate for the particular client.

F. These statements are representative of standards followed by members of the profession. Deviations from these statements could indicate that a lack of due care was exercised.

Income Tax Appeal Procedure

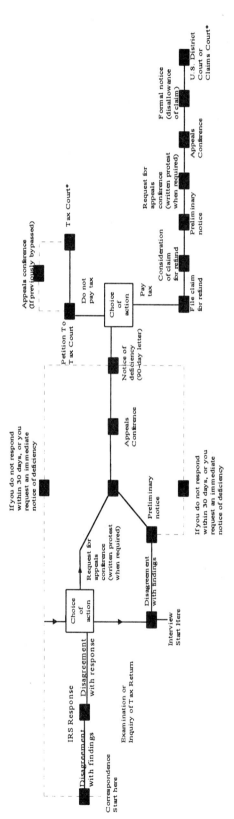

At any stage
□ You can agree and arrange to pay.
□ You can ask for a notice of deficiency so you can file a petition with the Tax Court.
□ You can pay the tax and file a claim for refund.

*Further appeals to the courts may be possible, except there is no appeal under the Tax Court's small tax case procedure.

Reproduced from IRS Publication No. 1 (10-90)

TEST FOR SELF-EVALUATION

True or False

T   F   1.   If a taxpayer agrees with the results of an IRS examination that he/she owes additional tax and signs an agreement form, the taxpayer will NOT be billed for additional interest for more than 30 days from the date the agreement was signed if the taxpayer pays the total amount due within 10 days of the billing date.
(IRS 95 4A-10)

T   F   2.   If a taxpayer does not respond to a 30 day letter OR if he/she does not reach an agreement with an Appeals Officer, he/she will receive a statutory notice of deficiency. A statutory notice of deficiency allows a taxpayer 90 days (150 days if mailed when the taxpayer is outside the United States) from the date of this notice to file a petition with the Tax Court.
(IRS 95 4A-12)

T   F   3.   If the proposed increase or decrease in tax resulting from an IRS examination, conducted at the taxpayer's place of business, exceeds $2,500 but not more than $10,000, the taxpayer or the taxpayer's representative must provide a brief written statement explaining the disputed issues within 30 days of the issuance of the 30 day letter.
(IRS 95 4A-17)

T   F   4.   In the case of taxes assessed after November 5, 1990, if the IRS has assessed the tax within the statutory period of limitation, the tax may be collected by levy or a proceeding in court commenced within 10 years after the assessment or within any period for collection agreed upon in writing between the IRS and the taxpayer before the expiration of the 10-year period.
(IRS 95 4A-29)

T   F   5.   By filing a Notice of Federal Tax Lien against a taxpayer, the Government is providing a public notice to the taxpayer's creditors that the Government has a claim against all of the taxpayer's property, INCLUDING property that the taxpayer acquires after the lien was filed.
(IRS 95 4A-30)

T   F   6.   The trust fund recovery penalty may be imposed against any person who is responsible for collecting or paying withheld income and employment taxes AND who willfully fails to collect OR pay them.
(IRS 96 4A-32)

T   F   7.   A taxpayer can only submit an Offer in Compromise if it is submitted based on doubt as to the liability owed and doubt as to the ability of the taxpayer to fully pay the amount owed.
(IRS 96 4A-33)

T   F   8.   Audrey's 1993 income tax return is under examination by the Internal Revenue Service. She agrees with several proposed changes by the examiner. Audrey thinks that she will owe additional tax of $3,000 and deposits a cash bond in that amount with the IRS. This deposit will stop the further accrual of interest on BOTH the tax and on the interest accrued to that point.   (IRS 96 4A-12)

T   F   9.   If you are filing a claim for credit or refund based on contested income tax issues considered in previously examined returns and do NOT want to appeal within the IRS, you should request in writing that the claim be immediately rejected.

(IRS 96 4A-10)

Fill in the Blanks

1.   When agreement cannot be reached between the taxpayer and the Appeals Division, the IRS issues a _____.

2.   The _____ defines the period of time during which one party may pursue legal action against another party.

3.   The position of Commissioner of the Internal Revenue Service is an _____ position.

4.   In addition to issuing Letter Rulings and Revenue Rulings, the IRS also issues _____, and _____.

5.   The Tax Committee of the AICPA has issued "_____," the purpose of which is to guide the conduct of CPA's in tax practice.

6.   "_____ of _____" is a term used to describe the possibility of winning or losing a tax issue if the case goes to court.

7.   An _____ in _____ gives the IRS the authority to negotiate a compromise settlement if there is doubt as to the amount or ability to collect a tax liability.

8.   _____ are additions to the tax liability and are not deductible as itemized or business expense items.

9.   The statement which is filed with the IRS District Office following an audit which recommends acceptance of adjustment of the tax return is known as the _____.

Multiple Choice

_____ 1.   With regard to the categories of individuals who may practice before the Internal Revenue Service, which of the following statements is CORRECT?
(IRS 96 4B-42)

    a.   Only enrolled agents, attorneys, or CPAs may represent trusts and estates before any officer or employee of the IRS.

    b.   An individual who is NOT an enrolled agent, attorney, or CPA, who signs a return as having prepared it for the taxpayer may, with proper authorization from the taxpayer, appear as the taxpayer's representative, with or without the taxpayer, at an IRS regional Appeals Office conference with respect to the tax liability of the taxpayer for the taxable year or period covered by that return.

    c.   Under the limited practice provisions in Treasury Department Circular No. 230, ONLY general partners may represent a partnership.

    d.   Under the limited practice provisions in Circular No. 230, an individual who is under suspension or disbarment from practice before the IRS may NOT engage in limited practice before the IRS.

_____ 2.   If an individual recognized to practice before the IRS by the Department of the Treasury knows that a client has NOT complied with the revenue laws of the United States with respect to a matter administered by the IRS, the practitioner is required to:
(IRS 96 4B-43)

    a.   Advise the client of the noncompliance.

    b.   Immediately notify the IRS.

    c.   Advise the client AND notify the IRS.

    d.   Do nothing until advised by the client to take corrective action.

_____ 3.   Gina disagrees with the results of an IRS examination of her tax return. She pursued the appeals procedures and disagreed with the Appeals Officer. If she wishes to appeal further, Gina may:
(IRS 96 4B-47)

    a.   Request a conference with a new Appeals Officer in a different district.

    b.   Wait for a notice of deficiency, NOT pay the tax, and petition the District Court.

    c.   Wait for a notice of dificiency, NOT pay the tax, and petition the Tax Court.

    d.   Submit a revised written protest that outlines the isssues and authority for the position taken.

_____ 4.   All of the following statements concerning the procedure for a written protest submitted by a representative to obtain an Appeals Office conference are correct except:
(IRS 96 4B-46)

a. A written protest is required when the tax due, INCLUDING penalties, is MORE than $10,000.

b. A written protest MUST contain the tax years involved AND a statement that the taxpayer wants to appeal to the Appeals Office.

c. A written protest MUST contain a statement of facts for EACH disputed issue and a statement of law or other authority relied upon for each issue.

d. A written protest MUST contain a declaration under penalties of perjury, signed by the taxpayer that the statement of facts is true and correct.

_____ 5. With respect to the small case procedure in the Tax Court, all of the following statements are CORRECT except: (IRS 96 4B-50)

a. Within 90 days of receiving a statutory notice of deficiency, the taxpayer must pay a filing fee AND file a petition form with the Tax Court in Washington, DC.

b. The total disputed deficiency (tax and penalties) for ALL tax years at issue must be $10,000 or less.

c. The decision of the Tax Court CANNOT be appealed to another court and CANNOT be used as a precedent for any other case or tax year.

d. The proceedings are conducted in accordance with such rules of evidence and procedures as the Tax Court may prescribe.

_____ 6. Mr. Alomar's 1993 income tax return was examined by the IRS and he agreed with the proposed changes. He has several ways by which he may settle his account and pay any additional tax that is due. All of the following statements with respect to this situation are correct except: (IRS 96 4B-49)

a. If he pays when he signs the agreement, the interest is generally figured from the due date of the return to the date of his payment.

b. If he does NOT pay the additional tax when he signs the agreement, he will receive a bill. The interest on the additional tax is generally figured from the due date of the return to the billing date.

c. If the bill is delayed, he will NOT be billed for additional interest for more than 60 days from the date he signed the agreement.

d. If he pays the amount due within 10 days of the billing date, he will NOT have to pay more interest or penalties.

_____ 7. If the IRS must seize (levy) your property, you have the right by federal law to keep all of the following except: (IRS 96 4B-74)

a. A limited amount of personal belongings, furniture and business or professional books and tools.

b. Unemployment and job training benefits and workmen's compensation.

c.   Salary or wages that have been included in a judgment for court-ordered child support payments.

d.   Your primary residence if the collection of tax is in jeopardy.

_____ 8.   With regard to the trust fund recovery penalty assessments for employers, all of the following statements are correct except: (IRS 96 4B-77)

a.   The penalty can be applied regardless of whether a taxpayer is out of business or without assets.

b.   The penalty is computed on unpaid income taxes withheld plus the employee's and the employer's portion of the FICA taxes.

c.   The two key elements that support an assessment of the penalty against an individual are responsibility and willfulness.

d.   The amount of the penalty is equal to the unpaid trust fund tax.

_____ 9.   Which of the following statements with respect to taxpayers' offers in compromise on unpaid tax liabilities is correct?   (IRS 96 4B-78)

a.   A taxpayer does NOT have the right to submit an offer in compromise on his/her tax bill but is given the opportunity in order to increase voluntary compliance with the tax laws.

b.   Doubt as to the liability for the amount owed must be supported by evidence and the amount acceptable under the offer in compromise will depend on the degree of doubt found in the particular case.

c.   Submission of an offer in compromise AUTOMATICALLY suspends the collection of an account.

d.   If the offer in compromise is made on the grounds that there is doubt as to the taxpayer's ability to make full payment on the amount owed, the amount offered must give sufficient consideration ONLY to the taxpayer's present earning capacity.

_____ 10.   All of the following statements with respect to effective record keeping are CORRECT except: (IRS 95 4B-52)

a.   Records that support the basis of property should be kept until the statute of limitations expires for the year that the property was acquired.

b.   Records of income should identify its source in order to determine if it is taxable or nontaxable.

c.   If an individual CANNOT provide a cancelled check to prove payment of an expense item, he/she may be able to prove it with certain financial account statements.

d.   Records should show how much of an individual's earnings are subject to self-employment tax.

SOLUTIONS

True or False

1. T (p. 16-14)
2. T (p. 16-11)
3. T (p. 16-11)
4. T (p. 16-24)
5. T (p. 16-7)
6. T (p. 16-22)
7. T (p. 16-13)
8. F (p. 16-14; interest stops only on amount remitted)
9. T (Figure 16-3)

Fill in the Blanks

1. 90 day letter: statutory notice of deficiency (p. 16-11)
2. statute of limitations (p. 16-23)
3. appointed (p. 16-4)
4. Determination Letters, and technical advices (p. 16-6)
5. "Statements on Responsibilities in Tax Practice" (p. 16-27)
6. "Hazards; litigation" (p. 16-11)
7. offer; compromise (p. 16-13)
8. Penalties (p. 16-16)
9. Revenue Agent's report (p. 16-10)

Multiple Choice

1. d (p. 16-25)
2. a (p. 16-25)
3. c (Figure 16-3)
4. d (p. 16-11)
5. b ($10,000 cap is tested year by year, not aggregated)
6. c (p. 16-14)
7. d (p. 16-7)
8. b (p. 16-22)
9. b (p. 16-13)
10. a (p. 16-7; records supporting the basis of property are relevant beyond the year of acquisition)

CHAPTER 17

THE FEDERAL GIFT AND ESTATE TAXES

LEARNING OBJECTIVES

After completing Chapter 17, you should be able to:

1.   Understand the nature of the Federal gift and estate taxes.

2.   Work with the Federal gift tax formula.

3.   Work with the Federal estate tax formula.

4.   Explain the operation of the Federal gift tax.

5.   Illustrate the computation of the Federal gift tax.

6.   Review the components of the gross estate.

7.   Describe the components of the taxable estate.

8.   Determine the Federal estate tax liability.

9.   Appreciate the role of the generation skipping transfer tax.

KEY TERMS

Alternate valuation date	Joint tenants	Taxable gift
Annual exclusion	Marital deduction	Tenants by the entirety
Disclaimers	Power of appointment	Tenants in common
Exemption equivalent	Probate estate	Terminable interests
Future interest	Qualified terminable	Unified tax credit
Gross estate	interest property (QTIP)	Unified transfer tax
Inheritance tax	Taxable estate	

OUTLINE

I.   TRANSFER TAXES

    A.   Nature of the Taxes
        1.   Transfer taxes are based on the value of the property transferred, not the income derived from the property.
        2.   The Unified Transfer Tax covers all gratuitous transfers.
            a.   the gift tax is a tax on transfers during the donor's lifetime.
            b.   the estate tax is a tax on transfers at or after death.
        3.   Persons subject to the tax
            a.   Federal gift tax
                1.   applies to all transfers of property by individuals who, at the time of the gift, were citizens or residents of the U.S.
                2.   applies to gifts of property located in the U.S. for individuals who were neither citizens or residents.
            b.   Federal estate tax
                1.   applies to the entire estate of decedents who, at the time of death, were U.S. citizens or residents.
                2.   applies to property located in the U.S. for decedents who were neither citizens or residents.
            c.   for nonresidents and/or non-citizens, application of these taxes may be different under treaties between the U.S. and various foreign countries.
        4.   Formulas
            a.   the gift tax

                    current year taxable gifts
              +   prior years taxable gifts
              =   total taxable gifts
                    tax on total taxable gifts
              -   tax paid or deemed paid on prior taxable gifts
              -   the unified tax credit
              =   tax on current year gifts
            b.   the estate tax
                    gross estate
              -   deductions allowed
              =   taxable estate
              +   post-1976 taxable gifts
              =   tax base
                    tentative tax on total transfers
              -   tax credits
              =   estate tax

B.   Valuation for Estate and Gift Tax Purposes
 1.   The fair market value of property on the date of transfer is generally the amount subject to the gift or estate tax.
 2.   An estate may elect the alternate valuation date if:
  a.   the estate is required to file an Estate Tax Return, and
  b.   the election would decrease both the value of the gross estate and the estate tax liability.
 3.   The alternate valuation date values all property six months after the date of death or on their date of disposition, the earlier.

C.   Key Property Concepts
 1.   Undivided ownership
  a.   joint tenants and tenants by the entirety have rights of survivorship.
  b.   tenants in common or community property interests pass to the estate or heirs.
 2.   Partial interests are interests in assets divided as to rights to the income or principal.

II.   THE FEDERAL GIFT TAX

A.   General Considerations
 1.   Under state law, for a gift to be complete, the following conditions must be present:
  a.   A donor competent to make the gift,
  b.   A donee capable of receiving and possessing the gifted property,
  c.   Donative intent on behalf of the donor,
  d.   Actual or constructive delivery of the property to the donee or donee's representative,
  e.   Acceptance of the gift by the donee.
 2.   Certain excluded transfers
  a.   transfers to political organizations
  b.   payments made on another's behalf for
   1.   tuition payments made to an educational organization
   2.   medical care

B.   Transfers Subject to the Gift Tax
 1.   Gift loans
  a.   A gift loan is any below-market loan where the foregoing of interest is in the nature of a gift.
  b.   The gift is determined as the difference between interest charged and the market rate.

        c.   Special limitations apply if the gift loan does not exceed $100,000, unless tax avoidance is a principal purpose of the loan. In such a case,

            1.   the interest element may not exceed the borrower's net investment income,

            2.   when net investment income is under $1,000, the interest element is disregarded.

    2.   Generally, the settlement of certain marital rights are subject to the Federal gift tax. An exception to the general rule is if, in settlement of their marital or property rights,

        a.   a written agreement between spouses is executed.

        b.   a final divorce is obtained within the three-year period beginning on the date one year before such agreement is entered into.

C.   Disclaimers

    1.   A disclaimer is a refusal by a person to accept property that is designated to pass to him or her.

    2.   The effect of the disclaimer would be to pass the property to someone else, thereby avoiding the payment of a transfer tax.

    3.   Care should be taken to satisfy the requirements of Section 2518 to avoid the application of a gift tax.

D.   Annual Exclusion

    1.   A donor may deduct the first $10,000 of gifts to each donee.

    2.   The gifts must be of a present interest, and may be doubled through gift splitting with one's spouse.

    3.   For gifts in trust the annual exclusion applies to each beneficiary of the trust as a separate individual.

E.   An exception to the future interest rule concerns gifts to minors. Provided the following conditions are met, the gift will be considered a gift of a present interest:

    1.   both the property and the income from the property may be expended by or for the benefit of the minor donee before he or she attains the age of 21;

    2.   if the property is not expended, it will pass to the minor at his or her attainment of age 21;

    3.   if the donee dies before reaching the age of 21, the property will pass to his or her estate, or as he or she may appoint under a general power of appointment.

F.   Procedural Matters.

    1.   Form 709 must be filed whenever the gifts for one calendar year exceed the annual exclusion, $10,000, or involve a gift of a future interest.

    2.   The due date is April 15 of the following year.

    3.   To elect gift splitting between spouses, Forms 709 must be filed.

III.   THE FEDERAL ESTATE TAX

    A.   The Gross Estate
        1.   The gross estate is composed of the value of all property in which the decedent has an interest at his death.
        2.   An exclusion from the gross estate for qualified family owned businesses is now available. The exclusion is the difference between $1,300,000 and the exclusion amount.
            a.   is intended to keep the business intact to benefit the deceased owner's family.
            b.   at date of death, the decedent was a citizen or resident of the U.S.
            c.   applies only when the value of the business interest exceeds 50% of the adjusted gross estate.
            d.   the decedent or a family member must have owned and materially participated in the business for at least 5 of the 8 years prior to death.
            e.   a qualified heir must materially participate in the business for at least 5 years in an 8 year period during the 10 years following the decedent's death.
            f.   tax savings are recaptured when,
                1.   the qualified heir ceases to materially participate.
                2.   the business is disposed of to outsiders.
                3.   the business is moved outside of the U.S. or the qualified heir losses his/her citizenship.
            g.   the exclusion is elective and is made by the executor. The election must include an agreement that the qualified heirs will accept liability for recapture tax consequences should they arise.
        3.   Adjustments for gifts made within three years of death, include
            a.   any gift tax paid on gifts made within 3 years of death
            b.   any incomplete transfers, property interests transferred by gift within the 3 years, and, in which the donor retained some rights:
                1.   retained life estate
                2.   revocable transfers
                3.   proceeds of life insurance
        4.   Survivorship annuities are included in the gross estate if any portion of the annuity is receivable after the decedent's death.
        5.   Certain property held in joint tenancy will be included in the decedent's estate unless it can be proved that the surviving co-owners contributed to the cost of the property.
            a.   funds received as a gift from the deceased co-owner and applied to the cost cannot be counted as funds provided by a surviving co-owner.
            b.   for married persons, one-half of the value of the property is included in the estate of the spouse who dies first.

6.   In joint ownership cases having equal ownership and disproportionate consideration, generally, gift treatment results.
- a.   for a joint bank account, a gift occurs when the noncontributing party withdraws funds provided by the other joint tenant.
- b.   for U.S. savings bonds, a gift occurs when the noncontributing party uses some or all of the proceeds for himself.

7.   Property over which the decedent possessed a general power of appointment is included in the gross estate.

8.   Life insurance proceeds on the decedent's life are included if:
- a.   receivable by the estate
- b.   receivable for the benefit of the estate
- c.   the decedent possessed an incident of ownership

B.   Taxable Estate

1.   Deductions are allowed for certain expenses, indebtedness, and taxes.
- a.   funeral expenses
- b.   administrative expense
  1.   commissions
  2.   attorney fees
  3.   accountant fees
  4.   court costs
  5.   selling expenses for asset dispositions
- c.   unpaid mortgages
- d.   claims against the estate, enforceable personal obligations of the decedent at the time of death
- e.   casualty or theft losses incurred while administering the estate

2.   Deductions are also allowed for
- a.   charitable contributions
- b.   transfers to the surviving spouse

C.   Computing the Federal Estate Tax
1.   Determine the taxable estate
2.   Add back post-1976 taxable gifts
3.   Compute the tentative tax
4.   Subtract available estate tax credits

D.   Estate Tax Credits
1.   Unified tax credit
2.   Credit for state death taxes
3.   Credit for tax on prior transfers
4.   Credit for foreign death taxes

E.   Procedural Matters
1.   Filing requirements parallel the exemption equivalent amounts.
2.   Form 706, if required, is due nine months after the date of death.
3.   An extension of time for filing may be requested.

IV.   THE GENERATION SKIPPING TRANSFER TAX

A.   The GSTT is imposed when a younger generation is bypassed in favor of a later generation.

B.   Generation skipping transfers are taxed at 55% however, a $1 million exemption is allowed.

TEST FOR SELF-EVALUATION

True or False

T F 1.   Mr. Hodges, a U. S. citizen, died on August 1, 1995. As the personal representative of the estate, you must file Form 706, United States Estate (and Generation-Skipping Transfer) Tax Return if the value of the GROSS estate at the date of death was $700,000.   (IRS 96 3A-13)

T F 2.   The gross estate includes property that was owned by a decedent at the time of death and was transferred at death by a will or intestacy laws.
                                                                  (IRS 96 3A-15)

T F 3.   Your taxable gifts are your total gifts reduced by the annual exclusion, the charitable deduction AND the marital deduction.   (IRS 96 3A-19)

T F 4.   An extension of time to file an INCOME TAX RETURN for any tax year that is a calendar year automatically extends the time for filing the ANNUAL GIFT TAX RETURN for that calendar year UNTIL the due date of the income tax return.
                                                                  (IRS 95 3A-18)

T F 5.   Mr. Antoine, a U.S. resident alien, died on July 1, 1994. As the executor of the estate, you must file an estate tax return if the value of the estate at the date of death was at least $100,000.   (IRS 94 3A-11)

T F 6.   Herman, as executor of the estate of his deceased father, must sell his father's house to make distributions to all beneficiaries. Herman pays $9,000 to paint and carpet the house to enhance its marketability. The $9,000 Herman pays is deductible from the gross estate to compute the taxable estate.
                                                                  (IRS 94 3A-13)

T F 7.   In January 1994, Bob gave an interest free loan of $10,500 to his son so that he could buy a boat. His son repaid the entire $10,500 in December 1994. In addition, Bob gave other gifts to his son during 1994 totaling $85,000. Bob must include an amount for the forgone interest on the boat loan on his gift tax return for 1994.   (IRS 94 3A-17)

T F 8.   If the alternate valuation method is elected in valuing the decedent's property, any property NOT disposed of within 6 months after the decedent's death is valued as of 6 months after the date of the decedent's death.   (IRS 93 3A-14)

T F 9.   During 1992, Barbara gave $5,000 to her mother, Julie; $6,000 to her father, Ben; and $3,000 to her Aunt Cheryl. Barbara must file Form 709, United States Gift and Generation Skipping Transfer Tax Return.   (IRS 93 3A-18)

Fill in the Blanks

1. A gift is the transfer of property from one person to another for less than _____ and _____ consideration.

2. The Federal gift tax is _____ in effect.

3. The deductions and exclusions which are allowed in arriving at the taxable gifts are _____, _____, and _____.

4. Gift splitting must be between _____.

5. The _____ comprises all property which is subject to the Federal estate tax.

6. _____ is a right that a husband has in his deceased wife's property.

7. An _____ is "one or more payments extending over a period of time."

8. The three things that can happen to a power of appointment are _____, _____ and _____.

9. Powers of appointment fall into two categories: _____ power of appointment and _____ power of appointment.

10. A _____ power of appointment is one in which the decedent could have appointment himself, his creditors, his estate, or the creditors of his estate.

11. The Federal estate tax is imposed on the decedent's right to _____ at death.

Multiple Choice

_____ 1. What amount of a decedent's taxable estate is effectively tax-free if the maximum unified estate and gift tax credit is taken, in 1997?   (IRS 96 3B-34)

    a. $0
    b. $10,000
    c. $192,000
    d. $600,000

_____ 2. Form 706, United States Estate (and Generation Skipping Transfer) Tax Return, was filed for the estate of John Doe in 1995. The gross estate tax was $250,000. Which of the following items is NOT credited against the gross estate tax to determine the net estate tax payable?   (IRS 96 3B-35)

a.   Unified Credit.
b.   Credit for gift taxes.
c.   Marital deduction.
d.   Credit for state and foreign death taxes.

_____ 3.   On June 15, 1995, Marlo made a transfer by gift in an amount sufficient to require the filing of a gift tax return. If Marlo did not request an extension of time for filing the 1995 gift tax return, the due date for filing was   (IRS 96 3B-37)

a.   December 31, 1995
b.   March 15, 1996
c.   April 15, 1996
d.   June 15, 1996

_____ 4.   For transfers by gift during 1995, one must file a gift tax return for which of the following?   (IRS 96 3B-38)

a.   a transfer of $18,000 to a son for which one's spouse has agreed to gift-splitting.
b.   A qualified transfer for educational or medical expenses.
c.   A transfer of a present interest in property that is not more than the annual exclusion.
d.   A transfer to one's spouse that qualified for the unlimited marital deduction.

_____ 5.   Valerie and Dino, who were married in 1992, made a gift to their son Michael on January 2, 1995. In July 1995, Valerie and Dino were legally divorced. Valerie married Scott on December 20, 1995. Which answer below best describes this situation?   (IRS 96 3B-39)

a.   The gift-splitting benefits are available to Valerie and Dino if Valerie consents.
b.   The gift-splitting benefits are NOT available to Valerie and Dino because they were divorced in 1995.
c.   The gift-splitting benefits are NOT available to Valerie and Dino because Valerie remarried in 1995.
d.   The gift-splitting benefits ARE available to Valerie and Dino because they were married at the time the gift was made.

_____ 6.   Jason died on October 1, 1995. The alternate valuation method was NOT elected. The assets in his estate were valued as of the date of death as follows:

Home	$300,000
Car	20,000
Stocks, bonds & savings	250,000
Jewelry	50,000

Dividends declared July 1, 1995, not paid as of October 1, 1995	1,000
Accrued interest on savings as of October 1, 1995	6,500

What is the amount of Jason's gross estate?   (IRS 96 3C-73)

a. $570,000
b. $620,000
c. $621,000
d. $627,500

_____ 7.   Ellie died on June 15, 1995. The assets in her estate were valued on her date of death and alternate valuation date respectively as follows:

Asset	Date of Death Valuation	Alternate Valuation
Home	$250,000	$300,000
Stock	$425,000	$450,000
Bonds	$200,000	$125,000
Patent	$100,000	$ 95,000

The patent had 10 years of its life remaining at the time of Ellie's death. The executor sold the home on August 1, 1995, for $275,000. If Ellie's executor elects the alternate valuation date method, what is the value of Ellie's estate?

(IRS 96 3C-74)

a. $895,000
b. $945,000
c. $950,000
d. $970,000

_____ 8.   Chris, who is single and a U.S. citizen, made the following gifts in 1995:

Cash to nephew	$100,000
Cash to sister	$100,000
Property to brother	$200,000
Cash to local university building fund	$100,000

Chris had not made any gifts in prior years. What is the amount of taxable gifts?

(IRS 96 3C-75)

a. $370,000
b. $470,000
c. $480,000
d. $500,000

_____ 9.   In 1995, Linda gave her daughter a gift of land that had a fair market value of $1,000,000. She made no gifts in years 1987 through 1994. In 1986, she used $121,800 of her unified credit to offset gift tax otherwise due. What amount of unified credit can Linda use to offset gift tax due on the 1995 gift?
(IRS 96 3C-76)

    a. $192,800
    b. $71,000
    c. $10,000
    d. $0

_____ 10.   During 1995, Wellington made the following gifts:

Cash to son Willis	$40,000
Land to wife Paula	100,000
Painting to niece Marlene	16,000

Wellington and Paula elect gift-splitting. Paula's only gift in 1995 was a $50,000 cash gift to her mother. What is the amount of the taxable gifts to be reported by Wellington in 1995?   (IRS 96 3C-77)

    a. $25,000
    b. $38,000
    c. $156,000
    d. $206,000

_____ 11.   All of the following provisions with respect to the election of the alternate valuation method for property included in the decedent's gross estate are correct except: (IRS 96 3B-33)

    a.   The election must be made on a return filed within one year of the due date, including extensions, for filing the return.
    b.   The election may be changed after filing the return by filing an amended return.
    c.   The election may be made only if it will DECREASE the value of the gross estate and the sum of the estate tax and the generation skipping transfer tax (reduced by any allowable credits).
    d.   The election applies to all of the property in the estate and does NOT preclude you from electing the special-use valuation for qualified real property.

_____ 12.   All of the following would be allowed as deductions from the Gross Estate in computing the Taxable Estate except: (IRS 95 3B-39)

a. Funeral expenses paid out of the estate.
b. Debts owed by the decedent at the time of death.
c. Income tax on income received after decedent's death.
d. Casualty and theft losses that occur during settlement of the estate.

_____ 13. Form 709, United States Gift (and Generation-Skipping Transfer) Tax Return is required to be filed for (IRS 95 3B-41)

a. a transfer of a present interest that is not more than the annual exclusion ($10,000)
b. a qualified transfer for educational or medical expenses
c. a transfer of a future interest that is not more than the annual exclusion ($10,000)
d. a transfer to your spouse that qualifies for the unlimited marital deduction.

_____ 14. All of the following are deductions allowed in determining the gift tax except:
(IRS 95 3B-42)

a. A gift to the state of Pennsylvania for exclusively public purposes.
b. The value of a gift made to one's spouse who is NOT a United States citizen.
c. A gift made to one's spouse, a United States citizen, in excess of $100,000.
d. A gift of copyrightable work of art to a qualified organization if you do not transfer the copyright to the charity.

_____ 15. Which of the following statements regarding gift splitting by married couples is CORRECT? (IRS 95 3B-43)

a. If only one spouse has made gifts during the year and the spouses consent to split the gift, the other spouse is always required to file a gift tax return.
b. If both spouses consent to split a gift of a future interest, both spouses must file gift tax returns only if the value of the gift is greater than $20,000.
c. A consent to split gifts may be made on an amended gift tax return after the due date of the original return.
d. If the spouses are divorced during the year, they still may split a gift made before the divorce so long as neither marries anyone else during that year.

_____ 16. Ms. Rose died on October 15, 1994. The assets which comprised her estate were valued as follows:

	10/15/94	02/15/95	04/15/95
House	950,000	900,000	800,000
Stocks	1,950,000	1,865,000	1,880,000
Bonds	500,000	500,000	540,000

The executor sold the home on February 28, 1995, for $900,000. The executor properly elected the alternate valuation date method. What is the value of Ms. Rose's estate?   (IRS 95 3C-79)

a. $3,220,000
b. $3,320,000
c. $3,265,000
d. $3,400,000

SOLUTIONS

True of False
1. T (p. 17-7; value of gross estate exceeds exemption amount)
2. T (p. 17-18)
3. T (p. 17-5)
4. T (p. 17-17; footnote)
5. F (p. 17-7; in excess of exemption amount)
6. F (p. 17-29; administrative expense)
7. T (p. 17-12)
8. T (p. 17-7)
9. F (p. 17-13; annual exclusion is $10,000 per donee)

Fill in the Blanks
1. full and adequate (p. 17-4)
2. cumulative (p. 17-5)
3. charitable, marital, and annual exclusion (p. 17-5)
4. spouses (p. 17-16)
5. gross estate (p. 17-18)
6. curtesy (p. 17-19)
7. annuity (p. 17-22)
8. exercise, lapse and release (p. 17-26)
9. general; special (p. 17-25)
10. general (p. 17-25)
11. pass property (p. 17-3)

Multiple Choice
1. d (p. 17-7; unified credit)
2. c (p. 17-6; marital deduction reduces gross estate not estate tax)
3. c (p. 17-17; April 15 of the following year)
4. a (p. 17-16; must file to elect gift-splitting)
5. d (p. 17-16; Valerie remarried)
6. d (p. 17-18)
7. c (the patent is valued at $100,000; 10 years = $10,000 per year, 6 mo. = 5,000)
8. a (p. 17-13, nephew 100,000 10,000; sister 100,000 -10,000; brother 200,000-10,000)
9. b (p. 17-7; 1995 unified credit 192,800 - 121,800)
10. a (p. 17-13; son 20,000-10,000; mother-in-law 25,000-10,000)
11. b (p. 17-7; irrevocable election)
12. c (p. 17-29; income received before death)
13. c (p. 17-13; future interest does not qualify for annual exclusion)
14. b (p. 17-34)
15. d (p. 17-16)
16. b (p. 17-7; 6 months from date of death or date of disposition, the earlier)

CHAPTER 18

FAMILY TAX PLANNING

LEARNING OBJECTIVES

After completing Chapter 18, you should be able to:

1.   Use various established concepts in carrying out the valuation process.

2.   Apply the special use valuation method in appropriate situations.

3.   Identify problems involved in valuing an interest in a closely held business.

4.   Compare the income tax basis rules applying to property received by gift and by death.

5.   Plan gifts so as to minimize gift taxes and avoid estate taxes.

6.   Make gifts so as to avoid income taxes for the donor.

7.   Reduce probate costs in the administration of an estate.

8.   Apply procedures that reduce estate tax consequences.

9.   Obtain liquidity for an estate.

KEY TERMS

Blockage rule	Entity buy-sell agreement	Special use value
Buy-sell agreement	Estate freeze	Step-down in basis
Cross-purchase buy-sell	Living Trust	Step-up in basis
agreement	Probate costs	

OUTLINE

I.   VALUATION CONCEPTS

    A.   Valuation in General
        1.   Fair Market Value is "the price at which property would change hands between a willing buyer and a willing seller, neither being under any compulsion to buy or sell and both having reasonable knowledge of relevant facts."
        2.   FMV is not determined by a forced sale price.
        3.   FMV is not determined by the sale price of the item in a market other than that in which the item is most commonly sold to the public.
        4.   FMV is based on what the general public would pay, sentiment should not play a part in the determination.

    B.   Valuation of Specific Assets
        1.   Stocks and bonds
            a.   traded on valuation date: mean between highest and lowest quoted prices on that date.
            b.   recently traded: the inverse weighted-average of the mean between the highest and lowest prices quoted on the nearest dates before and after the valuation date.
        2.   Notes receivable
            a.   unpaid principal plus accrued interest.
            b.   a lower value might be established due to:
                1.   a low interest rate
                2.   distant maturity date
                3.   proof of entire or partial worthlessness.
        3.   Insurance policies and annuity contracts
            a.   for a life insurance policy on the life of a person other than the decedent or an annuity contract issued by a company regularly engaged in selling annuities, the value is the cost of a comparable contract.
            b.   for noncommercial annuity contracts, special tables are issued by the IRS.
        4.   Life estates, terms for years, reversions and remainders involve using IRS tables.

    C.   Real Estate and the Special Use Valuation Method
        1.   §2032A permits an executor to elect to value certain classes of real estate at "current" use value.
        2.   All of the following conditions must be satisfied.
            a.   At least 50% of the adjusted value of the gross estate must consist of real or personal property devoted to the qualifying use.

        b.   At least 25% of the adjusted gross estate must consist of the real property devoted to qualifying use (qualifying property is considered at its "most suitable use" value for purposes of these tests).

        c.   A qualifying heir of the decedent is the recipient of the qualifying property.

        d.   The real property has been owned by the decedent or the decedent's family for five out of the last eight years, and the property was being used for its qualifying purpose during that time.

        e.   The decedent or a member of his family has participated materially in the operation of the qualifying purpose during that period of time.

    3.   The special use valuation procedure permits a reduction of no more than $750,000.

    4.   Estate tax savings are recaptured from the heir if the property is sold or withdrawn from its qualifying use within 10 years.

D.   Valuation Problems with a Closely Held Business

    1.   Goodwill may be present if the corporation's past earnings are higher than usual for the industry.

    2.   A discounted valuation may be justified if a minority interest is involved and the corporation has a poor dividend paying record.

    3.   The "blockage rule" permits a discount from the amount at which smaller lots are selling for when a controlling interest is held and the per unit value might fall if a large block of shares were marketed at one time.

    4.   A discount may be in order for lack of marketability of shares not traded in a recognized market.

    5.   Buy Sell Agreements and Valuation

        a.   In an entity agreement, the business buys the interest of the withdrawing owner.

        b.   In a cross-purchase agreement, the surviving owners buy out the withdrawing owner.

        c.   The purchase price will be included in the deceased owner's estate and will control for valuation purposes if:

            1.   the price is the result of a bona fide business agreement.

            2.   the agreement is not a device to transfer property to family members.

            3.   the agreement is comparable to other arrangements entered into by persons dealing at arm's length.

II.   INCOME TAX CONCEPTS

    A.   Basis of Property Acquired by Gift
        1.   Depends upon when the gift was made and whether it sold for a gain or loss:
            a.   after 1920 and before 1977
                1.   basis for gain is the donor's adjusted basis plus any gift tax paid.
                2.   basis for gain cannot be higher than FMV on the date of the gift.
                3.   basis for loss is the lower of the basis for gain or the FMV at the date of the gift.
            b.   after 1976
                1.   basis for gain is the donor's adjusted basis plus the gift tax attributable to any appreciation up to the date of the gift.
                2.   basis for loss is the lower of the gain basis or the FMV at the date of the gift.
        2.   The donee's holding period includes the holding period of the donor.

    B.   Basis of Property Acquired by Death
        1.   Generally property acquired from a decedent is valued at its FMV on the date of death or alternate valuation date and the holding period is automatically long-term.
        2.   The surviving spouse's half of community property takes the same basis as the half included in the deceased spouse's gross estate.
        3.   Under the §1014(e) exception, the original donor assumes the property with the same basis as existed in the hands of the deceased prior to his or her death. For section 1014(e), the following conditions must be satisfied:
            a.   The decedent must have received appreciated property as a gift during the one-year period ending with his or her death.
            b.   The property is acquired from the decedent by the donor or the donor's spouse.
        4.   Income in respect of a decedent is income which was earned by a decedent prior to his death but not reported on his final tax return due to his method of accounting.
            a.   For estate tax purposes income in respect of a decedent is valued at fair market value on the valuation date.
            b.   For income tax purposes, the decedent's basis and classification is transferred to the estate or heirs.

III.   PLANNING

    A.   A plan of lifetime giving can minimize transfer taxes and income taxes through use of the annual exclusion by
        1.   spacing gifts over several years.
        2.   making successive gifts of partial interests to transfer real property.

    B.   Gifts of property expected to appreciate in value removes the appreciation from the donor's gross estate.

    C.   Estate planning should consider reducing the probate estate through:
        1.   holding property in joint ownership with rights of survivorship.
        2.   naming a life insurance beneficiary other than the estate.
        3.   using a revocable, living, trust which at death becomes irrevocable.

    D.   The liquidity of an estate is often strained between the date of death and the final disposition of the estate assets. The following should be considered.

        1.   life insurance payable to the estate,
        2.   a carefully drawn will,
        3.   the judicious use of trust arrangements,
        4.   qualifying for the extension of time for the payment of death taxes.

TEST FOR SELF-EVALUATION

True or False

T F 1.   If a federal estate tax return does NOT have to be filed, an individual's basis in inherited property is the property's adjusted basis to the decedent at the date of death.   (IRS 96 1A-7)

T F 2.   On February 1, 1995, John Smith, a cash basis taxpayer, sold his machine for $5,000, payable March 1 of the same year. His adjusted basis in the machine was $4,000. Mr. Smith died on February 15, 1995, before receiving payment. The gain to be reported as income in respect of the decedent is the $1,000 difference between the decedent's basis in the property and sales proceeds.
                                                                              (IRS 96 3A-12)

T F 3.   There are provisions that allow additional time for paying the estate tax. The usual extension of time to pay is up to 12 months from the date the payment is due. However, if you can show reasonable cause why it is impractical for you to pay the full amount of the tax due on the due date, the IRS may extend the time for payment up to 10 years.   (IRS 96 3A-14)

T F 4.   Generally, any income generated by the property after the owner's death must be accounted for separately.

T F 5.   Generally, the income tax basis of property acquired from a person who died will be its fair market value on the date of death, or, if elected, on the alternate valuation date.

T F 6.   As it is possible to have a "step-up" in basis, it is also possible to have a "step-down" in basis for property received as the result of a death transfer.

T F 7.   When income must be included in the income tax computation and gross estate of a decedent, the individual is allowed a credit on his final tax return in order to avoid double taxation.

T F 8.   To determine your basis in the property you receive as a gift, it is sometimes necessary to add all or part of the gift tax paid on the property.
                                                                              (IRS 94 1A-11)

T F 9.   The only importance in properly determining the value of property is to correctly compute the possible gift or estate tax.

T F 10.   Due to the conservative nature of the IRS, taxpayers are required to use wholesale prices when determining the fair market value of property.

T F 11. Shares in a mutual fund should be valued at the redemption or bid price of the security.

T F 12. The value of property reflected on the estate tax return and subsequently accepted by the IRS is presumed to be correct in any case of future changes to that valuation and must be rebutted by the heir.

T F 13. The special valuation method allows certain classes of real estate to be valued at their "most suitable" use.

T F 14. Buy-sell agreements are useful tools in planning estate liquidity.

Fill in the Blanks

1. The special use valuation procedure permits a reduction in estate tax valuation of no more than $_____.

2. To qualify for the special use valuation method, at least _____% of the adjusted value of the gross estate must consist of real or personal property devoted to the qualifying use.

3. The concept that recognizes that the per unit value of shares may fall when a large number of shares are sold at one time is called the "_____."

4. To meet the requirements of section 6166, a decedent's interest in a farm or closely-held business must be more than _____ of his or her adjusted gross estate.

Multiple Choice

_____ 1. Donna received land as a gift from her grandfather. At the time of the gift, the land had a fair market value of $80,000 and an adjusted basis of $100,000 to Donna's grandfather. One year later, Donna sold the land for $105,000. What was her gain or (loss) on this transaction? (IRS 96 1C-55)

    a. $5,000
    b. $15,000
    c. $20,000
    d. No gain or loss

_____ 2. During 1995, Juan received a gift of property from his uncle. At the time of the gift, the property had a fair market value of $100,000 and an adjusted basis to his uncle of $40,000. Juan's uncle paid a gift tax on the transfer of $18,000. What is Juan's basis in the property? (IRS 96 1C-56)

a. $40,000
b. $50,800
c. $60,000
d. $128,000

_____ 3.   Mr. Hill inherited 1,000 shares of Pro Corporation stock from his father who died on March 8, 1995. His father paid $10 per share for the stock on September 1, 1975. The fair market value of the stock on the date of death was $50 per share. On September 8, 1995, the fair market value of the stock was $60 per share. Mr. Hill sold the stock for $75 a share on December 5, 1995. The estate qualified for, and the executor elected, the alternate valuation method. A federal estate tax return was filed. What was Mr. Hill's basis in the stock on the date of sale?

(IRS 96 1C-57)

a. $50,000
b. $60,000
c. $75,000
d. $150,000

_____ 4.   On June 1, 1995, Kirk received a gift of income-producing real estate having a donor's adjusted basis of $50,000 at the date of the gift. The fair market value of the property at the date of the gift was $40,000. Kirk sold the property for $46,000 on August 1, 1995. How much gain or loss should Kirk report for 1995?

(IRS 96 1C-67)

a.   No gain or loss
b. $4,000 short-term capital loss
c. $4,000 ordinary loss
d. $6,000 short-term capital gain

_____ 5.   In 1995, Daniel inherited 100% of Candy Corporation's outstanding stock from his mother. The stock had a fair market value of $250,000 at the date of death and was reflected on Candy's balance sheet as:

Cash	$250,000
Capital stock	$150,000
Accumulated earnings & profits	$100,000

Daniel immediately withdrew $50,000 out of Candy Corporation as a dividend distribution. Later in 1995, pursuant to a plan of liquidation, Daniel withdrew the remaining $200,000 out of Candy. For 1995, how much will Daniel be required to report as ordinary dividend income and capital gain or (loss)? (IRS 96 3C-63)

	Ordinary Dividend	Capital Gain or (Loss)
a.	$0	$0
b.	$50,000	($50,000)
c.	$100,000	($100,000)
d.	$50,000	($250,000)

_____ 6.   Mrs. Butler, a cash method taxpayer, died on July 31, 1995. A review of her records reflected that, as of July 31, 1995, she had received interest of $500 and wages of $80,000. Also, on stock that she owned, an $800 dividend was declared on June 20, 1995, and was payable on July 31, 1995. The dividend check was not received until August 3, 1995. What is the amount of income to be reported on Mrs. Butler's final income tax return?   (IRS 96 3C-71)

    a. $80,000
    b. $80,500
    c. $80,800
    d. $81,300

_____ 7.   Chester received a gift of stock having an adjusted basis of $11,000 and a fair market value of $7,200 at the time of the gift. Chester sold the stock for $9,000. What is the amount of Chester's capital gain or (loss)?   (IRS 95 1C-69)

    a. $9,000
    b. $1,800
    c. $0
    d.   ($2,000)

_____ 8.   With regard to the final return of a decedent, all of the following statements are correct, except: (IRS 94 3B-37)

    a.   On the final return of a deceased taxpayer, all income is reported on the accrual method regardless of the accounting method the deceased employed.
    b.   Medical expenses paid before death by the decedent are deductible on the final income tax return if deductions are itemized.
    c.   The death of a partner does NOT close the partnership's tax year before it normally ends.
    d.   Any credit that applied to the decedent before death may be claimed on the final income tax return.

SOLUTIONS

True or False

1. F (p. 18-5; FMV on date of death)
2. T (p. 18-17)
3. T (p. 18-29)
4 F (p. 18-17)
5. T (p. 18-15)
6. T (p. 18-15)
7. F (p. 18-17; transfer tax and income tax)
8. T (p. 18-14, 15)
9. F (p. 18-17; basis for depreciation, later disposition)
10. F (p. 18-2)
11. T (p. 18-4)
12. T (p. 18-18)
13. F (p. 18-6; current use)
14. T (p. 18-11)

Fill in the Blanks

1. $750,000 (p. 18-6)
2. 50% (p. 18-7)
3. "blockage rule" (p. 18-9)
4. 25% (p. 18-7)

Multiple Choice

1. a (p. 18-15; 105,000 -100,000 = 5,000)
2. b (p. 18-15; 60% of gift tax (appreciation) +donor's adjusted basis)
3. b (p. 18-15; 1,000 shares @ $60 per share, alternate valuation date, Sept. 8)
4. a (p. 18-15; donor's basis = gain basis, loss basis is lesser of FMV, 40,000 or gain basis, 50,000)
5. b (p. 18-15; $50,000 dividend is ordinary, basis $250,000 - proceeds 200,000 capital)
6. b (p. 18-17; dividend is IRD)
7. c (p. 18-15; gain basis, 9,000 - 11,000, loss basis 9,000 - 7,200)
8. a (p. 18-17; IRD)

CHAPTER 19

INCOME TAXATION OF TRUSTS AND ESTATES

LEARNING OBJECTIVES

After completing Chapter 19, you should be able to:

1. Use working definitions with respect to trusts, estates, beneficiaries, and other parties.

2. Identify the steps in determining the accounting and taxable income of a trust or estate and the related taxable income of the beneficiaries.

3. Illustrate the uses and implications of distributable net income.

4. Use the special rules that apply to trusts where the creator (grantor) of the trust retains certain rights.

KEY TERMS

Complex trust	Grantor	Reversionary interest
Corpus	Grantor trust	Simple trust
Distributable net income (DNI)	Income in respect of	Sprinkling trust
Expenses in respect of a decedent	a decedent (IRD)	

OUTLINE

I.   DEFINITIONS

    A.   A 'trust' usually refers to: an arrangement created by a will or by an inter vivos declaration through which the trustee takes title to property for the purpose of protecting or conserving it for the beneficiaries.

    B.   Typically, three parties are involved in creating a trust:
        1.   The grantor - transfers property which becomes the principal or corpus of the trust.
        2.   The trustee - manages the trust according to the terms of the trust document and applicable law.
        3.   The beneficiary - receives the benefits from the trust,
            a.   income interest - receives the accounting income,
            b.   remainder interest - receives the trust corpus at termination of the trust entity.
        4.   When the same individual is grantor, trustee and sole beneficiary, the trust is not recognized for tax purposes.

    C.   Each year trusts must be classified as either simple or complex.
        1.   A simple trust:
            a.   is required to distribute its entire accounting income each year,
            b.   has no qualified charitable organizations as beneficiaries, and
            c.   makes no distribution of corpus during the year.
        2.   A complex trust is any trust that is not a simple trust.

    D.   An estate is created upon the death of every individual to,
        1.   collect and conserve the individual's assets,
        2.   satisfy his liabilities, and
        3.   distribute the remaining assets to his heirs.

II.   NATURE OF TRUST AND ESTATE TAXATION

    A.   Taxable income of an estate or trust is taxed to the entity or its beneficiaries to the extent that each received the accounting income.

    B.   Filing Requirements
        1.   Form 1041, U.S. Fiduciary Income Tax Return is used by trusts and estates.
        2.   An estate must file if it has $600 or more gross income for the year.
        3.   A trust must file if it has $600 or more gross income and/or any taxable income.

4.   The return is due on the 15th day of the fourth month after the close of the entity's tax year.

C.   Tax Accounting Periods and Payments
1.   An estate may select any fiscal year or a calendar year.
2.   A trust, other than tax-exempt trusts, must use a calendar year.
3.   Trusts and estates having tax years ending 2 or more tax years after the death of the decedent, are required to make quarterly estimated tax payments.

D.   Tax Rates and Personal Exemptions
1.   Trusts and estates use a compressed tax rate schedule.
2.   Tax on net long-term capital gains are taxed at no more than 20%.
3.   The alternative minimum tax may apply.
4.   Trusts and estates are allowed a personal exemption.
     a.   simple trusts, $300
     b.   complex trusts, $100
     c.   estates, $600

III.   TAXABLE INCOME OF TRUSTS AND ESTATES

A.   Trust and estate taxable income computation involves 5 steps:
1.   Determine the accounting income of the entity.
2.   Compute entity taxable income before the distribution deduction.
3.   Determine distributable net income, (DNI), and the distribution deduction.
4.   Compute entity taxable income.
5.   Allocate DNI and its character to the beneficiaries.

B.   Entity Accounting Income
1.   Is the amount that the beneficiary of a simple trust or estate is eligible to receive.
2.   May be defined in the will or trust agreement, if not, state law prevails.
3.   Allocates specific items of income and expenditures to the income beneficiaries or to corpus.

C.   Gross Income
1.   Is determined similar to that of individuals:
2.   The basis of assets
     a.   acquired from a decedent = FMV on date of death or alternate valuation date.
     b.   acquired by gift = donor's basis
     c.   acquired by purchase = cost

3. Income in respect of decedent is included in the gross income of an estate or trust.

D. Ordinary Deductions
   1. Are determined similar to those of individuals, many are subject to the 2% of AGI floor.
   2. Are allowed for reasonable administration expenses.
   3. Are allowed for expenses in respect of a decedent.

E. Deductions for Losses
   1. Casualty or theft losses not covered by insurance.
   2. NOLs, where trade or business income is generated.
   3. Net capital losses are used only on the fiduciary income tax return.

F. Charitable Contributions
   1. Must be made pursuant to the will or trust agreement, and its amount must be determinable in the document.
   2. Must be made to a qualified organization.
   3. Generally, must be paid in the year claimed.

G. Deductions for Distributions to Beneficiaries
   1. DNI approximates current economic income and
      a. is the maximum amount of the distribution on which the beneficiaries may be taxed.
      b. is the maximum amount that can be used by the entity as a distribution deduction for the year.
      c. its composition carries over to the beneficiaries.
   2. DNI computation begins with the entity's taxable income before the distribution deduction, then:
      a. adds back the personal exemption,
      b. adds back net tax exempt interest,
      c. adds back net capital losses,
      d. subtracts any net capital gains allocable to corpus.

IV. TAXATION OF BENEFICIARIES

A. Distributions by Simple Trusts
   1. DNI limits the amount taxable to the beneficiaries.
   2. When there is more than one income beneficiary, the elements of DNI are apportioned ratably according to the amount required to be distributed.

B. Distributions by Estates and Complex Trusts
   1. Two-tier system

        a.   first tier distributions = income required to be distributed currently.

        b.   second tier distributions = all other amounts properly paid, credited, or required to be distributed.

2.   If first tier distributions exceed DNI, second tier distributions are not taxed.

3.   If first tier distributions do not exceed DNI, second tier distributions are taxed to the extent of remaining DNI.

C.   Character of Income

1.   Distributions are treated as consisting of the same proportionate classes of income as the items that enter into the computation of DNI.

2.   Special allocations are permitted to the extent required in the trust agreement and to the extent that the allocation has an economic effect independent of cash-flow and income tax consequences.

D.   Losses in the Termination Year

1.   An NOL incurred in the last year of the entity's existence is a deduction from AGI. It is passed through to the beneficiaries and deductible as a miscellaneous deduction, subject to the 2% of AGI floor.

2.   Carryovers of other losses, NOLs and net capital losses flow through to the beneficiaries in the termination year and may be used as deductions for AGI.

V. GRANTOR TRUSTS

A.   The creation of a reversionary trust is subject to the Federal gift tax. Also, if the grantor dies before the income interest expires, the present value of the reversionary interest will be included in his gross estate, and may be subject to the Federal estate tax.

B.   Section 674 provides that the grantor will be treated as the owner of any portion of a trust and taxed on the income therefrom, if he or she retains

1.   the beneficial enjoyment of the corpus and/or

2.   power to dispose of the trust income without the approval or consent of any adverse party.

C.   There are exceptions to the above rule which will not result in the income being taxed to the grantor. These include the power to:

1.   Apply the income toward the support of the grantor's dependents.

2.   Allocate trust income or corpus among charitable beneficiaries.

3.   Invade corpus on behalf of a designated beneficiary.

4.   Withhold income from a beneficiary during his or her minority or disability.

5.   Allocate receipts and disbursements between income and corpus.

D.   If certain administrative power are retained by the grantor or a non-adverse party, the income from the trust will be taxed to the grantor. These powers include:
1.   the power to deal with the trust income or property for less than full and adequate consideration.
2.   the power to borrow from the trust without adequate interest or security.
3.   the power to revoke the trust.

E.   A grantor is taxed on all or part of the income of a trust when, at the discretion of the grantor or a non-adverse party, without consent of any adverse party the income is or may be:
1.   distributed to the grantor or the grantor's spouse.
2.   accumulated for future distribution to the grantor or the grantor's spouse.
3.   applied to premium payments on life insurance policies on the life of the grantor or the grantor's spouse.

TEST FOR SELF-EVALUATION

True or False

T F 1. If the estate has unused loss carryovers or excess deductions for its last tax year, they are allowed to those beneficiaries who succeed to the estate's property.
(IRS 96 3A-18)

T F 2. A trust may be a simple trust for one year and a complex trust for another year.
(IRS 96 3A-20)

T F 3. A beneficiary of a COMPLEX TRUST must include in his taxable income the income that is required to be distributed, whether or not it is actually distributed during the tax year.
(IRS 95 3A-20)

T F 4. The beneficiaries succeeding to the estate's property are permitted to claim unused net operating loss carryovers or capital loss carryovers from the estate's last tax year.
(IRS 94 3A-16)

T F 5. A beneficiary of a complex trust must include in his taxable income the income that is required to be distributed only if the income is actually distributed during the tax year.
(IRS 94 3A-20)

T F 6. A beneficiary who succeeds to the property of the estate can claim the estate's unused net operating loss carryover and capital loss carryover existing upon termination of the estate.
(IRS 93 3A-15)

T F 7. Net operating losses are deductible by trusts, but NOT by estates.
(IRS 93 3A-16)

T F 8. The executor of Steven River's estate distributed the entire net estate to the beneficiaries before paying the estate's tax liability. John River received $3,000 as his share of the estate. John could be assessed up to $3,000 of the estate tax.
(IRS 93 3A-17)

T F 9. If an estate has unused loss carryovers for its last tax year, the beneficiaries succeeding to the estate's property are permitted to claim the losses on their respective returns.
(IRS 92 3A-12)

T F 10. If P, a cash basis taxpayer, is a beneficiary of an estate that must distribute all its income currently, P must report her yearly share of the distributable net income whether or not P actually received distributions during the year. (IRS 91 3A-26)

Fill in the Blanks

1. A trust involves three parties: a _____, a _____, and a _____.

2. A _____ is the transferor of the property who is the creator of the trust.

3. Beneficiaries fall into two categories: those entitled to _____ from the trust and those entitled to the _____ upon the expiration of the _____ interest.

4. The fiduciary return is due not later than the fifteenth day of the _____ month following the close of the entity's taxable year.

5. _____ is the maximum amount that can be used by the entity as a distribution deduction for the year.

6. Income required to be distributed currently, whether distributed or not, is classified as a _____ distribution.

7. Undistributed net income is the _____ net income of the trust, reduced by _____ and _____ distributions, plus any _____ paid by the trust on the remaining undistributable net income.

8. The creation of a reversionary trust is subject to the Federal _____ tax.

9. When an income interest in a trust is based on a beneficiary's life, he is known as a _____.

Multiple Choice

_____ 1.   All of the following might include income in respect of a decedent except:
                                                    (IRS 96 3B-30)
        a. The estate's return, if the estate receives it.
        b. The beneficiary's return, if the right to the income is passed directly to the beneficiary and the beneficiary receives it.
        c. The decedent's final return.
        d. The return of any person to whom the estate properly distributes the right to receive the income.

_____ 2.   In which circumstance must an estate of a decedent make estimated tax payments?
            (IRS 96 3B-31)

     a.   None, since an estate is NOT required to make estimated tax payments.
     b.   The estate has a first tax year that covers 12 months.
     c.   The estate has income in excess of $400.
     d.   The estate has a tax year ending 2 or more years after the date of the decedent's death.

_____ 3.   Rudy, a cash-basis taxpayer, received $50,000 in wages before his death. In addition, his stock portfolio paid $4,000 in dividends, $2,500 of which was paid to him before his death. By what date is Form 1041, U.S. Income Tax Return for Estates and Trusts, required to be filed?   (IRS 96 3B-32)

     a.   Form 1041 is NOT required to be filed.
     b.   9 months after death.
     c.   By the 15th day of the 4th month after the end of the tax year selected by the estate's personal representative.
     d.   By the 15th day of the 3rd month after the end of the tax year selected by the estate.

_____ 4.   A complex trust is a trust that   (IRS 96 3B-40)

     a.   permits accumulation of current income, provides for charitable contributions or distributes principal during the taxable year.
     b.   invests only in corporate securities and is prohibited from engaging in short-term transactions.
     c.   is exempt from payment of income tax since the tax is paid by the beneficiaries.
     d.   must distribute income currently, but is prohibited from distributing principal during the taxable year.

_____ 5.   The taxable income of estates and trusts is generally computed in the same manner as that of which type of taxpayer?   (IRS 96 3B-41)

     a.   Association
     b.   Individual
     c.   Corporation
     d.   Partnership

_____ 6.   The amount of the personal exemption allowed to a simple trust is
                                                            (IRS 96 3B-42)
      a. $0
      b. $100
      c. $300
      d. $600

_____ 7.   Which of the following is NOT a modification of taxable income used to determine distributable net income of an estate or trust?   (IRS 96 3B-44)

      a.   Capital gains are subtracted to the extent allocated to corpus and not distributed or set aside for a beneficiary.
      b.   The personal exemption is added back.
      c.   The net operating loss deduction is added back.
      d.   Tax-exempt interest is added.

_____ 8.   Phil, the grantor, set up two irrevocable trust: Trust K and Trust J. The income of Trust K is to be accumulated for distribution to Phil's spouse after Phil's death. The income of Trust J is to be accumulated for Phil's children, whom Phil is legally obligated to support, and the trustee has the discretion to use any part of the income for the children's support. Half of the income was so used in 1995. Based on this information, which of the following statements is correct?
                                                            (IRS 96 3B-45)
      a.   All the income from both trusts is taxed to Phil.
      b.   None of the income for either trust is taxed to Phil.
      c.   No income from Trust K is taxed to Phil and half of the income from Trust J is taxed to Phil.
      d.   All the income from Trust K and half from Trust J is taxed to Phil.

_____ 9.   Mr. Justin, a cash basis taxpayer, died on January 21, 1995. His estate received the following income and incurred the following expenses during 1995:

      Gain on sale of assets $10,400
      Dividend income $14,000
      Interest income $ 6,000
      Administration expenses $ 2,800

      The personal representative filed a statement waiving the right to claim the administration expenses as a deduction for federal estate tax purposes. What is the estate's taxable income for 1995?   (IRS 96 3C-72)

      a. $27,600
      b. $27,000
      c. $17,600
      d. $13,000

_____ 10. Trust W, a simple trust, has taxable interest of $5,000, tax-exempt interest of $10,000 and a short-term capital gain of $20,000. Capital gains are allocable to corpus. There are two equal beneficiaries. How much gross income does each beneficiary have from Trust W? (IRS 96 3C-78)

a. $2,500
b. $5,000
c. $12,500
d. $15,000

_____ 11. A simple trust has tax-exempt interest income of $10,000 and rental income of $15,000. There are fiduciary fees of $5,000 entirely allocable to the rental income. There is $2,000 of depreciation, but the trust is NOT required to set up a reserve. All the income is distributable to the beneficiaries. What is the trust's distributable net income? (IRS 96 3C-79)

a. $8,000
b. $10,000
c. $18,000
d. $20,000

_____ 12. Under the terms of the trust agreement, the income of the W Trust is required to be currently distributed to Ryan during his life. Capital gains are allocable to corpus, and all expenses are charged against corpus. During the taxable year, the trust had the following items of income and expenses:

Dividends from domestic corporations	$30,000
Taxable interest	$20,000
Nontaxable interest	$10,000
Long-term capital gains	$15,000
Commissions and miscellaneous expenses allocable to corpus	$ 6,000

The trust's distributable net income is: (IRS 96 3C-80)

a. $50,000
b. $54,000
c. $69,000
d. $75,000

_____ 13.   With regard to a trust, all of the following statements are CORRECT except:
(IRS 95 3B-44)

   a.   A trust is a separate taxable entity.
   b.   Generally, the trust is taxed on the income currently distributed on the income currently distributed and on the portion it has accumulated.
   c.   If income is required to be distributed currently or is properly distributed to a beneficiary, the trust is regarded as a conduit with respect to that income.
   d.   The income allocated to a beneficiary retains the same character in his hands as it had in the hands of the trust.

_____ 14.   Under the terms of the will of Jim Shaw, $9,000 a year is to be paid to his widow and $6,000 a year is to be paid to his son out of the estate's income during the period of administration. There are no charitable contributions. For the year, the estate's distributable net income is $10,000. How much must the widow include in her gross income?   (IRS 95 3C-77)

   a. $3,000
   b. $5,000
   c. $6,000
   d. $9,000

_____ 15.   Which of the following is a characteristic of a "simple" trust? (IRS 94 3B-44)

   a.   A trust in the final year of administration.
   b.   A trust which is partially liquidated during the taxable year.
   c.   A trust which is allowed a personal exemption deduction of $300.
   d.   A trust which distributes an amount out of corpus.

_____ 16.   Under which of the following situations is the trust's income NOT taxable to the grantor of the trust: (IRS 94 3B-45)

   a.   The grantor borrows the trust income and repays the loan with interest during the same year.
   b.   The grantor creates a trust and reserves the right to revoke it.
   c.   The grantor's spouse has a power, exercisable solely by herself, to vest the corpus or income of the trust in herself.
   d.   The grantor's spouse retains the power to control the beneficial enjoyment of trust.

_____ 17.   Trust D, a complex trust, is required to distribute $20,000 to its beneficiary under the terms of the trust instrument. The trust's distributable net income is $33,500. The $20,000 is deemed to have been paid from the following items of income:

Rent	$ 2,000
Taxable interest	14,000
Dividends	16,000
Tax-exempt interest	8,000
Total	$ 33,500

All expenses have been allocated. What is the trust's distribution deduction?

(IRS 94 3C-80)

a. $20,000
b. $19,000
c. $16,000
d. $15,000

SOLUTIONS

True or False

1. T (p. 19-26)
2. T (p. 19-5)
3. T (p. 19-23)
4. T (p. 19-26)
5. F (p. 19-23; whether or not distributed)
6. T (p. 19-26)
7. F (p. 19-16; estates can claim NOLs where trade or business income is generated)
8. T (p. 19-6; whoever receives the income is liable for the tax)
9. T (p. 19-26)
10. T (p. 19-22)

Fill in the Blanks

1. grantor; trustee; beneficiary (p. 19-4)
2. grantor (p. 19-4)
3. income; principal; income (p. 19-4)
4. fourth (p. 19-7)
5. distributable net income (p. 19-18)
6. first-tier (p. 19-23)
7. distributable; first and second-tier; income tax (p.19-28)
8. gift (p. 19-30)
9. life tenant (p. 19-4)

Multiple Choice

1. c (p. 19-13; definition of IRD)
2. d (p. 19-7)
3. c (p. 19-7)
4. a (p. 19-5; not simple, therefore, complex)
5. b (p. 19-9)
6. c (p. 19-8)
7. c (p. 19-18)
8. d (p. 19-31; Trust K, grantor's spouse, Trust J, legally obligated to support children)
9. b (10400 + 14,000 + 6,000 - 2,800 - 600 exemption)
10. a (p. 19-22)
11. d (p. 19-18; 10,000 + 15,000 - 5,000)
12. b (p. 19-18; expenses are deducted whether allocated to income or corpus)
13. b (p. 19-6)
14. c (p. 19-22; pro rata share is 60% of 10,000)
15. c (p. 19-5, 6)
16. c (p. 19-30; the grantor's spouse is treated as owner)
17. c (p. 19-18; DNI must be reduced by amounts not included in the trust's gross income)